KU-030-057

Doing ~~WITHDRAWN~~ Qualitative Research
Using Your Computer

A Practical Guide

■ ■

WS 2252562 9

S. 2008

WITHDRAWN

Doing Qualitative Research Using Your Computer

A Practical Guide

Christopher Hahn

Los Angeles • London • New Delhi • Singapore

UNIVERSITY OF CHICHESTER

© Christopher Hahn 2008

First Published 2008

Apart from any fair dealing for the purposes of research or
private study, or criticism or review, as permitted under the
Copyright, Designs and Patents Act, 1988, this publication may
be reproduced, stored or transmitted in any form, or by any
means, only with the prior permission in writing of the publishers,
or in the case of reprographic reproduction, in accordance with the
terms of licences issued by the Copyright Licensing Agency.
Enquiries concerning reproduction outside those terms should be
sent to the publishers.

SAGE Publications Ltd
1 Oliver's Yard
55 City Road
London EC1Y 1SP

SAGE Publications Inc.
2455 Teller Road
Thousand Oaks, California 91320

SAGE Publications India Pvt Ltd
B 1/I 1 Mohan Cooperative Industrial Area
Mathura Road
New Delhi 110 044

SAGE Publications Asia-Pacific Pte Ltd
33 Pekin Street #02-01
Far East Square
Singapore 048763

Library of Congress Control Number: 2007937353

British Library Cataloguing in Publication data

A catalogue record for this book is available from
the British Library

ISBN 978-1-4129-4692-6
ISBN 978-1-4129-4693-3 (pbk)

Typeset by CEPHA Imaging Pvt. Ltd., Bangalore, India
Printed in Great Britain by The Cromwell Press Ltd, Trowbridge, Wiltshire
Printed on paper from sustainable resources

300.
72
HAH

Contents

CHAPTER 1

Introduction, coding terminology, and the big picture

Science is organized knowledge. Wisdom is organized life.

Immanuel Kant

I **f, as Kant** suggests, science is organized knowledge, then qualitative researchers have a special challenge because of the nebulous nature of their raw data. A great deal of knowledge and wisdom is enmeshed in the stories of elders, open-ended interviews, field observations, folk art, pictures, and artifacts collected by qualitative researchers. But how can these data be organized and analyzed to create scientifically acceptable conclusions? Coherent and well-elucidated strategies are required to produce defensible results from free-form qualitative data. The science of qualitative research depends on the intelligent organization and analysis of rich and complex qualitative data without the time-tested statistical tools that dominate the world of quantitative analysis.

The qualitative researcher discovers the quality and character of lived experiences by collecting data that are not bound by the constraints of quantitative methods. Qualitative data do not have to measure a predetermined set of variables using a large population of randomly sampled subjects. That is the good news. The bad news is that qualitative data can be overwhelming unless they are carefully organized and distilled.

Only with intelligent analysis can scientific conclusions be drawn from the volumes of data that are usually collected during the course of a qualitative research project. This book is full of techniques, technological tips, and tools to help beginning, intermediate, and advanced qualitative researchers work smarter and faster without abandoning their qualitative method of choice.

Many prominent and well-respected scholars have wrestled with the problems and opportunities inherent to qualitative research. Over time these intellectual explorations into the qualitative world have produced wide-ranging and well-documented theoretical and methodological approaches to research problems commonly encountered by qualitative researchers. The practical focus of this book is possible because it builds upon the highly valued pre-existing body of qualitative research knowledge.

Qualitative methods are diverse

Investigators may use grounded theory, ethnography, case studies, focus groups, phenomenology, or creative mixed methods to guide their research designs. Data may be gathered from interviews, observations, participant-observations, field notes, public documents, photographs, audio-visual recordings, journals, artifacts, and sensations such as smell or taste. All of these methods and data gathering practices are supported by existing literature.

The step-by-step techniques and technological guidelines in this book focus on making qualitative researchers more efficient and their projects more valued by helping them more effectively plan, organize, and control their projects. These techniques must be used in tandem with the theoretical underpinnings of qualitative research. I encourage readers of this book to refer often to research methods texts. A tiny sampling of the qualitative methods literature follows so new investigators can get an introductory grasp of qualitative fundamentals.

Grounded theorists endeavor to develop solid hypotheses from the wide-ranging data they collect. The data are often collected through interviews and/or observations. In the words of Strauss and Corbin,

> In speaking about qualitative analysis, we are referring not to the quantifying of qualitative data but rather to a nonmathematical process of interpretation, carried out for the purpose of discovering concepts and relationships in raw data and then organizing these into a theoretical explanatory scheme (Strauss and Corbin, 1998, p. 11).

Case study researchers focus on a single case or multiple cases to

> understand complex social phenomena. In brief, the case study method allows investigators to retain the holistic and meaningful characteristics of real-life events – such as individual life cycles, organization and managerial processes, neighborhood change, international relations, and maturation of industries (Yin, 2003, p. 2).

Ethnographers immerse themselves in the everyday experiences of the people and objects of their study through fieldwork.

> First, the ethnographer enters into a social setting and gets to know the people involved in it; usually, the setting is not previously known in an intimate way. The ethnographer participates in the daily routines of this setting, develops ongoing relations with the people of it, and observes all the while what is going on. Indeed, the term "participant observation" is often used to characterize this basic research approach. But, second, the ethnographer writes down in regular, systematic ways what she observes and learns while participating in the daily rounds of life in others. Thus the researcher creates an accumulating written record of these observations and experiences (Emerson et al., 1995, p. 1).

Qualitative researchers, particularly those involved with fieldwork, may find a significant amount of meaning in artifacts, pictures, and other non-text items. Creswell (2003, p. 189) explains that qualitative researchers may

- Have participants take photographs or videotapes
- Examine physical trace evidence (e.g., footprints in the snow)
- Collect sounds
- Examine possessions or ritual objects to elicit views during an interview
- Collect smells, tastes, or sensations through touch.

Phenomenologists are driven by the quest to discover the objective and subjective reality of the phenomena being studied without the explicit objective of developing theory.

In phenomenological studies the investigator abstains from making suppositions, focuses on a specific topic freshly and naively, constructs a question or problem to guide the study, and derives findings that will provide the basis for further research and reflections. In phenomenological science a relationship always exists between the external perception of natural objects and internal perceptions, memories, and judgments (Moustakas, 1994, p. 47).

Qualitative research allows investigators to be dynamic and innovative. Qualitative methods evolve as new technologies and social forums emerge. For example, the Internet provides a good example of a qualitative method-ology that would not have been possible in the early days of qualitative research – online research.

In technologically-mediated environments, self, other, and social structures are constituted through interaction, negotiated in concert with others. The extent to which information and communication technology (ICT) can mediate one's identity and social relations should call us to epistemological attention. Whether or not we do research of physical or online cultures, new communication technologies highlight the dialogic features of social reality, compelling scholars to reexamine traditional assumptions and previously taken-for-granted rubrics of social research (Markham, 2004, p. 794).

The literature samples above illustrate the breadth of qualitative research. Qualitative data can be derived from many sources using numerous tech-niques and these data may facilitate insightful discoveries, but there is a price. Qualitative research is time consuming and the data are complex. Without thoughtful organization the researcher is likely to lose momentum and intellectual perspective. Without diligent project management qualitative researchers may forget critical data, spend far too much time looking for things they lost, and miss the most important themes that are embedded in their data.

At its core, this book is about the efficient organization and management of qualitative data using readily available tools. The researcher can more productively analyze data and write better conclusions if he or she intelligently uses the every-day technologies that have become available in the last few years. **This book will help you complete your projects on time and with less frustration by introducing you to efficient qualitative research techniques and problem solving ideas.**

This book is not the introduction of a new qualitative research method. For explanations of grounded theory, case studies, ethnography, phenomenology, focus groups, action research, online research, and other qualitative methods this book defers to the many excellent books and lectures available today. The researchers, professors, and authors who developed these leading methods of qualitative inquiry have provided us with well-developed theoretical, conceptual, and methodological directions.

The goal of this book is to enhance the quality, speed, and prestige of qualitative research by providing researchers easy access to innovative tips, techniques, and technologies.

Qualitative research is not homogeneous

Qualitative researchers are diverse. They employ different epistemological assumptions, research methods, methodologies, and designs to answer their research questions, but despite their differences qualitative researchers face common challenges.

⇒ Qualitative researchers generate an enormous amount of relatively free-form data such as interview transcripts, field notes from direct observations, documents, records, artifacts, pictures, and other non-quantitative information.

⇒ Organizing cabinets full of objects and hundreds (or thousands) of pages of qualitative data is not easy, but it is vital to the successful completion of the research project. Every project will be more efficient if the data are intelligently organized.

⇒ The examination of large volumes of data requires an orderly system of analysis that focuses on answering the project's research question(s).

About this book's voice

This is a practical how-to book, not a book about academic paradigms. It is a book that will be used by academics, but it is assumed that even the brightest scholars get frustrated by technological problems from time to time. I don't want frustration about technology to enjoin scholars from trying more resourceful techniques.

To encourage you to relax so you can be creative and innovative, I deliberately employ a relaxed literary style. I speak to you in the first person throughout this book. Because I am working on practical issues with you at your desk, in your study, and at your computer, I use an informal 'at home' voice rather than a more formal 'in the classroom' tone. Hopefully, the occasional light-hearted phrase or story will make you smile.

The terminology of qualitative coding

All major qualitative methods employ coding techniques to help organize the overwhelming amount of data that are frequently collected during qualitative research. In subsequent chapters the coding process will be explained in fine detail. This section is presented now to clarify possible confusion about coding terms.

It is assumed that most readers of this book are at least somewhat familiar with qualitative coding concepts, and that some readers are experts in one or more method of qualitative coding. Advanced qualitative researchers understand that there are significant differences in qualitative methods. An ethnographer writing field notes and gathering objects amasses a different type of data than a researcher conducting a case study. A grounded theorist is searching for a different type of conclusion than a phenomenologist.

Coding is the process of focusing a mass amount of free-form data with the goal of empirically illuminating answers to research questions. Coding moves in a stepwise fashion progressively from unsorted data to the development of more refined categories, themes, and concepts. The number of steps required to complete the coding process varies with the research method used and the amount of raw data, but qualitative coding commonly utilizes three or four steps.

The multidisciplinary approach of this book embraces and encourages the differences between various qualitative methods, but it also recognizes core similarities. No attempt is made to blend or homogenize different qualitative methods into a single method, nor is there an attempt to resolve all of the differences in terminology.

Qualitative coding Levels 1, 2, and 3 are descriptive terms to **broadly** represent core procedures used by the major qualitative research methods. These levels of coding do not precisely correspond with any existing method, but experienced researchers should be able to see the parallels between the coding levels described in this book and the coding steps in their preferred method. I encourage you to creatively use the *concepts* presented in this book and adapt them to your research needs.

Introduction to the levels of qualitative coding

Like a gold miner, the qualitative researcher sorts through large quantities of unsorted material

Like a miner panning for gold from streambed gravel, the qualitative researcher sifts through large amounts of data. The miner sees no gold when she first looks at a gold-bearing streambed, just a lot of rock, gravel, and sand. To find the gold the miner must systematically sift through piles of unsorted material to isolate the precious metal.

Like the miner, the qualitative researcher must progressively sort through mass quantities of freeform data to find answers to research questions.

The miner intelligently digs into carefully selected sites hoping to unearth nuggets hidden in unconsolidated gravel. The qualitative researcher focuses on data elements most likely to yield answers.

Qualitative coding terms

Generalized for descriptive purpose

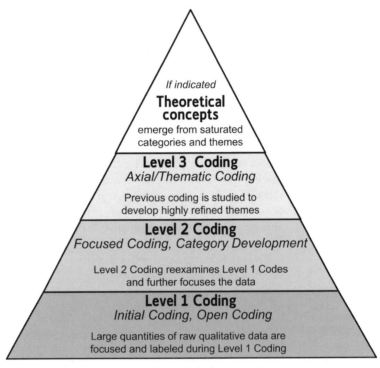

This illustration is best viewed from the bottom up as the data are progressively refined to arrive at categories, themes, and theories. The generalizations in this illustration are meant to broadly describe stages of the coding process while recognizing and upholding the vibrant differences between various qualitative methods.

Level 1 Coding

The experienced gold-panner goes through several steps to isolate precious nuggets of gold. First, large amounts of material that are obviously not gold-bearing are discarded with the shovel before the material ever makes it to the gold pan. Likewise, the first phase of qualitative coding (Level 1) is intended to significantly reduce the qualitative data to allow a more manageable focus. This first stage of coding is commonly called initial coding or open coding. A large nugget may be discovered at this early stage, but the real answers are expected to emerge later in the process.

Level 2 Coding

Once the streambed materials make it to the gold pan the miner's second step is to wash the lighter sand and gravel out of the pan (gold is heavy). The vast majority of material in the pan will be removed at this time.

Level 2 coding by the qualitative researcher starts with Level 1 codes. Level 1 coding identifies the data most likely to help answer research questions; the goal during Level 2 coding is to further refine the data. This step narrows the focus to a relatively few Level 2 codes. Level 2 coding is commonly called focused coding or category development.

Level 3 Coding

When the miner makes it to the third step she will see only a small amount of heavy black sand concentrate (mostly magnetite) at the bottom of her pan. She will look through the concentrate to occasionally find an obvious nugget, but she will not stop there. She will gently swirl the water to carefully remove the black sand, leaving only the heaviest material. Sometimes she will pick large gold flecks from the pan with a magnifying glass and tweezers.

Level 3 coding involves a very fine focus using the progressive convergence of ideas from Level 2 as the basis of inquiry. Themes are refined during Level 3 coding as ideas approach a critical density. Level 3 codes are generally refined enough to be used in reports and publications. Level 3 coding is commonly called axial coding or thematic coding.

Level 4 Coding Theoretical Development

Even though our miner was hard working, had a PhD in geology, and she used a systematic process to sift out precious gold she didn't find it necessary to develop a theory about the origin of gold deposits. She was happy to experience the phenomenon of finding gold; she did it well, and she grew rich.

Our miner's colleague, also with a PhD in geology, had a different philosophical orientation. He was less interested in experiencing the phenomenon of mining gold and more interested in developing a theory about the origin of gold deposits. Like this geologist, many qualitative researchers are interested in creating theories from the data they analyze. A final level of coding-related activity is necessary to ground qualitative theories in data that was originally unconsolidated.

Although not used by all qualitative methods, theoretical development reexamines previously discovered categories and themes, to explore, delineate, and develop themes that are so focused that they emerge as theories. Broadly applied, this process is called theoretical sampling, selective coding, theoretical saturation, and theoretical sorting. I call this step Level 4 coding.

The qualitative researcher does not discard material like the miner

The analogy between a miner panning gold and a qualitative researcher falls short in a couple of instructive areas. Unlike the miner who dumps most of the materials that are dug from the ground, the qualitative researcher preserves all valuable raw materials in their pre-coding state. Rather than throw out the unused data, the qualitative researcher tags, labels, and copies the most valuable data, but otherwise leaves the data intact.

In this book, techniques for storing large amounts of coded data in *Access* or *Excel* teach the qualitative researcher how to organize and store data for easy retrieval. By preserving the original data, while storing only selected data snippets in a database, the researcher can reexamine the data in situ if that is necessary to reevaluate and validate emerging themes.

> Choose the method that works best for your project

As mentioned earlier, this book endorses the use of the many fine qualitative research methods books that guide students and researchers through research problems on a level that is beyond the scope of this book. This book focuses on organizational and technological tips that are intended to support, rather than replace, existing research methods. Existing qualitative research methods frame the theoretical and methodological aspects of the research project; this book is a supplemental toolkit.

> The terminology:
> Level 1
> Level 2
> Level 3
> Level 4
> (theoretical concepts)

The coding terms used in this book are presented to make this book terminology-neutral for all qualitative researchers, regardless of their preferred research method. The terms (Levels 1, 2, 3, and 4) are not intended to replace the terms commonly used by established methods.

Throughout the book I refer to Level 4 coding as 'theoretical concept development.' This was done to provide a mental end game for the many qualitative researchers who are interested in developing theory.

I know that many other qualitative researchers are more interested in the exploration of phenomena than the development of theory. My apologies to all of you who fit into this category. Please substitute 'Level 4' for 'theoretical concept' as you progress through the iterative stages of data exploration.

The big picture – how this book can help you

> Piles and files of data can quickly lead to chaos if they are not intelligently managed. Disorganization gobbles time and degrades quality. Your research will produce better results if you carefully plan, organize, and control the project and its data.

Step 1: Invest planning and organizing time now to save a lot more time later

Any sizable qualitative research project generates reams of field notes, interview transcripts loaded with important quotations, and/or other text-based information. Qualitative projects might also involve artwork, artifacts, and other physical items.

All of these data that are critical to your success may be in computer files, on paper documents, in file cabinets, boxes, drawers, garages, and on the floor. This book helps you to develop your own system of organization. You are in charge of this process, so your files, papers, and objects will be stored in a system that works for your brain using the techniques that help you develop personalized data storage needs and opportunities. In the following chapters you will learn tips about the organization of data.

Step 2: Use available technology to improve coding and data analysis

Once your data have been efficiently stored you will need to analyze them to glean the answers to your research questions. This is when you will start to *really* appreciate the time and thought you put into your organizational system.

During the data analysis process you identify the most important snippets of your data as you code your text-based data. Different qualitative research methods have different approaches to data coding, but the basic principles are the same – the researcher must separate the wheat from the chaff. The most important information and physical objects must be identified, described, and labeled for future reference.

The first coding pass through your text data is a relatively fast-moving process. In the past many researchers printed their raw data and physically coded the transcripts and field notes. This book explains how to complete your initial/open coding *much* more efficiently in your word processor.

133.		What are the factors that allowed joint custody to work for you?
134.	*Being flexible* *Being forgiving* Being respectful	*Flexibility, forgiveness – of him and myself – keeping the kids as a priority and realizing it needs to be about them. And I think respect.* You have to be able to have some respect…Pete was never out there going through a midlife crisis making an ass out of himself with some goofy hairdo and clothes and a gold chain and being an embarrassment with some bimbo on his arm…so I wasn't having to sit at a program with him with some trophy girl thinking "what is he doing?" He's dated some pretty respectable people that if he's had somebody with him, they've been just fine. So that really helps because that helps you respect the other person, that they're working hard in life and a good citizen of America [laughing]

Original transcript/field note/object description data are retained in the right column; Level 1 codes and memos relating to the raw data are identified in the left columns of a specially formatted *Word* document.

Coding and theory development can move quickly but it should not be rushed. The mechanical procedure of coding is relatively easy because of the power of *Word*, *Excel*, and *Access*.

The illustration below shows a typical *Access* database record that has gone through the complete coding process. (If you choose to use *Excel* instead of *Access* for your advanced coding the data will be the same but the interface will be different.)

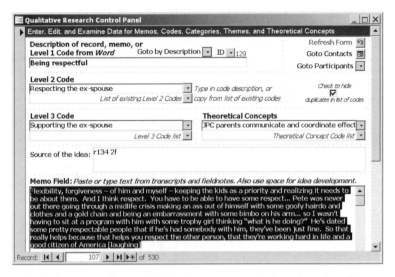

Each database record stores all code descriptions and selected text from the transcripts/field notes that correspond to the codes.

This book takes you through the creation of your *Access* or your *Excel* database in great detail. **I assume that you know nothing about databases,** so don't be scared by the word 'database.' Full *Excel* instructions are provided in Chapter 8.

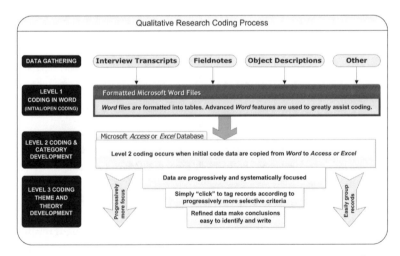

Intelligent use of *Word, Access,* and *Excel* can save the qualitative researcher an enormous amount of time and effort.

Step 3: Your data are at your fingertips when you write your results, conclusions and recommendations

At last, when it is time to write the final report, your most important data are at your fingertips and organized at all code levels. Writing the final report with data organized this well is enjoyable and efficient.

You will be able to paste your most important data (quotations, memos, object descriptions, and/or field notes) into your final report directly from *Access* or *Excel*. There is no need to leaf through individual word processing or paper files.

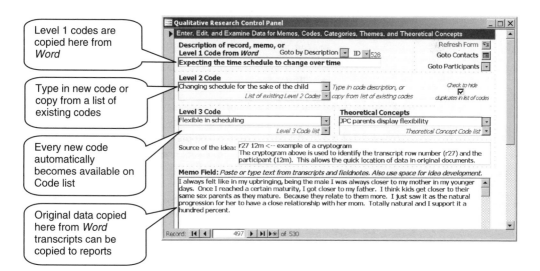

Level 1 codes are copied here from *Word*

Type in new code or copy from a list of existing codes

Every new code automatically becomes available on Code list

Original data copied here from *Word* transcripts can be copied to reports

Each Level 1 code record is associated with progressively more refined categories, themes, and theoretical concepts as the researcher proceeds through the coding levels.

When you write your report:

1. The results and conclusion sections gain a natural outline. Your most refined Level 3 codes and theoretical concepts serve as section headings. Level 3 codes almost always contribute data directly to the final report. Report writing is a relatively quick and efficient process.
2. With only a click or two of your mouse you can view all data that are associated with any given code, category, theme or concept. This allows a single-screen review of all the data (quotations, field note comments, etc.) associated with any code.
3. You will have all of the most important text data (quotations, field notes, object descriptions, etc.) at your fingertips. Quickly query and scroll through your choices, then copy and paste the most relevant data directly to your report

Level 1 Code	Coordinating parenting behaviors
Text Data from **transcript / *Word***	one of the reasons it has continued to work because when one person is willing - myself - and he may say this about me, I don't know this is just how I feel - has been willing to say ok we've got to be on one page - so we'll let it be your page. Cause I think it is important that parents whether they are together or divorced be pretty much on the same page.

Level 1 Code	Coordinating parenting behaviors
Text Data from **transcript / *Word***	the kids understand that both parents are on board all of the time and that they come first, and that other adult issues that we have going on come second.

Level 1 Code	Coordinating parenting behaviors
Text Data from **transcript / *Word***	Recognize that discipline, parenting is going to be shared, and you may by virtue of the divorce and joint custody not have a monolithic approach to parenting. Even if you discuss it with that person, it may not be monolithic in how it's approached. She may, by the virtue of the way she parents, who she is, and I may by virtue of who I am, may approach one particular context in a different way.

Data can be sorted and viewed in many convenient ways at any coding level using *Access* queries or *Excel* sorting. This illustration shows three quotations (of many) associated with the Level 1 code 'Coordinating parenting behaviors.' Data needed for a report/publication can be quickly reviewed, and then copied to the report.

from *Access* or *Excel*. There is no need to revisit the raw data files unless you want to reexamine the context of the data. It is amazing how fast report writing can be.

Microsoft Windows® and Microsoft Office® are helpful but not essential

Most of the ideas presented in this book can be developed and accomplished without any particular brand of hardware or software. For example, the formatting of interview transcripts to improve the effectiveness of coding can be accomplished in *WordPerfect*® or other full-featured word processing programs. *Word* is not required to get the job done. However, all of the examples are presented using *Word* commands and feature names.

Likewise, other database and spreadsheet programs can be used to execute the concepts described in this book. Determined and experienced software users will be able to adapt the ideas presented in this book to their research projects despite the lack of exact step-by-step instructions.

Virtually all of the commands illustrated in the book can be executed with any version of Microsoft® *Office* (*Office*). The examples in this book use the exact commands of *Office* 2003 and the Windows® XP operating system. These commands may be similar in other versions, but the reader should be aware of possible differences between versions.

You don't have to be a technology wizard

The tips in this book vary in their degree of technical difficulty. It is assumed that the vast majority of readers of the book are interested in getting the job done with a bare minimum of technical aggressiveness. For that reason detailed mission-critical commands are explicitly included in the body of the text. If you are a more advanced user you may be able to skip many of these detailed instructions.

If you are a raw beginner with the Microsoft *Office* programs, the Appendix introduces Microsoft *Office* Basics.

Microsoft *Office* basics are in the Appendix

Refer to the Appendix for Microsoft *Office* basics

Go to the Appendix to get basic help with fundamental Microsoft *Office* issues. The Appendix introduces *Word* basics, *Excel* basics, and *Outlook* basics. *Access* basics are included in Chapter 7.

Even though this book is written for non-aggressive computer users, a basic level of computer skill is assumed. This book is **not** a basic reference for Windows, *Word*, *Excel*, or *Access*. It is strongly recommended that early-stage readers purchase supplemental basic reference books, as needed, to augment this book.

The presentation of software commands

Main Menu

Edit   View   Insert   Format

⤺ Undo Typing   Ctrl+Z
↻ Repeat Typing   Ctrl+Y
✄ Cut   Ctrl+X
▣ Copy   Ctrl+C
▣ Office Clipboard...
▣ Paste   Ctrl+V

Second Level Menu

The *main menus* in Microsoft programs are quite uniform in their structure. After being selected (clicked on) the menu commands drop down below the main menu item displaying a new list of second level choices.

The picture to the left shows second level menu commands such as 'Undo Typing' and 'Repeat Typing.' Clickable menu command sequences are always shown in the same way in this book.

Main menu command ▶ Second level command.

For example, to copy selected data in an *Office* program you first click on 'Edit' from the main menu, and then you click on the second level menu command 'Copy.' This command sequence is summarized as Edit ▶ Copy.

Keyboard shortcuts

An often overlooked feature of Microsoft *Office* programs is their use of *keyboard shortcuts*. **These shortcuts save a lot of time when commands are repeated frequently**. Keyboard shortcuts require you to press two or more keys simultaneously. The shortcut keys are joined together by the plus sign (+).

To continue the example above, the keyboard shortcut for copying selected text requires you to press the 'Ctrl' and the 'C' keys simultaneously.

This is shown as Ctrl+C. When a menu command is illustrated that also has a helpful keyboard shortcut, the shortcut is shown in parentheses immediately after the menu command. The command for copying text to the clipboard is shown as Edit ► Copy (Ctrl+C). Sometimes, for frequently used commands only the keyboard shortcut is shown.

A third way to execute many often-repeated commands is to click on *toolbar* buttons. Many commands can be activated by clicking on the small button icons that were designed by Microsoft to represent the action to be performed.

The toolbar icon that executes the Edit ► Copy command is ▢. When an important command is used in this book that has menu selections, keyboard shortcuts, and toolbar icons all three methods of executing the command are often shown.

All three command techniques do exactly the same thing. Use the method that works best for you.

If you are technically aggressive

While most of the readers of this book are not assumed to be technically aggressive, I know that some readers are advanced. I fondly refer to these people as propellerheads. Some propellerheads will want to extend the ideas in this book through form customization, macros, and VBA programming.

When I include technically advanced material I will mark it with a propellerhead icon. The propellerhead symbol is included primarily as an anti-frustration device for non-propellerheads.

If you are feeling overwhelmed by software commands I recommend that you skip propellerhead material. Those of you who are not technically aggressive will be able to fully utilize the topics in the book without using advanced material.

All good qualitative researchers need to be thinkers

Pay particular attention to sections of the book that are marked by a big exclamation point. Skipping these sections could cause you to miss out on important topics that may be foundational to your understating of critical tasks and procedures.

Qualitative researchers do not rely on numbers and statistical programs to generate results, but they must think creatively and in depth. During your research process there will be times when you need to let ideas develop and resonate. This book is intended to be a catalyst for cogitation, but you are the one who does the thinking for your project.

Topics that require deeper thought are marked with the brainstorm icon. When you get to these sections you may want to take a walk, chat with a colleague, or do whatever you do to get into a good mental zone. It is fun to be a thinker; so, go ahead and have some fun!

Chapter summary

Even though their specific research methods may be different, all qualitative researchers face similar research challenges. All research projects must be planned, organized, and the data must be intelligently analyzed. The techniques in this book are not meant to supplant other research methods; they apply to researchers using grounded theory, ethnography, case studies, phenomenology, focus groups, action research, and/or creative mixed methods.

Qualitative researchers collect relatively free-form data through interviews, field notes, direct observations, public documents, records, artifacts, and pictures. These data are stored in cabinets full of objects and on hundreds (or thousands) of pages of text on a computer's hard drive. It is not easy to organize these data, but orderliness is vital to the successful completion of the research project.

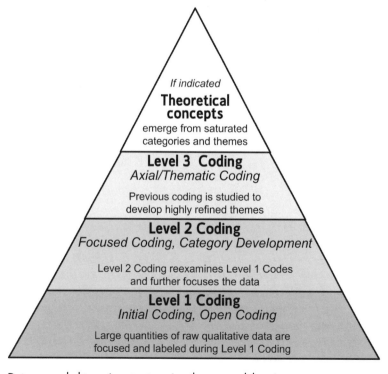

If indicated
Theoretical concepts
emerge from saturated categories and themes

Level 3 Coding
Axial/Thematic Coding

Previous coding is studied to develop highly refined themes

Level 2 Coding
Focused Coding, Category Development

Level 2 Coding reexamines Level 1 Codes and further focuses the data

Level 1 Coding
Initial Coding, Open Coding

Large quantities of raw qualitative data are focused and labeled during Level 1 Coding

Data are coded to arrive at categories, themes, and theories.

After transcribing text data, including field notes, recordings from interviews, public documents, and descriptions of physical objects, the data are formatted for coding in Microsoft *Word*. Level 1 coding takes place in *Word*. Level 2, 3, and 4 coding procedures are done in either *Access* or *Excel*. These successive levels of coding provide researchers with documented and well-organized answers to research questions. The coding results can be efficiently integrated into the final report.

After coding is completed, the conclusions of the study are apparent and the data are well organized. The final report can be written efficiently using the refined codes and the easily accessible primary data.

CHAPTER 2

Getting started – Planning your qualitative research project

Alice: *Would you tell me, please, which way I ought to go from here?*
The Cheshire Cat: *That depends a good deal on where you want to get to.*
Alice: *I don't much care where.*
The Cheshire Cat: *Then it doesn't much matter which way you go.*
Alice: *... so long as I get somewhere.*
The Cheshire Cat: *Oh, you're sure to do that, if only you walk long enough.*

From *Alice in Wonderland*

Presumably you have a better sense of direction than Alice. A long and winding road may be a romantic notion, but is not recommended for researchers who want to finish on time with a quality product. You probably have a good idea of when you want to finish your paper, article, thesis, or dissertation; and you have at least a general idea about your topic and research method. General ideas are enough to get you started, but those ideas must be fully developed by planning, organizing, and controlling the details of your project.

Develop your unique planning system

A successful research project requires careful planning. To get the project done on time and within the available budget it is important to think through the essential resources and tasks. If you leap into action on a research project without foresight you may end up wasting a lot of time by running into impasses that could have been avoided with adequate planning.

What could derail a research project? Lack of time, not enough money, the inability to recruit participants, travel restrictions to politically sensitive areas, failure to secure Institutional Review Board (IRB) approval, and many more things.

The most important tool during the planning stage is your brain. You must challenge yourself to mentally probe all elements of your project. The following sections explore topics to be considered as you ponder your upcoming research. Helpful tools are discussed, but there is no substitute for your own power of critical thinking.

Pen and paper

At the early planning stage a low-tech tool is often my preferred instrument – a simple notepad and pencil. Put your ideas on paper. Scribble your goals, a timeline, the amount of money you might need, sources of funds, possible roadblocks, and friendly allies. If you wake up in the middle of the night with a compelling thought, by all means, write it down in the middle of the night. Pencil and paper (or whiteboard and marker) may be all that you need to complete your project planning, particularly in relatively simple research settings.

Project management software

At the other end of the spectrum from pen and paper are comprehensive software tools that add professional power to project management. Project management software is for really big projects. Project management software programs can be employed to help keep the project team on time and on budget. These programs have not been reviewed for this book, but they are recommended for research projects that employ many researchers or multiple teams. For the most part, project management software is mature, tested, and effective. Microsoft offers a project management package as a part of the *Office* suite called *Project*, but this is just one of many desktop and Web-based project management packages. Spend time reviewing the features and benefits of project management software if your project is big enough to justify this type of software tool.

Outlook and Tasks

If you are working on a research project that is not big enough for project management software, but is too cumbersome for pen and paper, Microsoft *Outlook* (part of the *Office* suite) has an easy-to-use tool for organizing the planning process. *Outlook*'s project planning tool is simply called *Tasks*. **The *Tasks* module within *Outlook* allows you to set start dates, due dates, priorities, completion status, and reminders.**

At its simplest level, as shown in the illustration below, *Tasks* allows you to create a to-do list with active timelines. Start dates and due dates in *Tasks* can be viewed in several ways, and when a previously scheduled task comes due, *Outlook* will remind you with a sound and a pop-up message.

Tasks is an integrated program that allows the researcher to create simple or richly detailed project schedules. *Outlook* prompts the researcher with reminders when critical dates and times arrive.

● Task Timeline   By clicking in the 'Task Timeline' radio button the sample *Tasks* list shown above is transformed into a graphic timeline that can help you visualize the timing of your project.

Thu 30	Fri 1	Sat 2	Sun 3	Mon 4	Tue 5	Wed 6	Thu 7

_2 Establish Timeline Goals   _4. Select Research Method

_1 Start Research Project

_3. Review Research Methods

The Task Timeline is a visual aid to the management of a research project.

For instructions on starting *Outlook* refer to the Appendix

Opening *Tasks*
Go ► Tasks
(Ctrl+4)

Tasks is integrated into *Outlook*; therefore, to access the *Tasks* program you must first start *Outlook*. If you use *Outlook* for your e-mail client start *Outlook* the same way you start it when you check your e-mail. If you don't know how to start *Outlook* refer to the Appendix.

Now that *Outlook* is running it is time to start *Tasks*. This is done from the *Outlook* main menu. Click Go ► Tasks 🗓 Tasks   Ctrl+4

Once open, *Tasks* data can be entered and edited directly in the *Tasks* pane, or in the *Tasks* data entry screen. Both of these methods are illustrated below.

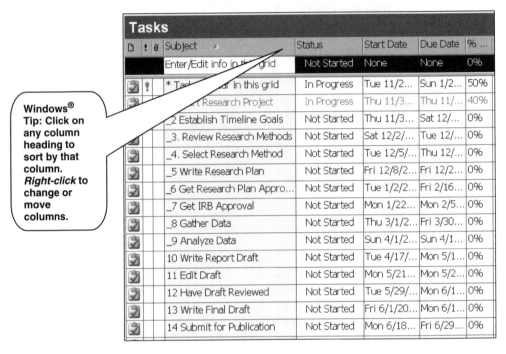

Windows® Tip: Click on any column heading to sort by that column. *Right-click* to change or move columns.

D	!	0	Subject ▲	Status	Start Date	Due Date	% ...
			Enter/Edit info in this grid	Not Started	None	None	0%
🗐	!		* Task in this grid	In Progress	Tue 11/2...	Sun 1/2...	50%
🗐			Research Project	In Progress	Thu 11/3...	Thu 11/...	40%
🗐			_2 Establish Timeline Goals	Not Started	Thu 11/3...	Sat 12/...	0%
🗐			_3. Review Research Methods	Not Started	Sat 12/2/...	Tue 12/...	0%
🗐			_4. Select Research Method	Not Started	Tue 12/5/...	Thu 12/...	0%
🗐			_5 Write Research Plan	Not Started	Fri 12/8/2...	Fri 12/2...	0%
🗐			_6 Get Research Plan Appro...	Not Started	Tue 1/2/2...	Fri 2/16...	0%
🗐			_7 Get IRB Approval	Not Started	Mon 1/22...	Mon 2/5...	0%
🗐			_8 Gather Data	Not Started	Thu 3/1/2...	Fri 3/30...	0%
🗐			_9 Analyze Data	Not Started	Sun 4/1/2...	Sun 4/1...	0%
🗐			10 Write Report Draft	Not Started	Tue 4/17/...	Mon 5/1...	0%
🗐			11 Edit Draft	Not Started	Mon 5/21...	Mon 5/2...	0%
🗐			12 Have Draft Reviewed	Not Started	Tue 5/29/...	Mon 6/1...	0%
🗐			13 Write Final Draft	Not Started	Fri 6/1/20...	Mon 6/1...	0%
🗐			14 Submit for Publication	Not Started	Mon 6/18...	Fri 6/29...	0%

Scheduling information can be entered directly into the Tasks list.

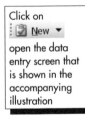

Click on
🗐 **New** ▾
open the data entry screen that is shown in the accompanying illustration

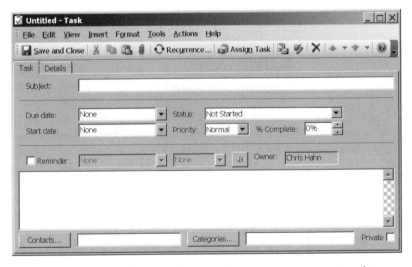

Task information can also be entered into the *Tasks* data entry screen. Start this screen by clicking N̲ew on the *Tasks* toolbar.

Tasks, pen and paper, whiteboard, and project management software are all effective planning tools. **Choose the planning tool that works best for your personal style and put it to use.** The last thing you want is to discover a serious and unforeseen obstacle three-quarters of the way through your research project that might have been preventable. Often these obstacles can be avoided if they are identified during the early planning process.

If you need further help with the nuts and bolts of the *Tasks* feature of *Outlook* it is recommended that you explore Microsoft's Help system or consult a reference book that focuses on *Outlook* or *Office.*

I encourage you to get used to using the Microsoft Help system. It will get you out of a lot of jams. From within *Outlook* press F1 or click on Help from the main menu. In the 'Search For' box type a word or phrase that sums up your dilemma. Keep trying if you do not get the results you want after your first try. Sometimes you have to be persistent and inventive.

> Press the F1 key or click on <u>H</u>elp from the menu to access Microsoft's Help System

Excel *as a planning tool*

Microsoft *Excel* is a powerhouse program that can be used in many different ways. For an introduction to *Excel* refer to the Appendix.

> *Excel* as a planning tool

A well-organized grid (rows and columns) can help make sense of complicated data. A collection of grids that we all learned to rely on at an early age was the trusty paper calendar. A calendar allows us to make sense of a jumble of 365 days by providing us with an easy to follow structure. Each week has its own row, each day of the week has its own column, and each month has its own page.

At its most basic level, an *Excel* worksheet is like a monthly calendar page. It is a single-page view of rows and columns. When the twelve monthly pages are combined we get a full annual calendar. Likewise multiple *Excel* worksheets can be combined to create something more comprehensive. The combination of worksheets is called a workbook.

Unlike a paper calendar, an *Excel* workbook is phenomenally adaptable, interconnected, editable, and expandable. The *Excel* template shown below is an example of how a spreadsheet can be used to help with the planning of your research project. This template is available for download at qrtips.com/chapter1.

One of the advantages of using *Excel* as a planning tool is its relative ease of use and its versatility. *Excel* can be configured to suit unique situations, limited only by your imagination. You are encouraged to take these incubator ideas and produce a planning tool that is meaningful to your project.

Change columns to suit your unique needs

Insert new rows as tasks are identified

Like monthly pages in a calendar, use worksheets to hold related planning information

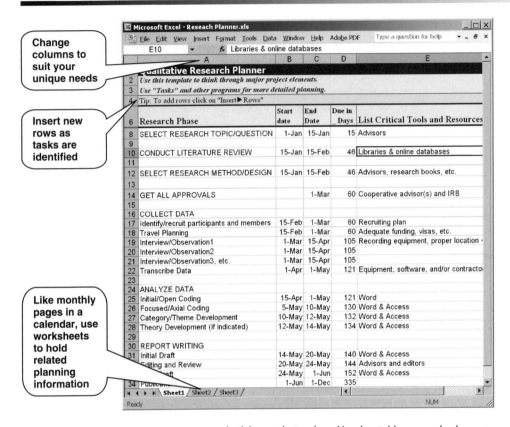

Research Phase	Start date	End Date	Due in Days	List Critical Tools and Resources
SELECT RESEARCH TOPIC/QUESTION	1-Jan	15-Jan	15	Advisors
CONDUCT LITERATURE REVIEW	15-Jan	15-Feb	46	Libraries & online databases
SELECT RESEARCH METHOD/DESIGN	15-Jan	15-Feb	46	Advisors, research books, etc.
GET ALL APPROVALS		1-Mar	60	Cooperative advisor(s) and IRB
COLLECT DATA				
Identify/recruit participants and members	15-Feb	1-Mar	60	Recruiting plan
Travel Planning	15-Feb	1-Mar	60	Adequate funding, visas, etc.
Interview/Observation1	1-Mar	15-Apr	105	Recording equipment, proper location -
Interview/Observation2	1-Mar	15-Apr	105	
Interview/Observation3, etc.	1-Mar	15-Apr	105	
Transcribe Data	1-Apr	1-May	121	Equipment, software, and/or contracto
ANALYZE DATA				
Initial/Open Coding	15-Apr	1-May	121	Word
Focused/Axial Coding	5-May	10-May	130	Word & Access
Category/Theme Development	10-May	12-May	132	Word & Access
Theory Development (if indicated)	12-May	14-May	134	Word & Access
REPORT WRITING				
Initial Draft	14-May	20-May	140	Word & Access
Editing and Review	20-May	24-May	144	Advisors and editors
...aft	24-May	1-Jun	152	Word & Access
Publica...	1-Jun	1-Dec	335	

Be creative in your scheduling with *Excel* workbooks. Add rows and columns to accommodate your planning needs.

Take time to think

You cannot optimize the tasks on your critical path if you do not take the time to think through the details. Through careful planning you can identify and accommodate actions that require priority.

All major elements of the research project, from the beginning to the end, must be visualized as well as possible. You can avoid unnecessary delays that might jeopardize the quality and even the completion of your project by taking the time to plan carefully.

The planning tool you use is up to you

The best planning system is one that you will use. The tools can be as simple as pen and paper; or you can track your thoughts in *Tasks*, *Word*, or *Excel*, or project management software: the choice is yours. Think things through, explore ideas, and then get started with your organized planning.

Steps in constructing your plan

After you have selected your planning tool it is time to build the plan. As you read through the sections below record your thoughts in the planning system you selected. Be sure to record the estimated time each task will take and a description of that task. Of course, your guesses about the time required will not be perfect. Don't let that stop you from trying to estimate the order of magnitude of the major tasks in your research project.

As you are thinking through all of the things that must be completed between the start and finish of your project, you may feel overwhelmed. Remember the story of the tortoise and the hare – keep going one step at a time and you will eventually finish.

It is important to prioritize your tasks to insure efficient progress. The most critical tasks must be identified and given special attention.

Think of the critical path as you plan your project

What is a *critical path*? Professional project managers utilize the Critical Path Method (CPM) to get their jobs done on time and to avoid unnecessary delays. Researchers can also use CPM's basic tenets to avoid scheduling pitfalls.

Sizable projects consist of many tasks. Sometimes tasks can be done in parallel, but other assemblies of tasks must be done sequentially. These assemblages of tasks are 'paths' that must be followed. That is, one task must be completed before the next task is started. Of all paths, the critical path is the assemblage of tasks that will delay the *entire project* if it is not completed on schedule. The following example will introduce CPM concepts.

Suppose you are going to do an ethnographic study of an isolated village in Nepal. The observations must be at least six months in duration to be considered valid. Because of visa stipulations, high-altitude weather, and the trekking distance from Katmandu this village is accessible to you for only six months of every year. You must arrive and leave on fixed dates.

The whole project will be compromised or delayed for an entire year if you don't get to the village on time because your project's validity depends on a full six-month data set. You cannot afford to make travel mistakes because of the consequences of travel delays; therefore, the critical path for the Nepal research project involves successful travel planning and execution.

If you do not think through 'critical path tasks' in your initial planning process you may spend ill-advised time on less critical activities. In this example, you cannot afford delays with your visa application or on-the-ground trekking arrangements in Nepal. Your entire project is at risk if your visa is delayed for a month, or if you have to spend an extra two weeks in Katmandu looking for equipment, supplies, or a guide.

Stepping outside the example, what are the critical path items for your research project? Think about committee approvals, IRB reviews, completing grant applications, and the logistics of your data collection.

Look for those tasks that will hold up the entire project if they take too long. Once you identify your critical path tasks give them the high priority they deserve.

If you are interested in learning more about CPM a search of the Web will yield a wealth of CPM information.

Create a written research plan

As you think through the foundational elements of your research project make notes and write memos about your planning ideas. Eventually, the research plan should be compiled into a single document that outlines the entire project.

If a research plan is required in an academic setting, for a grant, or in a corporation it is likely that a pre-specified format will be required for the research plan. If no specific format is required you can put together an informal seven-part research plan by creating a document from the thoughts that are generated as you think through Planning Ideas 1 through 7.

Planning Idea 1: Fine tune your research topic and research questions

Your project hinges on your research topic and your research questions. What is it that you want your research to accomplish? Without a clear goal your whole research project is likely to be fuzzy.

Why is it so important for you to fine tune every word of your topic and accompanying research questions? A poorly framed topic leads to sloppy questions that allow you to go down the wrong path when you plan and execute the research project because **research questions often determine the research method that is best suited for the study.**

The research question can dictate the research method

Throughout this book I provide examples from a study that I did relating to the attitudes and behaviors of parents who maintained long-term successful joint physical custodies after separation or divorce.

Initially I planned to use quantitative methods to conduct the research. I have a background in the hard sciences and I am a computer programmer. I like to work with statistics and quantitative methods.

At the early planning stages of the study I looked at the possibility of finding a large randomly sampled population of subjects that matched my selection criteria (a quantitative requirement). It soon became obvious that population sampling was my first roadblock. As it turns out, relatively few parents have maintained continuous joint physical custodies for at least five years, and it is difficult to randomly identify these individuals because access is generally through confidential sources like teachers, lawyers, and counselors.

My second quantitative roadblock was in the development of a solid set of hypotheses to test. While there were lots of studies that compared different types of custodies, there was a dearth of empirical studies that examined the inner workings of joint physical custodies. This made it difficult for me to adopt rational hypotheses to test based on existing studies.

Since I had major problems with my sample population and my testable hypotheses it was time for me to change the research topic or to consider qualitative methods. I chose to do the latter.

After I switched the study from quantitative to qualitative it was necessary to select the type of qualitative method to employ. To help me focus my thinking I refined the primary research question to 'How do parents successfully maintain long-term joint physical custodies?' Then I sampled the resources that were available to me.

After a sustained effort I identified and recruited 12 cases that met the selection criteria – long-term shared custody dual-home families where both parents agreed to participate in the study. But what analytic technique would I use?

Once again, I had to do some thinking. How did I want the end results to be presented? Did I want to study the phenomena related to the lived experience of parents maintaining joint physical custodies? Or did I want to create theory about what it takes to maintain joint physical custodies? I decided that I wanted the end result to be a set of hypotheses (theories) relating to the characteristics of the parents who were able to successfully maintain joint physical custodies. For the study I ended up using multiple cases to gather the data through interviews that were recorded, transcribed, and then analyzed using grounded theory methodology.

The point of this example is to illustrate the way in which the research topic and research questions dictate the fundamental approach of the research project. So, take time with your thinking process in the early stages. Focus on what you want your study to accomplish and the questions that you want it to answer.

If you are not able to precisely write down your topic then take it to the next level. Work with your advisors and associates to refine your ideas; expand your review of the literature; keep writing and rewriting your topic and questions. Work until you are satisfied with your research questions.

Planning Idea 2: A review of the existing literature can take time

Researchers want their work to add to the body of knowledge; therefore, it is incumbent on them to understand existing studies that relate to the proposed research topic. By venturing into libraries and probing on-line scholarly databases like ProQuest, LexisNexis, and EBSCOhost you will be able to frame your study within the existing body of published knowledge.

During the planning stage it is important to budget time for the literature review process.

⇒ How long will it take to gain access to physical and on-line libraries?
⇒ How long will it take for you to find and obtain the books and articles that you need?

⇒ How will you keep track of the information you find? Note: the organization of bibliographic data is discussed in more detail in Chapter 3.
⇒ How long will it take to read the material that you obtain?
⇒ How long will it take to write the literature review section of your report, thesis, or dissertation?

Once you have answers to the questions above enter them and an accompanying timeline into your planning tool.

Planning Idea 3: Choose the primary research method

It is a good idea to start thinking about your research method at the earliest stage of your project and to continue this thought process throughout your literature review, but the most serious research method decision making should be conducted after your topic and research questions are in place. To help you tackle the problem you will want to ask: How have other scholars approached problems similar to mine? What will be my technique for gathering data? How will I store the data? How will the data be coded and analyzed?

Data accumulates in the course of all qualitative research, sometimes at astonishing rates. But what qualitative research method should you use? Action research, case studies, ethnography, grounded theory, phenomenology, and creative mixed methods all have their strengths.

One significant consideration relates to how you will gather your data. Your plan must accommodate the tools, methodologies, and time requirements of the data collection techniques that are appropriate for your project. The strategies used to collect and analyze data vary according to the epistemological approach of the researcher.

Another consideration in the selection of your research method is the desired output of your study. What do you want the study to accomplish? Do you want to create theory? Do you want to identify participant preferences? Do you want to study phenomena? How do you want to characterize your study's participant populations? What research method best allows you to answer your research questions?

You may need to devote a considerable amount of time to reading books and articles about action research, case studies, ethnography, grounded theory, and/or phenomenology. Seek out talks with advisors and brainstorming sessions with colleagues. **Most of all, allocate time to think.** How long will it take you to choose your research method? Record this estimated time in your planning tool.

Planning Idea 4: Think through data-gathering strategies

The techniques used in qualitative research to gather data vary significantly, and gathering qualitative data can be the most time-consuming part of your research project. Will you be interviewing participants, observing native cultures, organizing focus groups, collecting data from existing documents, gathering artifacts, or something else?

The following list provides a brief overview of major types of data collected by qualitative researchers.

- in-depth/unstructured interviews
- semi-structured interviews
- structured interview questionnaires containing substantial numbers of open comments
- focus groups
- unstructured or semi-structured diaries
- action-oriented participation with the group being studied
- participant observation field notes
- technical fieldwork notes
- kinship diagrams, other anthropological material, and written descriptions of physical objects
- case study observation, participation, and notes
- minutes of meetings
- personal documents (e.g. letters, personal diaries, correspondence)
- press clippings
- photographs or any other type of visual material
- artifacts and physical objects
- written descriptions of artifacts, photographs, and other objects

Will travel be required for the collection of data? What voice and video recording equipment do you need? How much money is required? How can you gather your data without adversely impacting the results? Do you need to recruit co-researchers? How will you control the quality of your data if it is gathered by multiple researchers?

These, and other, questions must be explored as you plan the data-collection phase of your project. The detailed methodology that you use is very important! Your project will gain credibility if you follow and reference respected research methods. Review and read the leading research methods books related to your preferred approach. You are encouraged to be creative, but base that creativity on the experience of the scholars who took the time to write books and articles to pass along their knowledge.

Once you have a good idea of your data-collection techniques and you are able to estimate the amount of time it will take, enter those estimates in your project planning tool.

Planning Idea 5: Allocate time to analyze and process your data (if you are in a hurry, switch to a quantitative study)

Regardless of the method you choose, all qualitative research projects face similar data and time challenges. As a rule, qualitative research projects take more time than quantitative research projects. In part, because qualitative research projects accumulate a *lot* of data.

Qualitative data are richly complex. They are full of subtle nuances that allow the researcher to discover unexpected aspects of the lived experiences of constituents in their study. If the data were gathered intelligently, the answers being sought by the researcher will be waiting to be uncovered in the data. But, again, the data are complex.

Qualitative studies are not designed to produce statistically significant results; therefore, qualitative researchers are not limited by quantitative rules such as a large sample size, random sampling, defining a study by preconceived hypotheses, and using rigidly tested sampling instruments. Instead, qualitative techniques allow the researcher to poke into dimensions of discovery in ways that would not be allowable for quantitative researchers. In surprising ways great results can be extracted from piles of seemingly amorphous information through the process of qualitative coding. (Chapters 6 through 9 address the analytic process.)

The bad news is that qualitative data can appear at first glance to be daunting because of the piles of unstructured information. The data must be examined word-by-word, sentence-by-sentence, item-by-item and page-by-page. At each stage the researcher's observations, ideas, and thematic concepts must be recorded with the data, and in a memo format that can be easily recalled. This takes time!

My goal here is not to scare you; it is to let you know that you need to budget adequate time to complete the collection and analysis of your quantitative data. How can the qualitative researcher work through his or her data to produce valid results that are scientifically (although not statistically) significant? How can the qualitative researcher work through the mounds of data in a reasonable period of time? The answer lies in the organized reduction and focusing of qualitative data.

Invest in time to organize

The time you spend organizing is time well spent because it significantly accelerates the analysis phase of research. It is a big mistake to think that you are too busy to take time to organize. If you charge ahead – constantly creating and analyzing more data, but not maintaining your research system – you will create a real mess. That mess will almost certainly result in time-wasting inefficiencies. **One of the best investments you make may be the investment of the time it takes to keep your project organized.** (Chapter 3 discusses the organization of data in detail.)

After thinking through your data analysis techniques and the time it will take to keep your data organized, enter the related tasks and timelines into your planning tool.

Planning Idea 6: Budget time to write the report and get it published

Writing and reviewing the final report takes time. How many total pages do you expect? What tables must be prepared? What figures and illustrations must be created? Are you working with other researchers who will be co–writing the report? Do you need information from others before you can finish the report?

Think through these questions and try to think of others that will influence the amount of time it will take to complete the final draft. Enter your thoughts and timeline into your planning tool.

Planning Idea 7: Finally, go back and budget extra time for each step that requires approvals

Do you have a professor, an advisor, boss, or committee that needs to approve your research plan? If so you must allocate time to allow these people to read and comment on your plan. Are you working with human participants? If so it is likely that you will have to get approvals from your IRB. It is likely that your IRB is more removed and less accessible than your advisor or committee; therefore, the time it will take for them to get back to you may be less predictable. Delays related to approvals can be frustrating, but they are even more maddening if you don't budget time for these delays.

Unless you are really exceptional (and I hope you are) there is a good chance that revisions to your plan will be required by reviewers. Factor in time for these revisions.

Even though many universities and institutions set deadlines for reviewers, the delays imposed by approvals are often unpredictable. This uncertainty can be built into your project schedule by allocating a broad range of time for items that need third party review and approval.

> **Your project does not have to grind to a halt while you wait for approvals.** There are proactive tasks that you can do to prepare for future action as soon as the approvals are granted. Keep working during the approval process. This may be by networking with people who will be important in the next phases of the project, installing and learning required new software, making travel plans, expanding the scope of your literature review, and reading books and articles that you were too busy to finish when you were writing your research plan. If you have a tight schedule you cannot afford to waste time while your approvals are in someone else's hands.

Planning Idea 8: Prepare a financial budget

Your research project could be delayed or fail if you underestimate the amount of money your project will require or the time it will take to raise the money. The *Excel* worksheet below itemizes many of the expense items that you will need to consider. Take time with each category, and add new categories that are unique to your project.

Don't try to cut corners in your financial budgeting process. Assume that things will take longer and cost more than you would like, and plan accordingly.

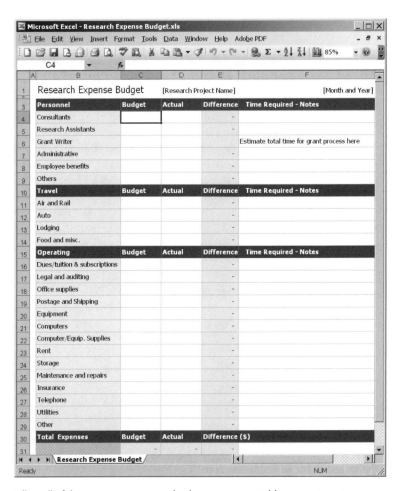

Fill in all of the categories as completely as you can. Add more categories as necessary. Enter the results in your research plan. A copy of this worksheet is available at qrtips.com.

As you think through the budget for your project, pay attention to the time it will take to raise the funds necessary to raise the money. This may be a critical path item. Enter fundraising time requirements in your project planning scheduling system.

Chapter summary

Research projects should be carefully planned and scheduled. Time spent in the early stages of the project may prevent unnecessary, perhaps critical, delays. It is not adequate to simply think about the time and resources needed to complete the project, all essential phases of the project should be written into a timeline.

Many different tools are available to the investigator as he or she produces the research plan. For simple projects a pen and paper may be adequate to record the essential steps that must be completed if the project is to be completed on time. Larger projects require more sophisticated software programs that may include *Word*, *Excel*, *Outlook*'s *Tasks* program, and/or specialized project management programs.

As the plan is developed the researcher focuses carefully on critical path tasks. These are the jobs that, if delayed, will delay the entire project. An awareness of critical path items allows the researcher to concentrate on the most time–critical tasks.

The project plan should include the researcher's best guess about the duration and expense of each major research phase including

- the development of the research topic and research questions
- the literature review
- the selection of the research method
- data gathering
- the analysis and coding of the project's data
- writing the final report, thesis, dissertation, etc.
- gaining approvals from advisors, employers, committees, institutional review boards, etc.
- the budgeting of monetary and other material resources.

When the plan is complete it should be reviewed by a third party. In some research settings the research plan is a requirement that must be fulfilled before the investigator may proceed. In these cases an advisor or supervisor will review the plan. In other cases the researcher may need to seek out reviewers. The suggestions and criticisms of reviewers should be taken seriously and plans revised accordingly. The experience of others can help the researcher avoid pitfalls during the course of a project.

CHAPTER 3

Organizing and controlling your research

> *The first rule of any technology … is that automation applied to an efficient operation will magnify the efficiency. The second is that automation applied to an inefficient operation will magnify the inefficiency.*
>
> Bill Gates

Physicists can measure entropy – the chaos, order, randomness, and disorder in a thermodynamic system. Entropy measurements are backed by fancy formulas that physicists can reliably calculate. Physicists have it easy.

A formula sounds so nice. Plug in the environmental variables, follow the rules, and out comes a reliable answer. There is plenty of chaos, order, randomness, and disorder in social and cultural systems, but scientists who study these systems do not have precise measurement formulas. The subtle nuances that create the lived experiences of humans are extraordinarily complex. Cause and effect is hard to measure because of the innumerable influences on individuals and groups. Each individual and group in the system is different because of their families, their educational experience, their culture, their social status … and the list goes on.

Like physicists studying entropy, quantitative social science investigators attempt to examine isolated variables, but in many cases this cannot be reliably done. Social scientists work in a world where the environmental variables are so overwhelming that quantitative research methods must sometimes give way to more open and unstructured investigations.

Qualitative investigators can embrace numerous unexpected variables without abandoning empirical rigor, and these efforts can pay off with startling insights. The end results of qualitative studies are not statistically significant with low p-values, but qualitative studies can deliver significant new trustworthy discoveries that help us understand and improve the human condition.

How does the qualitative researcher make sense of voluminous multi-faceted data? Despite the help provided in Chapters 6 through 9 of this book and in other texts, qualitative data will always present analytical challenges. To be dependable, qualitative studies must be backed by solid research methods and an orderly structure. Your research efforts will be more efficient and of higher quality if you carefully organize and control your work.

Through intelligent organization you will be able to quickly retrieve the pieces of paper, data, objects, and computer files that rapidly accumulate as your research gains momentum. **The last thing you want is to run into repeated delays and roadblocks that could easily have been avoided if you had better organized your project.** It takes time and energy to create an orderly system, and it is not a one-time activity. In fact, it takes routine and determined effort that can often seem boring and low in priority, *but the rewards will far exceed the effort expended.*

The tools and technologies described below allow you to move faster and think more clearly. You will no longer need to waste time shuffling memo cards, leafing through printed transcripts, or searching through disconnected computer files.

Create filing systems for everything

It drives me nuts when I lose my keys or I can't find my glasses. It is a frustrating waste of time to wander around my house to find these things that I absent-mindedly misplaced.

I may be a hopeless case with my car keys, and my propensity to let my mind wander while doing routine tasks remains a strong part of my cognitive makeup, but I organize my professional projects carefully. I simply cannot afford to waste undue time searching for misplaced items.

Organizing is work. I have to force myself to take time to reorganize *My Documents*, file my e-mails in the appropriate folders, enter reference citations into my bibliographic manager, and get the piles of paper from my desk to the file cabinet.

I admit, I am pretty good at letting internal self-talk convince me that just about any other research activity is more important than organizing. I am a filing procrastinator, but sometimes I just hit the wall. I find myself wasting time (with blood pressure rising) because the data or study that I need is lost in my needlessly disorganized system. When this happens I force myself to block out time to get things filed and organized. It usually doesn't take nearly as long as I think it will, and filing always increases my efficiency.

Take time to review the tools and procedures presented in this chapter. Seemingly small tips can significantly improve your productivity.

Manage text, audio, video, and other digital files with My Documents

Your computer may hold thousands of digital files. It is impossible to efficiently sort through this many random files; therefore, it is very important to carefully organize the files on your computer's hard drive and on your other digital devices.

Computer-based files can hold the vast majority of data for most qualitative research projects. In this section you will learn how to use *My Documents* so you can create uniquely named folders (and subfolders) that allow you to store your data in logical groupings. You will learn how to quickly move and rename individual files, and groups of files, to create a logical framework for your data. This framework, if maintained regularly, will help you efficiently find the data you need.

About digital file types

Individual software programs often have unique data formatting requirements. Software developers create customized data storage protocols to make sure the data stored by their programs match their design requirements and open properly. To identify their program's files, software developers give them unique extensions like .doc or .txt.

If you are not familiar with basic digital file types, the following list will help you make sense of the various file extensions you are likely to encounter during your qualitative research project. This section will tell you how to organize these files; subsequent chapters will help you use the programs that create the files during your research projects.

To look up any file extension go to http://filext.com/

⇒ **Text files** hold transcripts, drafts of reports, memos, letters, notes, e-mails, and more. Text files can be very simple or, like Word, they can include sophisticated formatting. (This book shows you how you can take advantage of some of the elaborate features of *Word*.) *Word* produces .doc files. The simplest type of text file uses the .txt extension. TXT files have no embedded formatting capabilities that allow bold, italics, or any other enhanced features. The cross-platform file format that includes many of the most popular text formatting features of *Word* and similar word processing programs is the Rich Text Format (rtf). RTF files are frequently used for document exchange.

⇒ The raw materials of many qualitative studies are the recordings of interviews and other field work. Technological advances have made digital recorders reliable, relatively inexpensive, and convenient. Chapter 5, 'Collecting your data' goes into these technologies in more detail.

⇒ All digital audio recordings are contained in **audio files** (mp3, wav, wmf, wma, etc.). Like all other digital files, audio files are stored on your hard drive, on a CD-ROM, a DVD, and on other digital repositories.

⇒ Interviews and other field work recorded using **digital audio-video** technologies are stored in files with extensions of avi, mpg, wmv, and mov.

⇒ **Illustrations** are created with various drawing programs like Microsoft *Paint*, Microsoft *Visio*, *CorelDRAW*, and Adobe *Illustrator*. Drawings created in these programs can be stored in standard image file formats like gif, tif, and jpg. **Photographs** are stored using the same file formats as illustrations, but they are edited with programs like Adobe *Photoshop*, *Paint Shop Pro*, and Google's *Picassa*.

⇒ PPT and PPS are files from Microsoft's popular slide show software *PowerPoint*.

⇒ PUB files are associated with Microsoft *Publisher.*

⇒ PDF files are readable across computer platforms; they are associated with *Adobe Reader.*

⇒ ZIP files have been compressed individually or in a group. These files must be 'unzipped' before they can be used. Several zip/unzip programs can be downloaded for free. Type 'free zip program' into your search engine (Google).

About *My Documents*

My Documents can help you save time by allowing you to organize your computer files by category and subcategory. These categories relate to your subject matter rather than the type of file. Becoming proficient with *My Documents* will help you with a lot more than research projects. It is important in virtually every aspect of Windows-based computing.

I know intelligent and competent people who have used computers for many years without moving any of their files outside of the root *My Documents* directory. They are frequently frustrated as they search for a document that they 'know is there' but cannot find. Sometimes they give up, thus losing valuable information after wasting precious time.

If you waste time looking for 'lost' files, take the time to review the tips in this section. **Your investment in 'organizing' and filing will reap great rewards in future efficiency.** This discussion is targeted at beginning and intermediate users of *My Documents*. I will try not to confuse you with parallel techniques that can be used to accomplish the same task. Instead, I will describe the favorite techniques that I have adopted and use every day.

If you are an old pro you may be perfectly happy with your current techniques, but you are encouraged to read on – perhaps you will pick up a couple of new tricks.

Technical note: *My Documents* is really just a special folder that is visible in a program called *Explorer.* Functions from *Explorer* are embedded in most Microsoft programs. For example, when you click on File ▶ Open in *Word* or *Excel*, the dialog box that pops up is really a special instance of *Explorer.* For the most part, that dialog box looks and behaves like a small version of *My Documents*. This means that most of the techniques you employ in *My Documents* can be used whenever you use a *Windows* program to open a file or 'browse' to find a file.

Starting *My Documents*

Windows places a *My Documents* icon on the desktop during all *Windows* installations, so unless you deleted the icon all you have to do is double-click on the *My Documents* icon. If you do not have a *My Documents* icon on your desktop you can get to *My Documents* in two other ways using the Start Menu

Double-click on the desktop icon to start *My Documents*

in the bottom left corner of the screen:

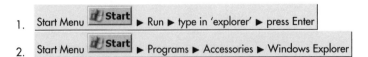

1. Start Menu ▶ Run ▶ type in 'explorer' ▶ press Enter

2. Start Menu ▶ Programs ▶ Accessories ▶ Windows Explorer

In both cases, remember that *My Documents* is really just a special directory in a *Windows* program called *Explorer*.

Setting up My Documents

First, some setup

Start *My Documents*.

A couple of one-time procedures follow.

Next, click on the Views icon on the *My Documents* toolbar (to the right of the Folders icon), then select Details. This view allows you to see a lot more information relating to each file like the time and date the file was last modified, the type of file, and the size of the file. You will want to change your viewing preferences to Thumbnails if you are looking at picture files, but I prefer that my default view is of details.

I really like to see the file extensions like .doc or .pdf when I organize files using *My Documents*; therefore, this one-time change must be made from the default *My Documents* settings.

Tools ▶ Select the View tab ▶ Make the changes shown in the picture

From the menu click on <u>T</u>ools, and then select the View tab from the Folder Options pane. As shown in the illustration below, check the item that says 'Display the full path in the address bar,' and uncheck the item that says, 'Hide extensions for known file types.'

Changing the settings to 'Display the full path in the address bar' is optional. If you do not check this *My Documents* will display a sometimes-confusing truncated folder name.

After you have done this click on OK at the bottom of the screen.

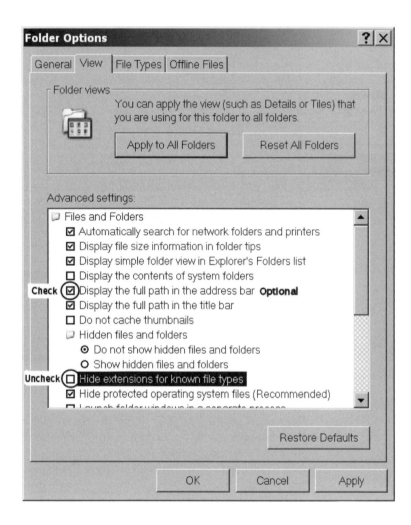

Create two
viewing panes
using 'Folders'

From the toolbar click on [📁 Folders]. Get in the habit of doing this every time you start *My Documents*. The program is more functional when two panes are available.

After this setup, you will have a *My Documents* screen with the attributes of the illustration below. This is the basic configuration that I use when I refer to *My Documents*.

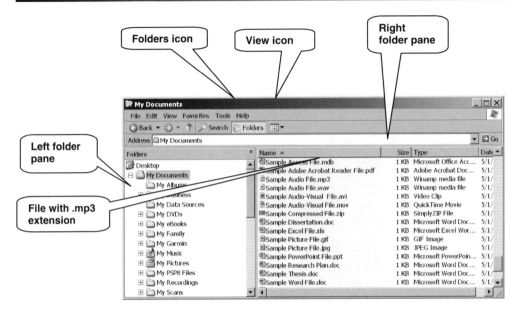

My Documents, shown in gray in the left pane, is the highest level folder. Multiple levels of folders can branch out below *My Documents*.

Strategies for file names, folder names, and folder organization

File names

File names and folder names can be descriptive and reasonably long, up to 255 characters. Give your file names that make sense to you so that they will help you recall the contents when you need them, say, a year from now. Do not assume that you will remember clever cryptographic schemes (designed to keep file names short) after a few months have passed.

A file name comes in two parts: the primary file name is followed by a period (.), and then an extension. File names look like this: 'file name.ext.'

You can use all alphanumeric characters, upper and lower case, spaces, and a lot of special characters. If you use a special character in your file name that is illegal you will get an error message. Simply change the special character to something legal.

For example, suppose you tried to create a *Word* file called 'Interview with ABC on 06/12.doc.' *Windows* will give you a reasonably straightforward error message letting you know that you used an illegal character, in this case the forward slash (/). To remedy the error, change the name to something like 'Interview with ABC on 06-12.doc,' or 'Interview with ABC on 06December.doc.'

Legal special characters include $ % ' - _ @ ~ ' ! ( ) ^ # &+ , ; = [ ].

Do not change the names of file extensions that are automatically assigned by software applications. Software programs recognize compatible file types by their extensions. (See *About digital file types* earlier in this chapter.) If you change the names of extensions you will destroy the ability of the software programs that created those files to recognize and open the files.

Folder names

The naming rules for folders are easy to live with; they are essentially the same as they are for files. The important thing to ponder when you name a folder is: what files are you going to put in the folder and what name will help you remember the contents of these files?

Spend time thinking about the organization of your files. How should your files be grouped? Which files belong together and which files should be separated? Do not make this a painful process. Think about the problem, make a decision, and then move files into the appropriate folders.

You can, and should, change folder names and file groupings as your project progresses. The time you spend with your project allows you to gain a deeper understanding of the subject matter. Your file and folder system should reflect the most insightful level of your thinking. Take action; do not be content with organizational ideas that made sense when you started your project that no longer fit.

Subfolders

All significant projects involve multiple tasks, files, data sources, and memos can be organized by creating subfolders.

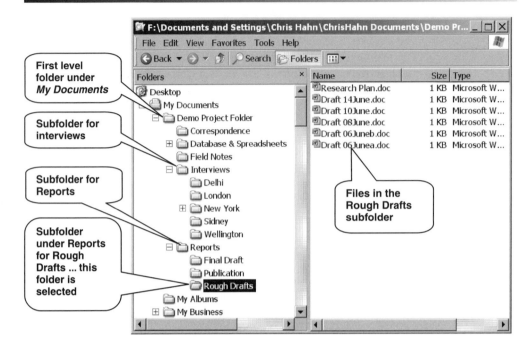

First level
folder under
My Documents

Subfolder for
interviews

Subfolder for
Reports

Subfolder
under Reports
for Rough
Drafts ... this
folder is
selected

Files in the
Rough Drafts
subfolder

Subfolders can be deeply nested to hold progressively more refined groupings of files. Use subfolders to organize the files in your project.

Creating subfolders

To create a subfolder, first click on the existing folder that will serve as the host folder for the new subfolder. In the picture above the Rough Drafts folder is selected.

Once the folder is selected click on File ▶ New ▶ Folder

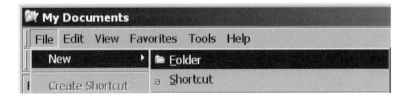

A new folder named 'New Folder' will appear in the right pane.

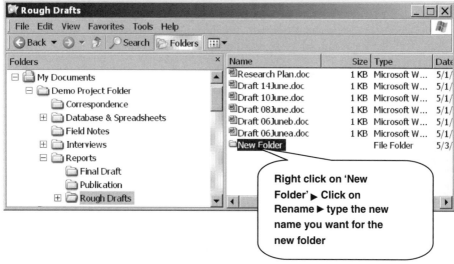

Copying and moving files between folders

After creating subfolders to hold subsets of your computerized files it is time to populate those folders. This can be done by either copying files from their original location or moving files from their original location. Files can be copied or moved one at a time or in groups.

No matter what technique you use, it is helpful to be able to see the source and the target directories. This is why I recommend creating a left 'folders' pane to accompany the right 'folders and files' pane. Click on the **Folders** icon every time you start *My Documents* to create the 'folders' pane.

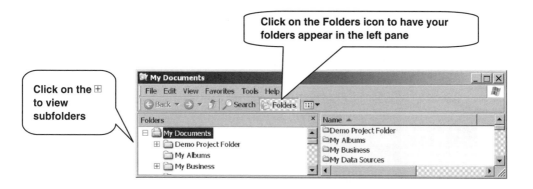

Some of the techniques for moving and copying files are faster than others. I personally use the keyboard shortcuts techniques almost exclusively because they are fast and because after so many years Ctrl+C/Ctrl+V (or Ctrl+X/Ctrl+V) are instinctive to me, but perhaps the other techniques will resonate better with your style. Whatever technique(s) you prefer, use them frequently to keep your files and folders in order.

Technique 1: Drag and drop a single file   The most visual of the file-moving techniques is drag and drop.

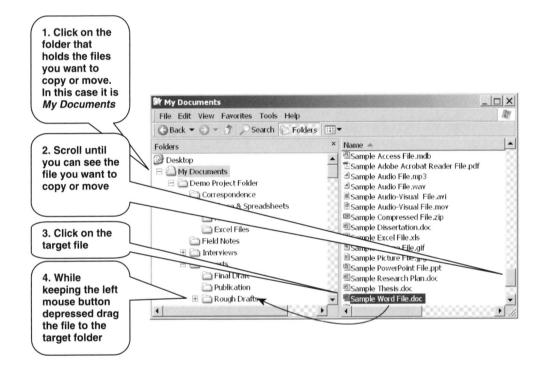

1. Click on the folder that holds the files you want to copy or move. In this case it is *My Documents*

2. Scroll until you can see the file you want to copy or move

3. Click on the target file

4. While keeping the left mouse button depressed drag the file to the target folder

As a default when you drag and drop, files are **moved** from one folder to another. **To copy a file, hold down the Ctrl key** when you drag and drop. Copying leaves the file in the original folder and puts a copy in the target folder.

The drag and drop rules are reversed if you are using *My Computer* (rather than *My Documents*) to copy or move a file to a secondary drive like (D:) or (E:) rather than to a folder on the same drive. The default action is to copy the file, not move it. To move a file while dragging and dropping to a different disk drive you must hold down the Ctrl key during the procedure.

Technique 2: Right-click   If in doubt, try right-clicking. This is a rule that has gotten me out of a lot of jams. Microsoft packs a lot of power into your mouse's right button.

Using all of the steps in Technique 1 work your way to the file you want to copy. Instead of dragging the file, right-click on the file. After right-clicking this menu will appear.

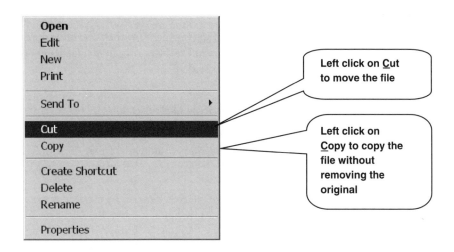

After clicking on Cut or Copy, *Windows* will store the file in your computer's memory until you want to paste it somewhere. Find the new location (folder) where you want the file to appear, right-click on that folder, then left-click on Paste.

From the source file Right-click ► Copy or Right-click ► Cut
To the target folder Right-click ► Paste

Note: The file that you Cut or Copied into your computer's memory (Microsoft calls it the Clipboard) will stay there until you (a) turn off your computer, or (b) use the clipboard for a different item by cutting or copying something else into the clipboard. This applies to Techniques 2, 3, and 4.

Ctrl+X to move the file or Ctrl+C to copy the file
On the highlighted target folder press Ctrl+V to paste
From the menu, Edit ► Cut to move the file, or Edit ► Copy to copy the file

Technique 3: Keyboard shortcut   Using all of the steps in Technique 1 work your way to the file you want to copy. Instead of dragging the file, left-click on the file, then press Ctrl and X at the same time to move the file, or Ctrl and C at the same time to copy the file.

Locate and click on the target folder. Once it is highlighted press Ctrl and V at the same time to paste the file.

Technique 4: Menu   This technique is identical to Technique 3, but instead of using Ctrl+X/Ctrl+V, or Ctrl+C/Ctrl+V, use the menu and select Edit ► Cut, and then Edit ► Paste, or Edit ► Copy, and then Edit ► Paste.

On the
highlighted target
folder use Edit ▶
Paste

Mix and match
Techniques 2, 3,
and 4

The keystrokes and menu entries discussed in Techniques 2, 3, and 4 can be used interchangeably. For example, you could Right-click ▶ Copy to place the file in the clipboard, and then you could use Ctrl+V or Edit ▶ Paste to paste the file.

Copying/Moving entire folders

Folders may be copied and moved using the same procedures described above for copying and moving files. They may be dragged and dropped or copied to the clipboard and pasted.

Copying/Moving multiple files

Groups of files may be moved or copied using the same procedures described above for copying and moving individual files. The only difference is that the multiple files to be moved or copied must be selected before the files are copied or moved.

To create a group of selected files from a list of files when the files are not adjoining in the list, start by holding down the Ctrl key. While the Ctrl key is depressed click on the files, one at a time, that you want to copy or move.

To select a group of files when the files are adjoining in the list, hold down the Shift key. While the Shift key is depressed click on the file at the top of the list, and then keeping the Shift key depressed click on the bottom file in the list. All files between the top file and the bottom file will be automatically selected.

Once the files are selected they may be copied or moved just as a single file can be copied or moved.

The organization of folders is also addressed in the Appendix in the section about using *Outlook* to organize e-mail messages. The techniques used in *My Documents* to create folders and move files are virtually identical to those in *Outlook*.

Bibliographic data

To be efficient, the researcher should record the citations and bibliographic details of research-relevant and referenced literature throughout the research process. Writing the literature review and final report will be a nightmare of lost details if references are not recorded and organized in a systematic manner throughout the project.

Especially for a poor typist like me, collecting and organizing references was one of the most frustrating parts of research – at least it was until I discovered EndNote. Epiphany is too strong a word, but I was sure happy to have most of the tedious and precise typing and organizing burden lifted from my jumbled fingers.

Personal bibliographic programs are among the most natural uses of software technology in research. These programs will

⇒ download citations from databases and catalogs like ProQuest and EBSCOhost
⇒ insert formatted citations into the body of your report if you are using *Word* or *Word Perfect* as your word processor
⇒ create a formatted bibliography/reference section at the end of your paper using most major publication styles specified by graduate schools and academic journals
⇒ reformat and renumber citations and the reference section of your paper if you insert, delete, or edit citations.

These features can liberate you from wasting hours of time-consuming and painfully precise typing.

EndNote, Biblioscape, and Reference Works are the leading software packages. They all have strengths and weaknesses, but they are all fantastic compared with managing references manually.

EndNote is the most popular program in the academic world and it contains many features. Biblioscape is less expensive than EndNote, but it lacks all of the high-powered features of EndNote. These features may not matter for many students. Reference Works is ideal for networks. It uses a client/server architecture so team members in larger projects have simultaneous use of the same bibliographic database.

Paper

Yes, important information still comes printed on paper. Articles, letters, guides, instructions, informed consent forms, survey instruments, approval documents, and more must be systematically stored. You want to be able to find those important pieces of paper when you need them. This is a low-tech process.

Step 1 – How big a box do you need? Start by estimating the volume of paper you need to file and organize and then buy an appropriately sized file cabinet, or if you want to save some money and be mobile buy 'bankers' boxes' instead of file cabinets. Bankers' boxes are corrugated cardboard filing boxes. While you are at the office store pick up some tabbed file folders.

Step 2 – Discard the paper you do not need. Recycle, shred, or otherwise toss out paper you do not need. There is no need to store and lug around useless (and heavy) paper.

Step 3 – Identify and label the file folders. Think through the divisions and subdivisions of your data and label the folders appropriately.

Step 4 – DO IT. This is the most painful step for me. It always seems as if something else is more important. Turn on some music (or whatever works for you) and get those piles of paper into the file folders and the file cabinet.

Step 5 – Maintain it. On second thought, this may be the most painful step for me. On a regular basis reorganize the system in response to your changing needs, and continue to get those piles into the folders. As you maintain your filing system remember Step 2, discard the paper you do not need.

Physical items

Physical items and artifacts collected during research should be cleaned, sorted, cataloged, conserved, packaged and organized. The techniques for conducting the physical and mechanical processes of artifact handling are beyond the scope of this book, but the system used to catalog physical items is discussed here because it can be integrated into the overall organization and database strategy of the project.

Collected artifacts should be labeled in a systematic manner, but the labeling method should not harm the artifacts by abrading, corroding, or obscuring important views of artifacts. Artifact labels generally include three cryptogram/numbers written one below the other: a) a site code, b) an accession number, and c) an inventory code.

a. Site code. If possible, create site codes that adhere to a standard naming scheme like the Smithsonian Trinomial system. This will make it easier for other researchers to understand your work. The Smithsonian Trinomial system establishes a single three-part (state-county-site) alphanumeric designation for each site. For example, the 44th site in Sioux county (SX) Iowa (Smithsonian state number 13) has a site code of 13SX44. (A listing of all Smithsonian State and County Symbols for Site Designations is available at qrtips.com/chapter3.)

b. Accession number. As each artifact is found it is given a sequential number. During artifact collection a master list of artifacts must be maintained to make sure that each artifact has a unique number and that artifact accession numbers are not duplicated. These lists might be sequential over all periods of time, or they might be broken down according to year and/or month.

c. Inventory code. Depending on the requirements for your project, the inventory code might identify an object's source of origin, date collected, description, etc. Document and preserve the inventory code system you devise so team members and later investigators can decode your naming system.

An explanation of the labeling system should be stored with the artifacts.

Once collected and labeled, an inventory of collected artifacts should be maintained, preferably in a computerized database. For relatively limited collections *Excel* is an ideal tool. (See the Appendix for *Excel* basics.)

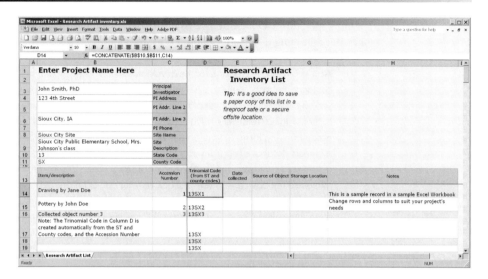

Items collected during research can be inventoried in an *Excel* workbook to keep a dynamic list of physical items. This template is available at qrtips.com.

Even more powerful than *Excel*, Microsoft *Access* is a great choice for physical item inventories. *Access* allows the use of data entry forms and relational database power for larger and more complex situations with multiple investigators and with third-party data entry personnel.

See the Appendix for an introduction to *Access*.

Develop your contacts and keep them in a database

People are the lifeblood of qualitative research. They are the participants and group members being studied; and they are the advisors, colleagues, research assistants, and the authorities that you communicate with every day. Can you easily edit your contact information? Can you 'mail merge' e-mail messages and hard copy mailings into reports? Can you easily backup your contacts?

If you can quickly and reliably find phone numbers, e-mail addresses, and mailing addresses, congratulations. If not, you may want to consider upgrading your method of keeping track of contact information.

There are many ways to efficiently keep track of contacts using newer technologies including personal digital assistants (PDAs), cell phones, computers, and online directories. If you are successfully using one of these tools there may be no reason to switch to a Microsoft *Office*-based software program like *Outlook*, but you may want to occasionally synchronize your contacts with *Office* because it backs-up your contact data and it facilitates mail merge operations. *Office* offers several methods of keeping track of contacts, but the following discussion will focus primarily on *Outlook*.

1. *Access* is a terrific platform for the development of a powerful and fully featured contact database. With *Access* you can add all of the features you want, and you can start with a nice template from microsoft.com. The downside to *Access* is that it takes relatively advanced skills to customize the database and its accompanying forms to your unique needs. For this reason I mention *Access* as a contact database program only in passing. If you want advanced and highly customized features, and if you are a proficient *Access* user I recommend it, otherwise my advice is to use *Outlook* as your contact manager.

2. Many people think of *Outlook* as an e-mail program, but within *Outlook* is a module called *Contacts*. *Contacts* is fully featured and powerful without any customization; and if necessary, *Contacts* is highly customizable. *Contacts* can be used for mail merge and e-mail merge functions. This is the recommended solution that will be explained in more detail below.

3. *Word*'s Mail Merge wizard (Tools ▶ Letters and Mailings ▶ Mail Merge) allows you to create and maintain a database that contains most of the basic contact data that are commonly used. This 'recipient list' is actually an *Access* file with an .mdb extension. This method of recording contact information is not recommended as a primary contact maintenance system because of its limited and overly simplified interface.

Using **Outlook's 'Contacts'** *to manage names and addresses*

Start *Contacts*

For instructions on starting *Outlook* and a discussion of its e-mail functionality refer to the Appendix.

Once *Outlook* is running, start *Contacts* in one of three ways:

1. Press Ctrl+3
2. From the menu select Go ▶ Contacts
3. Click on the Contacts button on the left sidebar

Create a new contact entry

To create a new contact database directly in *Outlook* enter your first contact by clicking on the 🔳 New ▼ icon on the toolbar, or by using the menu – File ▶ New ▶ Contact , or by using the shortcut key combination of Ctrl+N .

The basic entry form will look like this.

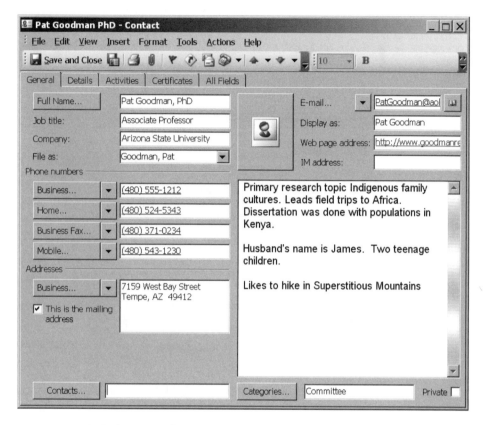

Outlook's Contact form.

Fill in the information that you have about this contact. There are many more fields available if you have specific information that is associated with this contact. These data fields are accessible by using the tabs on the new contact form.

These tabs allow access to additional data fields.

If you still do not find appropriate fields for your data after exploring all of the tabs you can create user-defined fields.

After completing the new contact form click on ▣ **Save and Close**. Repeat this process as often as necessary to populate *Contacts* with all of your important 'address book' information.

Contacts allows you to view your contact records in a number of ways. By clicking on ◉ **Address Cards** the view below will appear.

Viewing your contacts

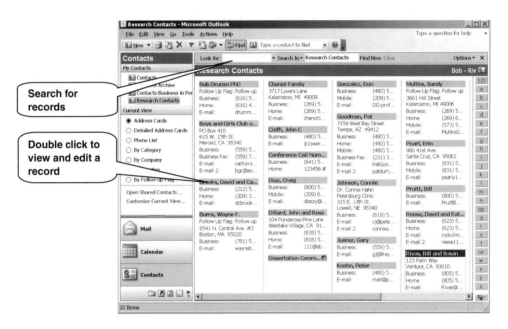

Contacts in Address Card View mode.

The same data can be examined in the phone list view shown below.

New folders can be created using File▶ New ▶ Folder

Click on column headings to sort by that field

Columns and other settings are customizable

Contacts in Phone List View.

Take the time to explore the features of *Contacts*. You are likely to discover other useful tools to enhance your ability to keep track of your contacts.

Import and Export. *Outlook* is the industry standard

A significant advantage of using *Contacts* is that many handheld PDAs including Palm and BlackBerry, cell phones, and other devices will synchronize their address books with *Outlook*'s *Contacts*. This means that you can enter information into your PDA and electronically routinely transfer the information to *Contacts*, and vice versa.

If you are switching to *Contacts* from a different computerized address book the odds are pretty good that you will be able to import those data to *Contacts*. From the menu use File Import and Export, or refer to the documentation from your existing 'addresses' or 'contacts' device.

Use mail merge for personalized group letters and e-mailings

Mail merge and e-mail merge can be done in *Outlook* and *Word*

The Appendix describes *Outlook*'s standard e-mail functionality. You are encouraged to go there to get started and to learn how to create e-mail files and folders.

A more advanced topic and one that can save you a lot of time, is the mail merge function. Built into *Outlook* and *Word* are interfaces that allow you to merge selected records from your *Outlook* or *Access* contact database to a form letter. The form letter can be e-mailed or printed.

Mail merge is helpful when you need to send a standard letter to many people, and you want that letter to be personalized. **Rather than send a bulk letter that says 'Dear Participant,' you can address the letters to each participant by name and include personalized information.**

Sending bulk e-mails

We are all familiar with getting bulk forwarded e-mails from well-meaning friends. Sometimes they are funny and interesting, other times they aren't. The most disturbing thing to me about these e-mails (from well-meaning friends) is seeing how many of these forwarded e-mails expose the identity of other recipients to complete strangers.

It is okay to fill up the 'To...' field of the e-mail messages with close mutually acquainted associates, or trusted family members; but with rare exceptions, it is bad form to include the e-mail addresses of lots of unacquainted people in the 'To...' field.

In the course of your research there will be occasions when you will want to send bulk e-mails. It is an expedient way of communicating with groups of people, but use good taste and acceptable techniques.

1. **Send the message only 'To' yourself, and put all of your intended recipients' e-mail addresses in the 'Bcc' field.** This is the simplest way to forward e-mails to a list in a manner that conceals the identity of the other recipients.

    To see the Bcc field in *Outlook* click on the 'To...' button from the New Mail Message window (the window you use to compose new mail messages). A 'Select Names' window will appear that shows the Bcc field. Paste or type the list of e-mail addresses in the Bcc field.

   If you have 100 recipients, an identical e-mail will go to all. Each recipient will see that the message is 'From:' your e-mail address, and the message is 'To:' your e-mail address. The recipient will not see the distribution list.

2. **The gold standard – Mail Merge.** To create a truly custom e-mail message for each recipient use *Outlook*'s mail merge feature. Mail merge creates individualized e-mail messages for each recipient. Instructions for doing this are below.

   If you have 100 recipients, a customizable e-mail will go to each recipient. The 'From:' field of the e-mail will display your e-mail address, but the recipient will see that the message is only 'To:' him or her. The recipient will not see the rest of the distribution list. Instructions for using mail merge follow.

Some database knowledge is helpful during mail merges

Tech Aggressive

> This discussion of mail merge techniques uses database terms like 'field' and 'record.' Refer to the Appendix for a review of these concepts. Also, since this is a more advanced topic, I will make some assumptions about your technical aggressiveness and your willingness to do some problem solving if at first you don't succeed.

When to mail merge directly from *Outlook*

You can mail merge from *Contacts* in *Outlook* or from *Word*. The process is very similar because *Word's* software functions drive the mail merge process. The difference is the initial interface to the records you are going to use as the source of the mail merge data. You can end up with the same results from either program, including customized e-mail messages and printed documents.

> Initiate your mail merge from *Word* or *Outlook's Contacts*

If you are going to use *Outlook's Contacts* as your data source I suggest that you start your mail merge in *Contacts*. I make this statement even though you can start in *Word* and perform merges using *Contacts* data. I have experienced occasional problems with merges using *Contacts* data that started in *Word* because these merges sometimes use database field names that do not match *Contacts'* address list field names. This may cause the merged data to display improperly. Again, this problem goes away if you simply start these merges in *Contacts*.

If you are going to mail merge using records held in *Access* (this includes *Word* address lists), *Excel*, comma delimited text files, and more, I recommend that you start with *Word*.

Mail merge techniques

Mail merge is the key to professional looking group e-mails and letters. There is a learning curve, some trial and error is necessary, and you must be willing to explore extensions of the ideas presented in this section. But if you are determined to learn the process the end result can be very pleasing. You will gain respect from the recipients of your communiqués and you will save time. Mail merge is a skill that can help you for years to come.

I suggest that you test the process a couple of times by mail merging some letters and e-mails to yourself and maybe a couple of friends before putting your newly acquired skills to work in the real world.

The mail merge command structures for both *Outlook* and *Word* are very similar so only one set of instructions is provided below.

Differences will be mentioned if they are significant. The most significant difference between merges from initiating the mail merge in *Outlook* or *Word* occurs at the beginning of the process when you select the contact records to be merged.

Word can mail merge using the following records.

Word	(.doc) A *Word* document file consisting of a single table.
Access	(.mdb) A database table or query.
Web file	(HTML) A Web page file consisting of a single table.
Text file	(.txt) A text file that includes columns separated by commas or tabs, and rows separated by paragraph marks.
Outlook	A contact list created by *Outlook*. These records may be selected.
Contacts	In *Contacts* before starting the mail merge wizard; or if the wizard was started from *Word*, *Contacts* records may be selected after the wizard is started.

Records are not pre-selected from a list before the mail merge process is initiated in *Word*. The records to be merged are selected from a database table, database query, spreadsheet, or contact list after you start the mail merge wizard. To get going, start a new *Word* document.

From the menu of either *Word* (or *Outlook*'s *Contacts*) select ‾Tools ▶ Letters‾ and Mailings ▶ Mail Merge…

> The mail merge wizard starts using the same menu commands in *Word* or *Contacts*

The mail merge process is fundamentally the same in *Word* and *Contacts*. The wizard is mostly self-explanatory; and normally, I would not step you through a perfectly good wizard, but there are some confusing decision points in this process that require instruction. I will not explain the many variations that are possible; you are encouraged to explore these variations on your own.

> Starting mail merge from *Contacts*

The mail merge process that starts in *Contacts* includes one more step than the *Word* process. Since the *Contacts* wizard is the longest, this wizard is used to demonstrate the mail merge process in this section.

The following demo starts by showing a typical contact record. The data in this record are used to illustrate data involved in the mail merge process. You may want to refer back to this illustration after you see the completed merge.

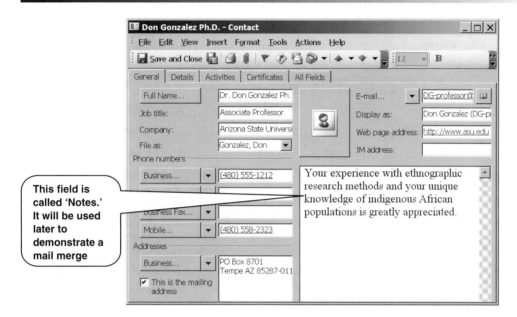

This field is called 'Notes.' It will be used later to demonstrate a mail merge

Typical address record from *Contacts*. You will see these data in the merged document later in this section.

When you start the mail merge wizard from *Contacts* it works best to start with pre-selected data records. You can determine which contact records will be eventually merged in a remarkably simple manner: by selecting those records from the *Contacts* list before the wizard is started.

Select records in *Contacts*

With *Contacts* in Phone List view, hold down the Ctrl key, and then one at a time click on the records you want to include in the mail merge. In this example, merged documents will be created for the currently selected records of contacts Gonzalez, Goodman, and Koehn.

In *Contacts* pre-
select the records
to be merged

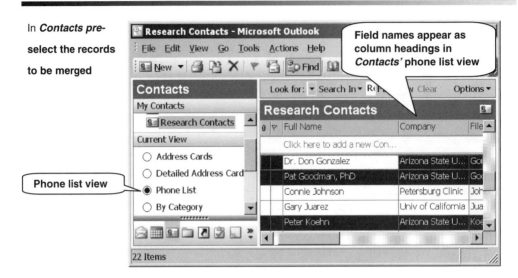

Three records are selected.

There are several other methods of selecting groups of records used by *Word*
and *Contacts*. You are encouraged to discover these techniques by exploring
the mail merge interface and by using Microsoft's Help system (press F1).

Step 1: Start the
mail merge
wizard in
Contacts

While the records are still selected, start the wizard Tools ▶ Letters and
Mailings ▶ Mail Merge...

The following screen will appear (only when started from *Contacts*).

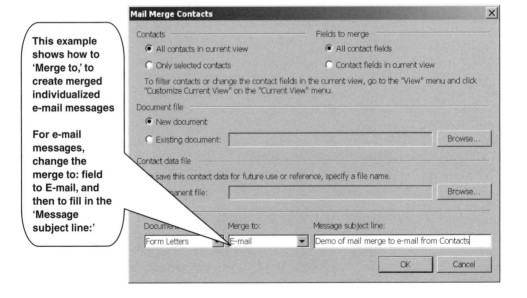

This example
shows how to
'Merge to,' to
create merged
individualized
e-mail messages

For e-mail
messages,
change the
merge to: field
to E-mail, and
then to fill in the
'Message
subject line:'

Step 2: Start the mail merge wizard in *Word* Warning, non-intuitive step: A blank *Word* document will appear

After finishing the form above by clicking OK you may be puzzled when a blank *Word* document appears. This is a common point of confusion. At this point **you will need to start the mail merge wizard again**, this time from within *Word* by using the same menu entries, Tools ▶ Letters and Mailings ▶ Mail Merge...

Even though you have started the mail merge wizard for a second time, the system has not lost track of your original starting point in Contacts.

Step 3: Select recipients

If you pre-selected a list from *Contacts* you do not need to do anything more at this step, click on Next.

If you started from *Word* choose 'Use an existing list' to use any data type except *Contacts*, then click on

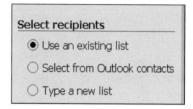

 Browse... to select the data source. Click on Next to continue after you have selected the data source.

Step 4: Write your letter

Now that the data records are selected you finally get to write your message. This message is written in *Word* (a *Word* screen appears automatically) and can use the formatting features of *Word* like bold, underline, and italics (unless you intend to send this as a plain text e-mail).

To display the merged contents from your data records you must insert the merge fields at the spot in your document that you designate for the merged data. The wizard provides two special merge fields called AddressBlock and GreetingLine. The sample letters below show the purpose and use of these merge fields.

«AddressBlock»
«GreetingLine»
As my research planning has progressed I wanted to take a moment and thank you for the valuable role you are playing on my committee. 'Notes' The revised draft of my research plan should be ready by next week.

Thank you,

Michelle Nielson

Alternative formatting is shown below that produces the same result using the "More items" technique instead of the Address block... and the Greeting line... technique.

«Courtesy Title» «First Name» «Last Name» «Suffix»

«Job Title»

«Company»

«Address 1»

«Address 2»

«City» «State» «Postal Code»

Dear «Courtesy Title» «Last Name»,

As my research planning has progressed I wanted to take a moment and thank you for the valuable role you are playing on my committee. «Notes»

To see the source of the «Notes» data refer to the 'Typical address record from *Contacts*' illustration on page 55

The revised draft of my research plan should be ready by next week.

Thank you,

Michelle Nielson

Step 5: Preview your letters

When you are all done with writing your letter click Next to continue.

If you have problems …

At this point troubleshooting may be required if your data does not appear as it should. Try using different fields and matching fields. Toggle back and forth between 'Write your letter' and 'Preview your letters.'

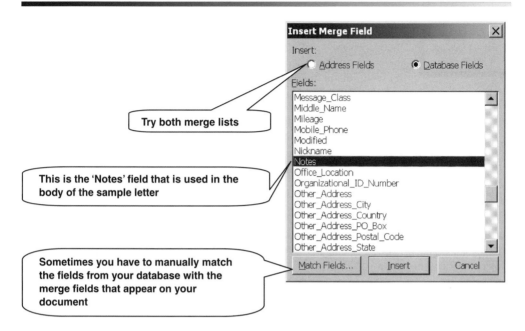

The preview screen should show data merged from your contact records.

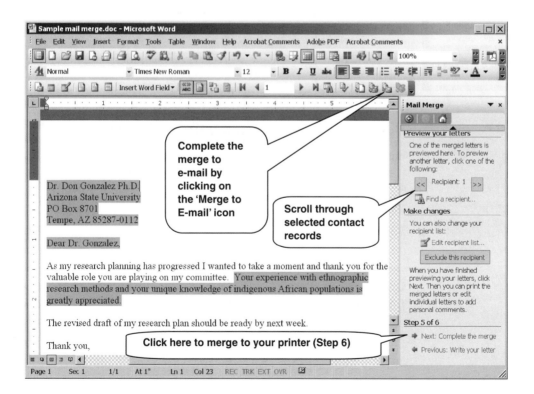

Step 5a: Merge to E-mail. *Warning, non-intuitive step.*

To complete the merge to e-mail you should break away from the mail merge wizard because the wizard leads primarily to the printer. Proceed directly to the e-mail screen by clicking on the **'Merge to E-mail' icon** shown in the illustration above.

After clicking on the 'Merge to E-mail' icon you will see the following window.

The message subject line you completed in Step 1 should appear here. It can be changed as needed

Leave the setting at 'All' to send to the originally selected list

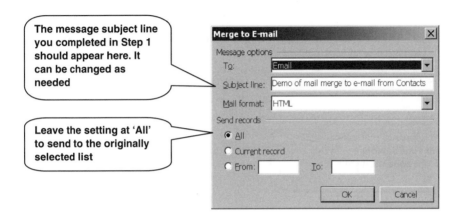

Check the Sent Items folder in *Outlook* to verify that the e-mails have been sent

After all of the preceding steps, the mail merge is over after a few blinks of the screen. How do you know that it worked? Go back to *Outlook*, and look at the 'Sent Items' folder in the Mail module. If the mail merge worked each of the merged e-mails will be available for your review in the sent folder.

Step 5b: Merge to Printer

If you want to complete the mail merge process with printed documents instead of e-mail proceed to the mail merge wizard's Step 6 by clicking on 'Next: Complete the merge,' and then click on Print on the final page.

Hone and use your communications skills

It is not enough to be technologically competent. Great techniques will get you nowhere unless you put them to work in a sensible way. Lack of effective communication is one of the reasons that there are so many brilliant students who permanently get stuck at the ABD (all but dissertation) stage.

During your research project you must reach out to those who are important to your project, keep these people informed, and keep on keeping these people informed.

Work diligently with your department, committee, and Institutional Review Board

The people who sit on your committees and on the IRB can make your research project or break it. Period. So treat all of these people with respect and keep them up to date about your progress.

In an academic setting you often have established deadlines for reporting the progress of your project. At the bare minimum, make sure you get your progress reports in on time. If there is a reason you cannot make the deadline at least let your boss, committee, or advisor know why. Be honest and be regular in your communiqués.

Your committee will appreciate your enthusiasm if you stay in touch. Quick updates are helpful as relevant information emerges that may be of interest to your committee members. Keep your memos brief, but keep the flow of information alive and personalized. Use the telephone, meet in person, send letters, and send e-mails. Again, mail merge is often a helpful vehicle.

Seek out experts in the field

> Reach beyond the requirements to build your professional network

When you read a great article that directly relates to your research, or when you hear a great conference presentation, take the time to try to contact that expert. You will be surprised at how often you will get positive feedback.

If you are at a conference where you can meet the presenter personally, try to set up a meeting. Simply walking up to the front of the room at the end of a presentation might allow you to establish a meaningful alliance.

E-mail is an especially good way to contact people in your field whose work you respect. Send a short note explaining your appreciation for this person and explaining why it is important to your research. Do not be surprised when you get responses. If the responses are positive keep the dialogs going in a manner that is constructive for all parties. You might be able to establish collaborations with the most influential people in your field.

Phone calls are free through the Internet

When you use Skype, NetZero, and other similar services, computer-to-computer voice phone calls are free anywhere in the world. This makes complex international research collaborations possible when the budget is small. If you are not familiar with these services use Google or another search engine to look up 'Computer-Based VoIP Providers' or 'Internet telephone.'

Controlling your progress

Creating a plan and getting organized are the best steps you can take to get a good start on your research project, but your project can get derailed if you do not control your progress. The balanced management of a project requires planning, organizing, **and controlling**. Controlling means that you should regularly check back at the details of your original plan, timetable, and budget to see if you are on track or getting derailed.

Maintain your task list. If it is a big project your project management software will hold all of your planned activities and timetable. This software must be maintained and corrective action should be taken if your progress significantly deviates from your plan. If you have a relatively small project, remember to check back with your task list to make sure that you have not forgotten to do something important or that you are not spending an inordinate amount of time on a low priority task.

Track your budget. You do not want your research project to fail because you run out of money. If money is an issue, do a regular accounting to compare your budget with your actual expenditures. If you are over budget take remedial action.

Control personnel. If you are using the services of other people to get your research project done, then do regular reviews of the performance of these people. If they are doing a good job, let them know. If they are not performing up to your standards, help them improve. If they are failing you may have to let them go and replace them with someone more motivated and/or capable. If you fail to control your personnel you can jeopardize the entire project.

Pay the most attention to the tasks that are so critical that they can delay the entire project

In Chapter 2 the concept of a 'critical path' was presented during the planning phase of the research project. The concept is so important that it bears repeating.

The critical path is the chain of tasks that controls the timing of the entire project. If any of the tasks on the critical path takes too long, the completion of the entire project will be delayed.

Once the project is underway you should continually control your progress by making sure that your critical path tasks get the attention they deserve. If you spend too much time on a task that is tangential, and if this tangential task delays an activity on the critical path, then you have delayed your entire project. The delay is not because you have been lazy. After all, you have been busily working. The problem is that you have not been working intelligently.

Pay attention to your critical path tasks throughout your project. You will have a much better chance of getting it done on time. Refer to your plan regularly. If you are falling behind, adjust and then work smarter.

Use your filing system

Good advertisers know that a single exposure to a sales pitch is far less likely to get you to buy their product than repeated exposures to the same message. Therefore, one of the adages of the advertising industry is 'repeat, I repeat, repeat your message.'

In this spirit, at the end of this section on organizing and controlling I will repeat – keep going back to your filing system. Continually revise and improve the directory structure on your computer and move your files to the most appropriate folders. Likewise, keep those piles of paper off your desk and in your file cabinet or bankers' box. The time you spend keeping your files in shape will be one of the best time investments you can make. It will keep you from wasting time during the perpetual search as your blood pressure rises, 'now where did I put that *^#&#! file?'

Chapter summary

Business students taking their first management course soon learn that the principles of management are planning, organizing, and controlling. These principles apply to research projects just as they do to the management of a large construction job. Chapter 2 focused on planning; this chapter explored techniques for organizing and controlling your research project.

A good builder would not build a house directly on top of unconsolidated gravel because the house would lack structural integrity. Before framing the house the builder takes time to lay down a solid foundation. Qualitative researchers can learn from the experienced builder because loosely consolidated data are the raw material of qualitative research.

For the qualitative researcher a coherent system of organizing and filing data serves as a foundation for the construction of a high quality research project. Order must be brought to amorphous non-quantitative data. Text files, scanned pictures, photographs, audio files, audio-visual files, and most other qualitative data are stored in cabinets, on computer drives, and other media. These files and objects must be intelligently organized.

For Windows users digital file organization revolves around *My Documents* and *My Computer*. Files should be named in a descriptive manner and then grouped in folders. Folders should be descriptively named and then further organized using a system of subfolders to create logical affinities between topics and data types.

All extensive research projects include a review of the literature related to the project. References to the literature are precisely noted in the body of the final report and in a bibliography. References can be organized using software programs like *EndNote, Biblioscape,* and *Reference Works*. These programs take away a tedious task from the researcher – the precise typing and strict organization of in-line references and the bibliography.

Physical artifacts and other non-digital objects collected during research should be cleaned, sorted, cataloged, conserved, packaged and organized. Artifact labels should allow current and subsequent researchers to quickly identify the artifact's collection site, its accession number, and an inventory code.

Names, addresses, e-mail addresses, phone numbers and other contact information for the people associated with the research project should be stored and organized with care. This can be done with Microsoft *Outlook,* personal digital assistants (PDAs), cell phones, and/or bound paper address books. Most PDAs and many cell phones can synchronize their data with

Outlook to create a backup mechanism for your contacts and to facilitate mail merge operations.

Your work is not done after you have created a system of file organization, reference management, artifact storage, and contact management. The systems of organization you have created must be maintained. As your project grows you will find that refinements, changes of course, and unexpected events will require the modification of some of your plans and systems. Your project will be more efficient if you take time to make necessary changes – and if you do your filing on a regular basis.

CHAPTER 4

Backup your data

If you have built castles in the air, your work need not be lost; that is where they should be. Now put the foundations under them.

Henry David Thoreau

One hundred and fifty years ago Thoreau was contemplating great ideas – his castles in the air – at Walden Pond. He put a foundation under these ideas in writings that influenced Mahatma Gandhi, John F. Kennedy, Leo Tolstoy, and many more.

In the twenty-first century most scholars use computers to help them capture their ideas. When we have recorded our ideas and saved them on our hard drives we may feel like our 'castles in the air' now have foundations, but without secure backups those foundations are weak.

Why would a book about qualitative research techniques and tools devote a whole chapter to backing up your data? The following near-disaster story will help you understand.

As I completed my graduate coursework I wrote many papers related to the topic that would eventually become the focus of my dissertation. Associated with these papers was a large collection of bibliographic references and journal articles.

My aging laptop computer was an invaluable repository of this careful work. This vault of accumulated knowledge was my lifeblood as I prepared for comprehensive exams and constructed my dissertation proposal. This same laptop stored the audio files and typed transcripts of my dissertation interviews. Everything was snugly tucked away on my laptop's hard drive.

After returning from a flight to interview research participants I started my computer, checked my e-mail, and was about to review my recently collected data when I heard a disturbing ker-plunk, ker-plunk, ker-plunk – and then my screen went dead. I tried not to panic.

My entire hard drive was irrevocably damaged and broken parts were rattling around inside the computer. It was a fatal physical crash. The data carefully collected over the years was gone. All of my software programs were useless, even the operating system. The computer was dead, and this was my only computer.

This could happen to you!

When you use computers and digital technology to boost efficiency and enhance research techniques, your computer files are your lifeline. If the files are lost your project is gone. Your castle in the air did not have a foundation.

After I recovered from the shock of hearing ker-plunk, ker-plunk, ker-plunk my mind quickly raced to my backup systems. Were they good enough? Would they be complete? Would they work?

At the time I had two backup systems: a complete backup to an external hard drive and a '*My Documents*' weekly backup on a DVD disk. Luckily, my backup system worked. I didn't lose it all.

What if you hear ker-plunk, ker-plunk, ker-plunk? Or what if your laptop gets stolen? What would happen to your project?

If you feel comfortable with the answer then jump to the next chapter, but if you felt a tinge of panic take this chapter seriously.

Onsite and offsite backups

External hard drives, CD disks, memory sticks, and DVD disks can rescue you in the case of an internal hard drive failure. External hard drives usually remain physically attached to your computer through a cable, and removable CD and DVD disks are frequently stored in your home or office. Most of the time this is good enough, but what if fire, theft, or a natural disaster occurs? Everything stored in a single location could be lost.

Your backup system should include off-site repositories for your data. If you find it impractical to keep off-site backups of your complete hard drive, including your programs and operating system (*Windows*), at least keep off-site backups of your project-related files. Techniques are discussed later in this chapter.

Backups to external hard drives

Large external hard drives are now readily available at all computer and office supply stores. When you buy one, and you should, make sure the capacity of the external hard drive is bigger than the internal hard drive on your computer. External hard drives are very inexpensive relative to the value of the data you have at risk. External hard drives plug into the USB port on your computer. Installation is simple – plug it in.

If you do not know the size of your internal hard drive, start *My Computer*. The primary internal hard drive is usually labeled with a name followed by (C:). Look for your hard drive's size in the 'Total Size' column. If your *My Computer* display does not have a Total Size column, right-click on the drive letter, and then select Properties.

Many external hard drives come with backup software. Look at this software 'feature' when you purchase an external hard drive. Make sure the backup software does a complete image (ghost) type of backup. This type of backup protects against the worst case scenario – an absolute hard drive failure. **If your hard drive utterly crashes you want to be able to *completely* restore all of your programs, all of your data files, and all of your settings** (including the registry) directly from the backup files on your external hard drive.

You should purchase a commercial brand of backup software if you are not satisfied with the features of the backup software you own (you own at least one backup program). Microsoft offers a backup utility under Programs ▶ | Accessories ▶ System Tools|. I have never had a good experience with this backup utility from Microsoft, but it is already installed on your Windows computer.

To find a backup software program that works for you, search the Internet (Google, etc.) for 'backup software reviews.' Because I have not personally reviewed the many choices on the market I cannot say which program is best. I personally use Acronis True Image. This program automatically makes daily full-system backups.

Backups to CD and DVD disks

A standard CD disk holds 650 to 700 MB of data; a DVD holds 4.4 to 4.7 GB of data. This is a lot of storage space. You can store hundreds of text-based books on a CD, and about seven times that amount of data on a DVD. CD and DVD disks (optical disks) are portable and are readable on almost all computers, so they are ideal backup media for your most important data. For most of us, our most important files are in the *My Documents* folder.

Optical disks can store files in *My Documents*, they are portable, and they can easily be archived off site. Optical disks are not optimal for complete system backups because of their limited capacity (see 'Backups to external hard drives').

Your computer probably already has CD writing capabilities, and it might have the ability to write to DVD drives. If you do not have a DVD writer built into your computer, external DVD writers can be purchased at reasonable prices. These devices install easily and plug into a free USB port.

When you purchase CD or DVD disks for backups I recommend that you spend a little extra money and get the RW (rewritable) variety of optical disk. Rewritable disks allow you to write *and* erase files. This allows you to do backups to the same disk over and over again.

The trickiest part of copying (backing up) your files to a CD or DVD is finding the software to do the job. Some extra steps are necessary when you use *My Documents* or *My Computer*, and I have found that these utilities are problematic when copying to optical disks.

I recommend the purchase or free download of software that will make this task of writing to CD or DVD disks easy. Search the Internet (Google, etc.) for 'CD writing software' or 'DVD writing software.' There are several free choices. I use Roxio Easy Media Creator, a program that I find useable even though it has some glitches. If you use this software, the optical disk writing features are in the 'Data' section of the program.

USB flash memory sticks

USB flash memory sticks are best used, like optical disks, for copying/backing up *My Documents* and specific project files. One of the major advantages of using memory sticks vs. CD or DVD disks is the ease of use of these tiny USB devices. Also, memory sticks can be purchased that have significantly more capacity than standard CD and DVD drives.

Simply plug a memory stick into one of your free USB ports and it will be recognized as a drive on your computer. Use the *My Documents* techniques starting on page 41 of Chapter 3 to copy (backup) selected files and folders to the memory stick.

Memory sticks are so portable that many people hook them onto their key rings. Keeping your most important files with you at all times solves some of your off-site storage needs in case of a localized computer disaster.

A problem with always carrying your most important files is security. Confidential data must not be compromised. Standard memory sticks can be made more secure with password protection, and for more security you can buy memory sticks that biometrically recognize your fingerprint. (Yes, these really exist. Agent 007 must be beaming.)

Backups to off-site servers

At the minimum, your most important *My Documents* and project files should be stored off-site to protect from fire, flood, theft, and other potential disasters. This can be done at little or no cost to you.

E-mail files to yourself

Free Web-based e-mail services with Yahoo, Hotmail (now *Windows* Live), Gmail, and others come with at least 2 GB of storage. You can use these e-mail services to store your most important files. To use one or more of your e-mail accounts as backup repositories, send messages to yourself and attach mission critical files. As soon as your e-mail account receives the e-mail message with the attached data you have created a bombproof storage repository.

Your e-mail messages, with backup file attachments, are stored in a secure e-mail server. These files are stored far from your site; in fact, you will probably not even know where in the world your files are stored, but you can access them from virtually any location through the Internet.

Other than the price you pay for monthly Internet services, this is a free backup solution for your mission critical files. Go to Yahoo, Google, Windows Live, and other similar free e-mail sites to create accounts.

A variation on the concept of e-mailing files to various personal e-mail accounts is to upload *Word* and *Excel* files to Google *Docs and Spreadsheets* (docs.google.com). This is an especially attractive solution if you are interested in using the multi-user features of *Google Docs and Spreadsheets*.

Online backup services

Online Internet-based backup services for off-site data storage are readily available at reasonable prices. The advantage of these for-fee data storage services is that your files can be automatically backed up. Every day at a specified time your most important files can be backed up to extremely secure servers.

Search the Internet (Google, etc.) for 'online data storage,' or for 'off site data storage.'

Backups through a local network

If you work in an office with a local area network or a wide area network, there is a good chance that your files are automatically being backed up. Many universities and companies have arrays of servers and other media that routinely backup all of the files on the network, including your computer's files. If your organization does not have an automatic backup system in place you can still do backups through the network by copying mission critical files to another computer on the network. Check with your system administrator for details.

Fireproof safe

Small fire resistant safes protect paper and software during a fire for approximately 30 minutes and the safe helps keep them dry. These safes are relatively inexpensive and available at most office supply stores. The purchase of a fireproof safe large enough to protect your most important paper files, computer disks, and interview tapes is highly recommended.

Remind yourself to do backups

Write the 'backup task' in your paper calendar, set up recurring appointments in your *Outlook* calendar, or stick Post-it notes wherever you will see them. In other words, do not forget to implement your backup system.

Chapter summary

Don't be a loser. That is, don't risk losing your hard work, your data, your analysis, your literature, your references, and your report. You can protect against disasters by backing up your data.

Multiple layers of backups should be maintained. The first line of defense is an external hard drive attached to your computer. This external hard drive should be configured to completely mirror or ghost your computer's internal hard drive, thus allowing the easy restoration of your operating systems, all of your programs, and all of your files in case of the catastrophic failure of your computer's hard drive.

To guard against the complete destruction of your office because of fire, flood, theft, etc. an off-site backup of at least your most important files should be maintained. This can be done by e-mailing files to yourself, paying for an online backup service, or simply copying your most important files to removable media (CD, DVD, memory stick, external hard drive) and storing the removable media in a secure off-site location.

CHAPTER 5

Collecting your data

I never guess. It is a capital mistake to theorize before one has data. Insensibly one begins to twist facts to suit theories, instead of theories to suit facts.

Sir Arthur Conan Doyle

"Perhaps when a man has special knowledge and special powers like my own, it rather encourages him to seek a complex explanation when a simpler one is at hand." *Aah yes! One has to admire the confident wisdom of Doyle's great detective.*

The Adventure of the Abbey Grange

Sherlock Holmes explored obscure nooks and crannies to find the data that allowed him to solve magnificently complex cases. As qualitative researchers, we should keep in mind that 'genius is an infinite capacity for taking pains.'

A Study in Scarlet

All **good researchers** take pains when they collect their data, but unlike quantitative researchers who embark on their research to prove or disprove hypotheses (as Doyle put it – theorizing 'before one has data'), qualitative researchers are open to discoveries that are not limited by pre-existing hypotheses. Qualitative researchers get to savor complexities that would not be allowed in strictly quantitative studies.

With so many types of qualitative data it is impossible to specify one 'best' way to collect data. There must be a great deal of flexibility about how qualitative researchers proceed with data collection, but there is no room for sloppiness. Data collection must be carefully planned, executed, and controlled to gain scholarly respect. Your methodology should be completed and described in a manner that allows your peers and supervisors to understand the care and precision that went into the collection of your data.

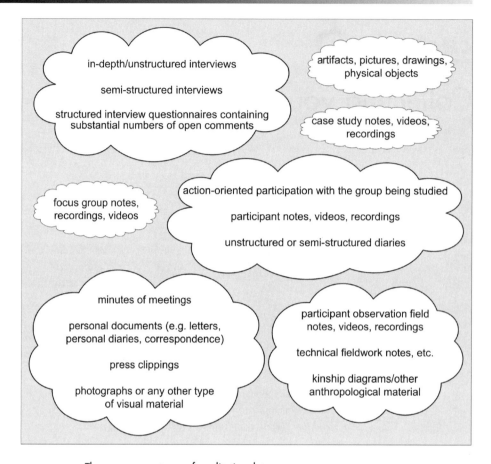

in-depth/unstructured interviews

semi-structured interviews

structured interview questionnaires containing substantial numbers of open comments

artifacts, pictures, drawings, physical objects

case study notes, videos, recordings

focus group notes, recordings, videos

action-oriented participation with the group being studied

participant notes, videos, recordings

unstructured or semi-structured diaries

minutes of meetings

personal documents (e.g. letters, personal diaries, correspondence)

press clippings

photographs or any other type of visual material

participant observation field notes, videos, recordings

technical fieldwork notes, etc.

kinship diagrams/other anthropological material

There are many types of qualitative data.

Preparing for interviews and fieldwork

All qualitative research methods have core commonalities that are explored below, but it is beyond the scope of this book to explain the nuances of each major qualitative method. You are encouraged to study one or more of the leading methods books in your area of specialization (ethnography, grounded theory, phenomenology, focus groups, case studies, etc.) so you can understand the fundamentals of your research method.

The focus of this section is on data–gathering techniques that are broadly useful for qualitative researchers. In one way or another, all qualitative research methods involve the accumulation of data that must eventually be analyzed and coded. These data may be transcripts from interviews or video recordings, they may be derived from documents written by others, and they may be researchers' written observations in the form of field notes, descriptions, and memos.

Recording interviews, cases, and participant interactions

Taking notes during an interview or observation causes a split in the researcher's focus. Part of your brain is directing your eyes and fingers to write down something you just heard while another part of your brain is listening to what is being said while you are writing. This is a fundamental conflict.

The solution to this problem is to use audio and/or video recorders to capture words and actions. When you record your interviews and other data collection activities you free yourself to be in the moment.

Record your data collection activities on electronic media whenever it is feasible. The data you collect are so important that redundant (backup) recorders are strongly recommended. I like to take it even a step further – record your data collection activities using two different types of media; say, digital *and* analog (cassette tape) audio recordings, or videotaping *and* audio recording. Whatever equipment you choose, test and practice your recording techniques before conducting a real-life data recording session.

It is impossible to overstate the importance of keeping your data secure. After they are created, store your data recordings in fireproof safes, and keep your primary and backup recordings in different locations. If your data is confidential in nature, make sure you adhere to all of the security commitments you made to your Institutional Review Board (IRB) and your participants. Keep the recording media safe from fire, theft, vandalism, unauthorized eyes, and other hostile elements.

Tape recorders, video recorders, and transcription equipment

Digital recording is the technique of choice because the files can be electronically backed up, e-mailed, and edited. Weak digital recordings can be enhanced and boosted using readily available software. Techniques like this are not as accessible for physical media like cassette tapes.

In our digital world, cassette recorders are still valuable, especially as backup recorders. Transcription playback equipment is readily available for cassettes and mini-cassettes at office supply stores, so do not throw out perfectly good equipment that you already have.

Selecting digital recorders

An amazing number of choices are available to capture voice recordings to digital files. To get the job done inexpensively you might not have to look farther than the microphone in your MP3 player or cell phone. I have recorded numerous interviews with the tiny microphone in my MP3 player without losing a word.

The rapid rate of technological advancement and change makes it imprudent to mention name brands and specific models because new products regularly enter the market. A bit of research on the Internet will lead you to viable recording equipment solutions. For information on specific equipment conduct a Web search for 'mp3 voice recorder,' 'cell phone voice recorder,' or 'digital voice recorder.'

Recording telephone interviews and conference calls

Telephone conversations and recorded conference calls (that can be transcribed) do not work into all research plans, but data gathering through the telephone is appropriate in many situations. Phone-based data collection can greatly expand the geographic scope and lower the cost of a research project. Telephone interviews lose some of the nuances that are more observable during in-person interviews, but they also offer privacy. Participants may be more relaxed talking with you on the telephone from their home than they would be in a face-to-face interview.

As with in-person interviews, telephone interviews should be recorded. It is unethical to record phone conversations without permission. If you are going to gather data through the phone, all participants should be informed of your intention to use recording equipment when the call is scheduled, and again at the time of the call.

It is possible to create primary and backup recordings of phone interviews and conference calls by (a) using a conference call service to record the call, and (b) making a backup of the call directly onto your computer with inexpensive audio capture equipment and software.

The primary call recording technique

The best sound quality will likely come from conference call recordings. FreeConferenceCall.com provides this free service in Austria, Belgium, France, Germany, Ireland, Italy, the Netherlands, Spain, Switzerland, the UK, and the USA.

Similar services may also be available in the countries listed above and in other countries. Search the Internet for 'conference calling' or 'conference call recording' to identify a system that works for you. Since I have never had a reason to dislike FreeConference, I have not tested other systems.

To use the FreeConference system sign up for a FreeConferenceCall.com account. You will be given a dedicated phone number, an access code, and a subscriber PIN. These identification items are necessary to utilize the FreeConference services.

To conduct a conference call, all parties must call the specified telephone number, and then enter the PIN when prompted. The service automatically connects all of the callers.

Recording the phone call (even if it is just two people) does not happen automatically with FreeConference. During a conference call, the host can initiate the recording by pressing 9 at any time. After the call is completed, log into the host account to download the recording. If you do not want to have your participants pay long distance fees for the phone calls you can upgrade your account so all of your participants may dial-in with a toll-free number.

Services like this provide you with inexpensive and high quality recordings of telephone-based data collection. Practice the techniques before using them with participants.

The backup call recording technique

Hardware to record phone calls at your site can be expensive (professional dictation quality) or inexpensive. This discussion will focus on the inexpensive solution.

The reason that I call this a 'backup' technique is that the sound quality captured with inexpensive hardware can be marginal with some phone connections. The biggest problem is that the sound input from the participants (from remote telephones) is weaker than the input from the local telephone that is connected to the recording device. The disparity in input signals makes it difficult to set an optimal recording level.

Phone calls and many other audio sources can be captured by your computer and other recording hardware devices that accept input through 3.5 mm/1/8th inch mini plugs (tape recorders and mini disk players). Data capture through these telephone recording devices emanates from a telephone wall jack or a phone handset, depending on the type of device you choose. Search the Internet for 'digital audio capture' or 'telephone recorder adapter' to find sources of these telephone audio-capture devices.

The simple hardware described above must be accompanied by digital recording software. An Internet search for 'audio capture software' will provide several viable software choices, some of which are free. Use the instructions that come with the program you choose. Make sure the software you choose provides output to common formats like .wav and .mp3.

After the recording session

Immediately after a recording session (interview, focus group, etc.), take some time to organize your materials while all of the details of the interview are still fresh in your mind.

1. Check the tapes to make sure everything worked technically.
2. Review your notes to see if any additions or changes should be made.
3. Prepare your files and tapes for transcription and get the file/tape to the transcriptionist if you are not doing your own transcription. File the backup in a safe/fireproof place.
4. Send thank-you letters or e-mails to all participants. Mail merge works well for this if there are numerous participants.

Researcher observations and descriptions

It is not always possible or appropriate for researchers to capture the verbatim words of participants or members of the study. Often, the researcher must describe an ethnographic scene, the behavior of a focus group, or the importance of an artifact using his or her skills as an observer–writer. In these situations written field notes and documents are data. These data, compiled from multiple observations and descriptions, become the raw material for subsequent qualitative coding and analysis.

Emerson, Fretz, and Shaw (1995) offer implications for writing field notes with a focus on ethnographic research. The four points below, based on their suggestions, are broadly applicable to all qualitative data that are created from the written or dictated words of the researcher.

1. What is observed, written down, or dictated as data is inseparable from the observational process.
2. The researcher should give special attention to the indigenous meanings and concerns given to situations, interactions, and objects.
3. Field notes written or dictated at the time of an observation are an essential grounding for subsequent analysis and reporting.
4. Field notes should capture the in-situ social interactions and physical context of the people and situations being studied.

Transcription

To advance to the next step in the analysis of your data, a written copy of the words collected in audio and/or video recordings is essential. For data originally captured in audio or audio-visual format, tools are available to make the transcription process efficient.

Transcription playback equipment, and software for digital audio files

Traditional cassette tape-based transcription is done with a tape player controlled by a foot pedal. The foot pedal allows the hands-free ability to start (play), stop, rewind, and fast forward the tape. After playing a section by pressing a pedal with your foot, the transcription equipment automatically rewinds a bit so you can check the words and phrases you typed before you advance to the next phrase.

Fine tuning is possible. For example, you can adjust the amount of automatic rewind that takes place when you release the pedal. I recommend that you borrow or purchase transcribing equipment if you are transcribing a sizable amount of text from cassette tapes. This type of equipment is commonly used by secretaries, medical assistants, and court personnel who professionally transcribe voice recordings, so this equipment is available at most office supply stores.

The playback of digital audio files requires no special physical equipment because there is no mechanical tape, but the needs of the transcriptionist are the same. Software and foot pedals are available for computer-based digital audio and video files that duplicate time-tested transcriptionist tools, but you may find that foot pedals are not necessary for your computer-based transcription projects because transcription software can put foot pedal power on your keyboard. The same play, stop, auto rewind, and fast forward features built into tape playback equipment are available in transcription software. Because transcription software is visible on your computer screen, you can transcribe without diverting your hands or eyes from the keyboard or monitor.

Here is the best part; perfectly usable digital audio file transcription software is freely available. The company in Australia that makes Express Scribe gives the program away via free downloads in the hope that they will promote the purchase of their companion product Express Dictate. Conduct a Web search for 'transcription software' to find Express Scribe and similar programs. Optional foot pedals are available.

The audio tracks of video recordings (using standard formats like .mov, .wmv, and .avi) can also be transcribed using readily available for-fee software. Search the Web for 'transcribe video files,' or if you want to get more specific about the output from your video recorder, include the specific file type in your search, for example, 'transcribe mov files.'

Voice recognition transcription software

I was an early adopter. I tried to use voice recognition software in the early days of personal computers. It was pretty awful and not worth the trouble. I confess that I have not been brave enough to use newer incarnations of voice recognition, but I know people who have. The following is a paraphrased quote from a colleague.

"I have finished my interviews, but what helped me transcribe data? I have a point and speak program that allows me to speak and transcribe data into a word processor (*Word*). I am using audio tapes of my interviews and transcribing them into *Word* documents by repeating the contents of my tapes into a microphone. The program has performed well!" He used a product called Dragon Point and Speak.

A major problem with voice recognition software is that it requires familiarity with one voice at a time. This rules it out for transcribing an interview or other multi-party recording directly from a tape or audio file. To use the transcription software to transcribe an interview you have to speak the entire interview (the words of *all* participants) into the software.

Editing digital audio files

A nice advantage of collecting your audio data in digital files is the ability to edit and enhance the quality of the recordings. It is possible to boost a very weak voice so that it becomes understandable. Audio editing software ranges in price from free to moderate. Search the Web for 'audio editing software' or 'audio editing software reviews' to locate and select a product that works for you. You will not need advanced music editing features to edit voice recordings.

Audio file conversion can (a) help reduce the size of your audio files (.wav to .mp3 or .wma), and (b) convert your files to a format that can be read by your transcription software. Software to convert audio files is available free or for a moderate fee.

I have been able to shrink file sizes by converting files from stereo. WAV format (44 kHz, 2 Channel 16 bit) to mono WMA format (32 kbps, 1 channel). The size can be reduced, extraordinarily, to about 3% of its original size without noticeable degradation of quality.

Search the Web for 'audio file type conversion' or 'audio file converter.'

Doing your own transcriptions and working with transcriptionists

To transcribe your own files, or not to transcribe your own files? That is the question. Some people have strong opinions on both sides of this argument. Since I have done my own transcription work and hired transcriptionists I understand the rationale for both approaches.

The main arguments for doing your own transcription are that you will save a lot of money, guarantee confidentiality, and you will grow much closer to your data as you transcribe. Transcribing is a pre-coding immersion into your data.

The main argument for hiring a transcriptionist is that you can move much faster and cover more material because you are not bogged down by the tedious process of transcribing. Consider your budget, your timelines, confidentiality requirements, the amount of data that are in your project, and the preferences of your advisors when you make your decision to transcribe on your own or hire someone to do the transcription.

Digital files and the Internet have created world-wide availability of transcription services. The lowest cost English language transcription services tend to be in India. On the other hand, because of subtle phrasing and detailed instructions you want to pass on, it is often nice to work with a local transcriptionist. Search the Web for 'transcription services' if you want to use an online transcriptionist.

Whatever path you choose, do not compromise on the quality of your data. If you are doing your own transcription, hold yourself to high standards. If you are hiring a transcriptionist, carefully check his or her work. Refer back to the original recording if you are in doubt about any word or phrase.

Formatting your transcript (transcriptionist instructions)

Transcription can be done with any text-editing software, but there are advantages to using *Word*. If you use *Word* to transcribe your audio data

(a) you will not have to import your transcripts into *Word* for coding, (b) you can use AutoComplete to accelerate typing, and (c) you can use macros to accelerate typing.

No matter what software is used during transcription, use this simple rule while transcribing: **create a new paragraph every time a new person starts speaking.**

For example,

> (new paragraph) Interviewer: How is the weather today?
> (new paragraph) Participant 1: I feel like I want to run away.
> (new paragraph) Participant 2: So do I.
> (new paragraph) Interviewer: Why?

The creation of a new paragraph every time a different person speaks is important to the subsequent formatting of the document for Level 1 coding. The detailed techniques for this formatting process are described in Chapter 6.

While recommended, it is not necessary to type in identifiers like Interviewer, Participant 1, and Participant 2 if the structure of the conversation or interview makes the identities of the speakers self-evident. If you chose to identify each speaker at the beginning of each paragraph a code can be established for each speaker; such as, 'I,' 'P1,' and 'P2' for Interviewer, Participant 1, and Participant 2.

Using 'Macros' and 'AutoComplete' for repetitive tasks during transcription

Suppose you are doing research on the Djaberadjabera aboriginal group in the Kimberly region of Western Australia. You know you are going to have to type Djaberadjabera a lot of times. (Just the thought of this makes me worry about carpal tunnel syndrome.)

Now suppose that you could type Djaberadjabera simply by pressing Ctrl+D (a macro). Or just start typing the first characters D-j-a-b, and then the whole word pops up to be automatically inserted using the auto complete feature of *Word*. You could save a lot of time and frustration in the course of transcribing extensive interviews and writing subsequent reports.

Macros

Tools ► Macro ► Record New Macro

Macros record all of your keystrokes and mouse clicks. Use them to complete repetitive activities. It is a good idea to create a macro whenever you find yourself repeating the same phrase, big word, or sequence of commands over and over again. Make a macro if you find yourself getting annoyed with repetitive keyboard and mouse motions. After making a couple of macros you will be able to create them with ease. To make a macro:

Be prepared to type the phrase and/or execute the commands that you want to record before creating a new macro. Then, from the menu select <u>Tools ▶ Macro ▶ Record New Macro</u>. In the Macro name box, type a name for the macro.

By default the new macro will be available in all documents. If you want the macro to be available only in the current document, click in the 'Store macro in' box, click on the file name of the current document.

In the Description box, type a description of the macro if you want to change the default description.

I strongly recommend that you assign the macro to a shortcut key, so click on the 'Keyboard' icon. In the 'Press new shortcut key' box, press the key sequence that you want to use when you execute the macro (for example, <u>Ctrl+W</u>) and then click Assign. Click 'Close' to begin recording the macro. At this point all of your keystrokes are being recorded so **press only the keys and click only the commands you want recorded.**

Perform the actions you want to include in your macro. When you record a macro, you can use the mouse to click commands and options, but not to select text. Use the keyboard to type in words or phrases. *To select text use keyboard commands. For example, you can use F8 to start selecting text – press the arrow keys to select text – press F9 to stop selecting text.*

To stop recording your macro, click 'Stop Recording' on the small toolbar that appeared on your screen when you started recording the macro.

To execute the macro, press the shortcut key combination you selected before you started recording the macro.

AutoComplete/AutoText

AutoComplete will finish typing a long word or phrase for you.

Highlight (select) the word you want to store as an AutoText entry. I selected <u>Djaberadjabera ▶ Insert ▶ AutoText ▶ New (Alt+F3)</u>.

To use AutoComplete, the word or phrase must contain at least four characters because *Word* inserts the entry only after the first four characters have been typed. After typing the first four letters of the AutoComplete string *Word* inserts the selected text in the Create AutoText window that appears. Make changes as necessary, and then click on OK.

Now, give it a try. After typing the first four letters of the word the entire word will appear. For example, when I type 'Djab' AutoComplete causes a box like the one below to pop up on the screen.

Press Enter when this box pops up to insert the AutoComplete word.

typing the first Djaberadjabera (Press ENTER to Insert)
For example, when I type Djab

Editing and assigning keyboard shortcuts

From time to time you may want to edit and assign keyboard shortcuts, not just for the macros you make, but for virtually every other *Word* command, AutoText, or toolbar choice. You can also use the following procedure to look up the keyboard commands previously assigned.

From the menu, Tools ▶ Customize ... the following box will appear.

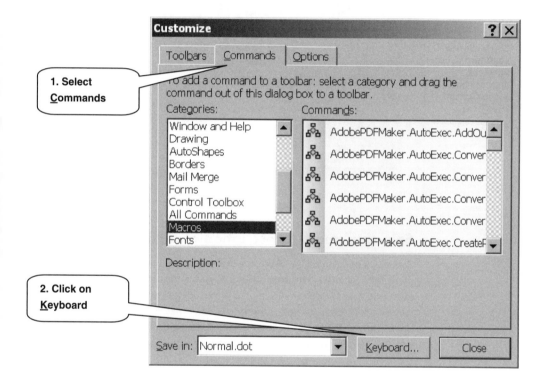

You can assign keyboard shortcuts to any command. This example shows the Ctrl+E shortcut that I use to execute a macro I made that types the word '*Excel*' in italics.

There is no straightforward way to get a list of all of the keyboard shortcuts you have made. To take a look at the keyboard combinations assigned to specific macros, scroll through the macros and look at the entries in the 'Current keys:' box.

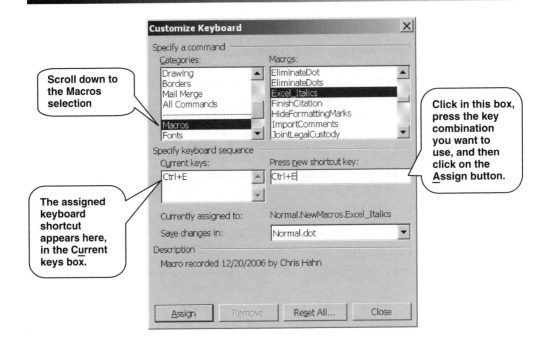

Scroll down to the Macros selection

Click in this box, press the key combination you want to use, and then click on the Assign button.

The assigned keyboard shortcut appears here, in the Current keys box.

Selective audio transcription of digital files

Advances in technology make it possible for the researcher to deftly review and precisely mark locations in digital audio files to one tenth of a second. Without mechanical rewinding to slow down the process, the researcher can instantly jump to audio file bookmarks that are named with substantial descriptions. With the help of audio transcription software it is nearly as easy to review data in audio files as it is to review traditionally typed transcripts.

Qualitative researchers can use selective audio transcription in certain circumstances to identify and bookmark Level 1 codes (see Chapter 6) and other relevant passages without transcribing the entire audio file. Using this technique, only the text directly associated with codes is transcribed.

During selective audio transcription Level 1 codes are written as bookmarks in the audio transcription software (Express Scribe). Each Level 1 code is later copied into a *Word* code document. The verbatim text (quotation) that inspired the Level 1 code must be typed and transcribed in the *Word* code document adjacent to the Level 1 code.

This technique is described in more detail in Chapter 6. It is mentioned in passing here to make readers aware that selective audio transcription is an option for some projects, particularly where recordings have a high ratio of non-relevant chatter to code-quality data.

Naming transcript and code document files

Once you have collected data and transcribed it you have a collection of precious objects. In Chapter 3 broad strategies for file names, folder names, and folder organization were considered, but specific naming schemes for data files and transcripts were not discussed. An orderly system of naming your files can save you time and facilitate efficient searches in the analysis stage.

When you look at a sizable list of files in *My Documents,* specific files can be hard to find if the list of file names is random and unsorted. Generally it is not a good idea to get too clever with the cryptographic naming of files because longer descriptive names jog the memory better after time has passed, but it is a good strategy to develop long-name systems that facilitate easy sorting in *My Documents.*

By the time you start collecting data you will have a very good idea of the number of participants or sites you expect, their geographic locations, their sex, their approximate ages, affiliations with groups, and other identifying characteristics. To identify the files associated with specific participants or sites, a binomial or trinomial naming system will create order. This example can be expanded to facilitate the naming of files associated with any type of data including transcript files, audio files, audio-visual files, scanned illustrations, press reports, and photographs.

A binomial naming system has two primary naming components. For example, the third female participant from the University of Nebraska might get a binomial name of p4F-sUN (participant 4th Female, school University of Nebraska), or 4F-UN, or simply 4fUN. For more complex situations create a trinomial system.

It is a good idea to name your cryptogram files in a way that allows them to be sorted alphabetically in a folder in *My Documents.* The following example uses extremely simplified binomial filenames that start with a participant number (the first part of the binomial) and include only a single letter (the second part of the binomial.).

The name of all files directly begins with the participant number according to the time they entered the study. The letter that follows indicates the participant's sex (but other identifying characteristics could be used, such as state or social group). This example will use 'm' for male or 'f' for female.

Sequential filenames using this simplified binomial system would appear in a list as 1f.doc, 1m.doc, 2f.doc, 2m.doc, etc. Again, I keep the names very simple here because I want to illustrate a quirk in the Windows sorting system in *My Documents.*

 Warning

My Documents sorts numbers as text

The Windows naming schema will corrupt the simple system described above if you have more than 10 participants. Windows filenames are sorted as 'text' even though they might start with a number. Why is this important? Because your files will look like the list below on the left if you do not modify your filenames.

An unmodified list of numerical filenames looks like this in *My Documents*	A modified list of numerical filenames sorts properly in *My Documents*
1f Transcript 1.doc	_1f Transcript 1.doc
10f Transcript 10.doc	_2f Transcript 2.doc
11f Transcript 11.doc	_3m Transcript 3.doc
12m Transcript 12.doc	_4f Transcript 4.doc
2f Transcript 2.doc	_5m Transcript 5.doc
3m Transcript 3.doc	_6m Transcript 6.doc
4f Transcript 4.doc	_7f Transcript 7.doc
5m Transcript 5.doc	_8m Transcript 8.doc
6m Transcript 6.doc	_9m Transcript 9.doc
7f Transcript 7.doc	10f Transcript 10.doc
8m Transcript 8.doc	11f Transcript 11.doc
9m Transcript 9.doc	12m Transcript 12.doc

If you want your filenames to be sorted numerically, and you have more than 10 files, put an underscore (_) in front of single-digit numbers to insure that they are sorted properly. The text that follows the initial numeric part of the cryptogram can be descriptive and as long as you like, the key to the sorting order is the beginning 1 or 2 characters in the filename. This system is shown in the right column above.

When the transcript files are transformed into code document files, as described in Chapter 6, the transcript files should be saved under new and more descriptive file names, such as

_1f code document 1.doc
_2f code document 2.doc
_3m code document 3.doc, etc.

You will save a lot of time throughout the duration of your research project if you invest time in the creation of a file naming system and if you take time to regularly maintain the filing system.

Chapter summary

The qualitative researcher has a considerable amount of creative freedom when deciding how to collect the project's data, but creativity must not be accompanied by sloppiness. The researcher's goal is to collect data that can be systematically categorized in a manner that withstands careful scrutiny. The open-ended and free-form nature of qualitative data requires the qualitative researcher to gather data with integrity and scientific rigor.

Participant interviews, focus groups, and other data sources that are collections of verbatim spoken words should be recorded, preferably using digital technology. Observational and descriptive data collection techniques require the researcher to write (or record) field notes and memos that directly relate to the research topic.

Because the final product of the study is a written report, the data relevant to the study must be described and/or transcribed into written words. During transcription there are techniques available in *Word* to speed the data entry process including the creation of macros, the use of AutoComplete, and the use of keyboard shortcuts. The completed transcripts are formatted to create code documents for subsequent analysis.

Transcript files, audio files, audio-visual files, scanned pictures, and other data files that are created during the data collection process should be named in an orderly manner that allows the researcher to identify and return to the files during later research stages. Naming schemes that use binomial and trinomial components are recommended. The *Windows* file system allows long file names so there is no reason to cause confusion by using unnecessarily cryptic file names.

CHAPTER 6

Level 1 coding

The important thing is not to stop questioning. Curiosity has its own reason for existing. One cannot help but be in awe when he contemplates the mysteries of eternity, of life, of the marvelous structure of reality. It is enough if one tries merely to comprehend a little of this mystery every day. Never lose a holy curiosity.

Albert Einstein

F **inally, the data** are collected, described, and transcribed! By the time you get to this point in your research project you probably have mixed feelings of excitement, exhaustion, pride, and (perhaps) apprehension about the next step. Level 1 coding is the first step in the cerebral process of sifting through your data to gain the insight necessary to answer your research questions *based on the data.*

The data coding process is iterative. It consists of multiple stages that prepare and format raw data so that they are available for evaluation, synthesis, and analysis. The goal of the coding process is to focus ideas and to organize data that exemplify concepts, categories, and themes. Level 1 coding is the first step; it reduces qualitative data to a much more manageable focus. Level 1 coding is also known as initial coding or open coding.

Coding can be done in an orderly step-by-step manner, but it always requires the researcher to do some serious thinking. The main research instrument of qualitative research is the researcher, that's you. You don't have to be an Einstein but you are going to have to think. Now for the good news – this process can flow easily and result in well-organized data.

The software programs in Microsoft *Office* including *Word, Excel,* and *Access* are designed to be broadly modifiable by the end user. Chapters 6, 7, and 8 of this book show you how to construct your own coding and analysis system. The tutorial lessons build on a downloadable generic template that can serve as a standalone program or as a springboard for your creative customization.

The end result will be your own qualitative research system. The goal is to use your computer to eliminate unnecessary inefficiencies, thus freeing you to work faster and think more deeply. As an added bonus you are likely to learn some new software skills that will be applicable to your everyday work for years to come.

Data coding in Microsoft *Word* – creating the code document

Introduction to the code document

The first formal analytic pass through your memos, field notes, and transcripts takes place during Level 1 coding. The process starts with raw unformatted text and ends with a well-organized *code document* that includes a Table of Contents, a Table of Codes, an Index, Level 1 code descriptions, and highlighted original text data that corresponds with each Level 1 code.

Reading carefully through lengthy text documents takes time, and coding requires more than simply reading. It takes concentration to decide when Level 1 codes must be created and which corresponding passages of text must be highlighted during this first coding step. This is true whether you do your coding the traditional way (on paper) or with this computer-based system.

The investment of the time required to create a well-formatted code document is significant, but it is time well spent. The code document created in *Word* during the Level 1 coding process will greatly accelerate later stages of analysis and writing. To give you a boost and to allow you to learn from an actual *Word* file, a template for a code document is provided at qrtips.com/chapter6.

The creation of the code document requires several steps:

⇒ Saving the transcript text to a code document file in *Word*
⇒ Converting the entire transcript to a three-column table; all paragraphs become individual rows
⇒ Carefully reading through the transcribed data to identify, create, and mark your Level 1 codes
⇒ Marking and preserving the verbatim data that inspired the individual Level 1 codes
⇒ Creating a Table of Contents for the Code document
⇒ Creating a Table of Codes for the Code document
⇒ Creating an Index for the code document.

Converting the transcript to a code document

It does not matter what text editor or word processor was used to create the transcript, but what does matter is that a new paragraph was created every time the conversation shifted from one person to another. If your transcripts do not have paragraph breaks every time a different person starts speaking, I suggest that you take time to edit the transcript. It should go fast, simply press Enter after each section of text that represents a shift from one speaker to the next. Full transcription instructions are included in Chapter 5.

Open the transcript file

If the transcript was created in a program other than *Word*, it is time to make the transition to *Word*. Open the file using *Word* – File ▶ Open. Browse to find the location of the transcript file that will be used as the base for your code document.

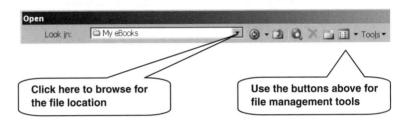

If your transcript file is not in a format that is initially recognized by *Word* as a *Word* document (such as .txt), change the setting in the File ▶ Open dialog box so that 'All Files' are displayed.

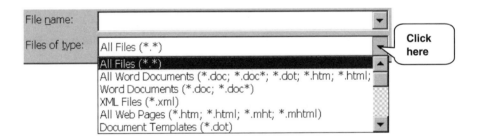

Use 'Save <u>A</u>s' to create the code document

After you open the transcript file in *Word*, immediately save the document using a new file name. This will preserve the original transcript file, and create the code document in *Word*'s native format.

File ▶ Save <u>A</u>s...

Save the file as a *Word* document (.doc). Name the file according to a logical naming scheme (see the *Naming transcript and code document files* section of Chapter 5). Store the new file in a special folder for code documents (see the *My Documents* section of Chapter 3).

The new file you created is the core of your code document, but several more steps are required to optimize it.

Format the code document with row counters and a column for Level 1 code descriptions (without touching the transcript data)

Formatting the code document is a dramatic process that requires several steps. These steps might seem tedious at first, but all the steps are straightforward. Code document formatting moves quickly after you have done it a couple of times, and the rewards of working with a nicely formatted code document are far greater than the effort required to set up the file.

1. Open the newly created (still unformatted) *Word* code document. A greatly abbreviated sample is shown below.

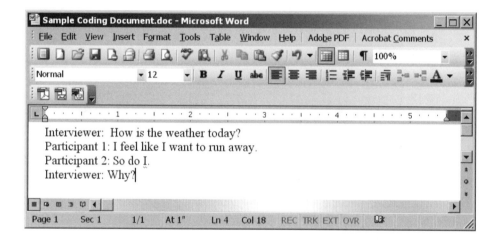

2. Select everything in the entire document by pressing Ctrl+A (everything in the document will be selected).

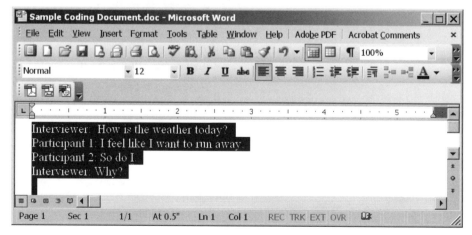

3. (a) Convert the entire document into a table. Table ▸ Insert ▸ Table. (b) While the entire document is highlighted you can change other settings. In this example the line spacing is changed from single line spacing to 1.5 line spacing.

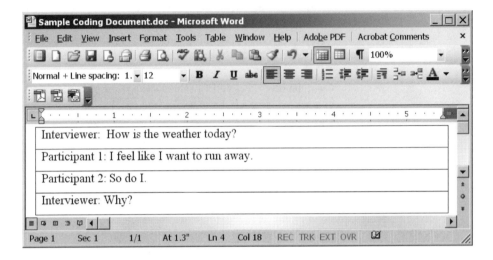

4. Create a new column to the left of your text data. Click within the table so the table has the focus, and then select Table ▸ Insert ▸ Columns to the Left. You will eventually type Level 1 codes in this column.

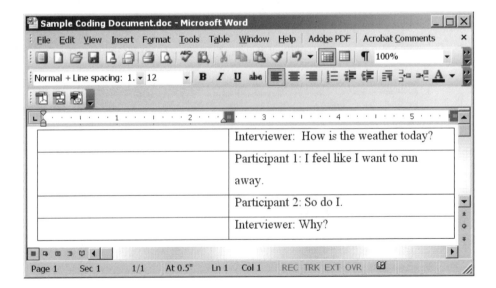

5. Resize the new column by placing the mouse pointer on the border between the two columns. When the pointer changes to the double arrow icon, press and hold the left mouse button, and then resize the column by sliding the mouse to the left.

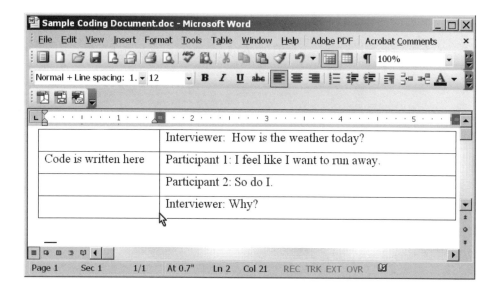

6. Now, after clicking in the left column to give it the focus, create another column to the left of your new column – Table ▶ Insert ▶ Columns to the Left. Resize the new (far left) column so it is just big enough to hold 2 or 3 numerical digits.

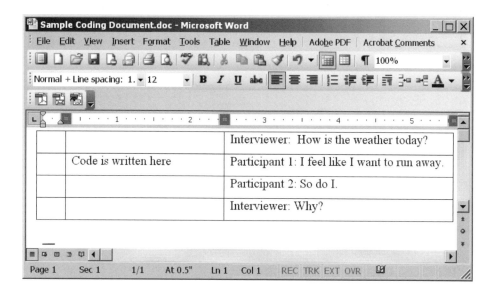

7. Click in the far left (newest) column. Select Table ▶ Select ▶ Column. The entire far left column should become black after it is selected. While the column is selected, click on the numbering icon on the toolbar ⊞, or select Format ▶ Bullets and Numbering ▶ select the Numbered tab ▶ click on one of the numbered lists.

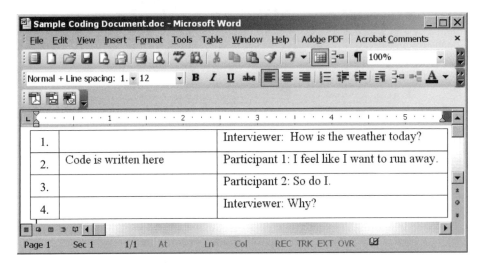

The numbered left column allows you to positively identify the location of each Level 1 code and its accompanying data

Optional formatting to improve readability

8. Select the far left column – Table ▶ Select ▶ Column. While it is selected, click on Format ▶ Paragraph. I recommend the settings shown below.

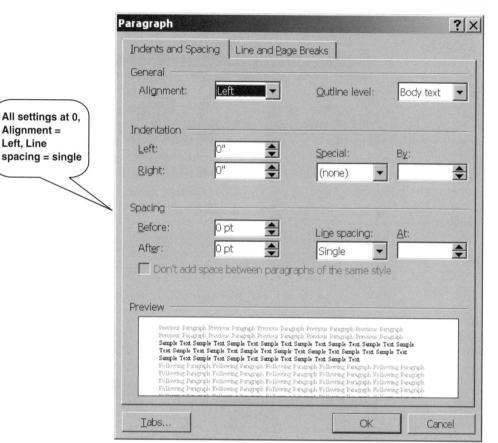

All settings at 0, Alignment = Left, Line spacing = single

Press OK when your settings changes are completed.

9. Use your mouse to select the top number in the left column. Change the font to something smaller, I suggest 8 pt. Format ▶ Font ▶ Font tab, then change the Size to 8 and then press OK. All of the numbers in the list will change.

10. Now we will change the font size in the middle column. Click in the middle column where the codes will be written, and then select Table ▶ Select ▶ Column. Change the font size to 8 (or whatever you prefer).

The final result looks like this:

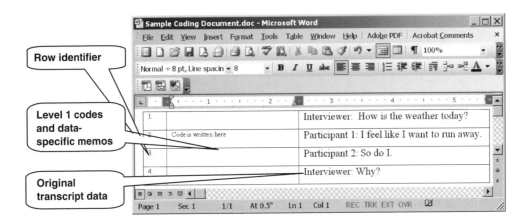

Row identifier

Level 1 codes and data-specific memos

Original transcript data

You are now ready to begin Level 1 coding. Take the time to fine tune the appearance of your code document as your needs change throughout the project.

Remember to save your document, Ctrl+S.

Reading, thinking, and identifying – create your Level 1 codes and memos

Now that the structure of your code document is in place it is easier to visualize the Level 1 coding process.

Overview

1. Read through the formatted code document.
2. When you come to a passage that is relevant enough to inspire a Level 1 code, write a code description in the middle column.
3. In the right column, use text effects (colors, bold, etc.) to mark the section of text that inspired the creation of the Level 1 code.
4. Each row will be identifiable because of the sequential numbering already entered in the far left column.

What is a code? How do you know what text passage is relevant enough to justify a Level 1 code? How do you phrase the code description? What is the proper way to think through the process of identifying codes? These are questions that relate to the core of your research method.

In general, a Level 1 code is a thought captured in a phrase that can help answer your research questions. This phrase (and the supporting raw text) is a small puzzle piece. It takes many Level 1 codes, all directly inspired by the data, to provide the foundation for higher level analysis. Eventually, Level 1 codes are used to develop categories and themes.

Method-specific fundamentals and details are mission critical, but beyond the scope of this book. Consult with your advisors, refer to research methods books that relate to your specific qualitative method, and interact with other scholars. The deep thinking process that allows categories, themes, and theories to emerge should be framed by the experience of scholars in your field. Type Level 1 codes into the middle column of the code document.

Level 1 codes are created rapidly without undue deliberation or an immediate attempt at duplication or categorization. The main question is: can the data that inspired the code be used, even in a small way, to support a theme that helps answer your research questions?

What is a memo? As you are quickly working your way through a code document, ideas and facts frequently appear that explain participant demographics, sequential events, discrete incidents, actions, and proceedings. These are important things to note because they provide structure to the study and are important when you describe the context of the study. Memos are different from codes because they provide an understanding of the context and framework of the study rather than research-question-specific phrases to be used in category and theme building.

Use a memo to identify facts, events, and any other ideas that are important to the study. What are the ages of your participants? What are their living conditions? Where do they live? What is their favorite holiday? These questions might not help you directly answer your research questions, but they provide descriptive scaffolding for your study. **Write memos in the middle column of the code document** (the same area used for Level 1 codes). There are no rules about the style or length of these memos.

As you will see later in this chapter, in 'Writing memos and creating a Table of Contents for the memos,' these memos can be conveniently organized into a table of contents by marking them with Heading styles. This Table of Contents makes it easy to find and revisit the sections in your data that related to memos.

> A key point to understand before you start coding is that you need to record Level 1 codes *and* memos in the middle column when you make your first pass through the code document.

Identifying, creating, and marking Level 1 codes

By the time you make your first pass through the document you undoubtedly will have a lot of data to read, so **the pace of Level 1 coding should be rapid**. Your goal is to identify sections of the document that are directly relevant to the categorization of ideas related to your research topic. Once you identify these sections your job is to create Level 1 codes or write memos.

Quickly move through sections of transcript data which are off topic. These sections generate no codes and few memos.

Create and write down Level 1 code phrases (codes) when you find a section in the text that speaks to you and might help answer one or more of your research questions. Stop to create a Level 1 code whenever a data segment supports a possible topic-related category.

How should you write your code? Stay close to the data. Let the passage of text help create your words. Do not spend too much time getting the phrasing perfect. Each Level 1 code phrase can be different. *Level 2, Level 3, and Level 4 coding gives you plenty of opportunity to refine code language and group together codes into categories,* so do not waste time over-analyzing your codes during Level 1 coding.

| A tip from grounded theory – use gerunds |

I find a rule espoused by Glaser (1978) and Charmaz (2006) to be helpful during all phases of coding: the use of gerunds. Gerunds, loosely defined, end in 'ing.' Even though present participles also end in 'ing,' do not worry about the technicalities of using verbal nouns (gerunds) or non-finite verbs (participles). Instead, think of the meaning you want to put into the Level 1 codes you create. You might find that words ending in 'ing' will help because they give a sense of action and sequence.

| How and where should you write your Level 1 codes? |

Write your codes in the middle column of your code document in the same row as the data that generated the idea. After you write your code, mark the code and its accompanying text data with the same formatting features. This formatting allows the code to be quickly correlated with the data. *Word* has a lot of ways to identify and format text.

Marking and preserving verbatim data used to develop individual Level 1 codes

133.		What are the factors that allowed joint custody to work for you?
134.	*Being flexible* *Being forgiving* *Being respectful*	*Flexibility, forgiveness – of him and myself – keeping the kids as a priority and realizing it needs to be about them. And I think respect.* You have to be able to have some respect…Pete was never out there going through a midlife crisis making an ass out of himself with some goofy hairdo and clothes and a gold chain and being an embarrassment with some bimbo on his arm…so I wasn't having to sit at a program with him with some trophy girl thinking "what is he doing?" He's dated some pretty respectable people that if he's had somebody with him, they've been just fine. So that really helps because that helps you respect the other person, that they're working hard in life and a good citizen of America [laughing]

As the example above shows, the codes and the data that led to the code idea are marked in *italics* for the top two codes, *'Being flexible'* and *'Being forgiving.'* The bottom code, 'Being respectful' is marked with the gray color.

Choose from the many formatting features of *Word* to identify and mark text including footnoting, [commenting] , coloring, highlighting , and *styling* **text**. Be creative in applying these tools to mark and annotate significant parts of the data.

Let *Word* organize the document for you

For smaller projects the code table may be sorted by column in lieu of building a Table of Codes or Table of Contents, Table ▶ Sort.

You will save yourself a lot of wasted time in later stages of your project if you learn and apply the features of *Word*'s pre-programmed Table of Contents, Table of Codes (Table of Authorities), and Index selections. These features are all special *Word* fields that allow you to condense and summarize the results of the memos, comments and codes you created while doing your Level 1 coding. These features are all accessed through the same menu sequence, Insert ▶ Reference ▶ Tables and Index.

It takes time to learn these features, and some advanced techniques are required, but an organized listing of your most important findings makes the effort worthwhile.

⇒ The Table of Codes is an **alphabetical** listing of all Level 1 codes that you create in the middle column of the code document.

⇒ The Table of Contents is a **sequential** listing of all comments and memos that you make in the middle column of the code document.

⇒ The Index is an alphabetical listing of all key words and phrases that you mark in the body of the transcript text.

Creating a Table of Codes for the code document

As you rapidly progress with Level 1 coding it soon becomes clear that many of your codes group together alphabetically. At later stages of Level 1 coding it is nice to take a look at your emerging list of codes in an efficient manner. An alphabetical list of codes at the beginning of each code document is valuable during coding and when you write your final report.

What is the tool in *Word* that creates an alphabetized table? The *Word* 'Table of Authorities' is the answer. The Tables of Authorities is used by lawyers to mark legal citations, but the tool works just fine to create a qualitative research Table of Codes. Even though I use the term Table of Codes in this book, use the term Table of Authorities if you are searching Microsoft's Help system (F1).

The process of making a Table of Codes is a bit convoluted to explain, but the process is fast once you get a little practice. Shortcut keys are helpful when creating Tables of Codes.

Abbreviated instructions for the creation of Table of Codes entries:

A full explanation follows, but so you can understand that the creation of each Level 1 code entry is very fast, this is a summary of the keystrokes needed to create a Level 1 code entry. Do this every time you type in a new Level 1 code. Type the code text in the middle column of the code document ▶ Highlight the code text you just typed ▶ Press Alt+Shift+I ▶ Press Enter twice ▶ Press Ctrl+Shift+8.

The following illustration gives you an idea of what a Table of Code looks like.

Table of Codes – Level 1 codes focus on actions and processes. Write code in left column. Select text, then press ALT+SHIFT+I to mark index entry. *Uses Word's Table of Authorities feature. Ctrl+N to hide formatting marks that become visible when a code is marked. Ctrl+. To eliminate dots, etc. Ctrl+R reveals the codes.*

2 parents being important	72
Being consistent for the kids	14, 81
Being flexible and gracious	74
Being flexible with money	27
Both parents are important	11
Both parents need to be cooperative	35, 45, 70
Checking in with kids to see if change is needed	5
Commitment to parenting is foremost	69
Conferring with the kids about house	72
Different chore loads	23
Disciplining in coordination	23
Flexible scheduling	8
Listening to the kids	81
Living nearby	9
Maintaining traditions the first year	83
Parents communicating working together	20
Relying on ex for decisions	24
Relying on faith	13
Respecting ex	15
Respecting the kids rights	69
Seeing the importance of both parents	5
Staying on the same page	22
Struggling to disengage emotionally	41
Worked out the holidays amiably	7

Right-click in the table (or Error message) above to update the field after new initial codes have been created.

A Table of Codes can be very colorful if font colors are used to establish the correlation between the transcript data and the Level 1 code.

Detailed instructions for the creation of Table of Codes entries

You should mark each new Level 1 code for the Table of Codes immediately after the new code is written.

In the example below, the Level 1 code is *Both parents are important*, and the accompanying transcript data are marked in italics (and blue).

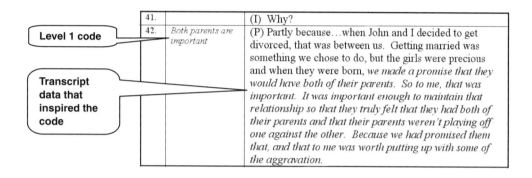

Level 1 code

Transcript data that inspired the code

| 41. | | (I) Why? |
| 42. | *Both parents are important* | (P) Partly because…when John and I decided to get divorced, that was between us. Getting married was something we chose to do, but the girls were precious and when they were born, *we made a promise that they would have both of their parents. So to me, that was important. It was important enough to maintain that relationship so that they truly felt that they had both of their parents and that their parents weren't playing off one against the other. Because we had promised them that, and that to me was worth putting up with some of the aggravation.* |

Step 1

| 42. | Both parents are important |

Highlight code text

Step 2

To mark the selected text, press Alt+Shift+I, *or from the menu select* Insert ▶ Reference ▶ Index and Tables ▶ select the Table of Authorities tab ▶ Mark Citation. You will get a window that looks something like this.

Press Alt+Shift+I

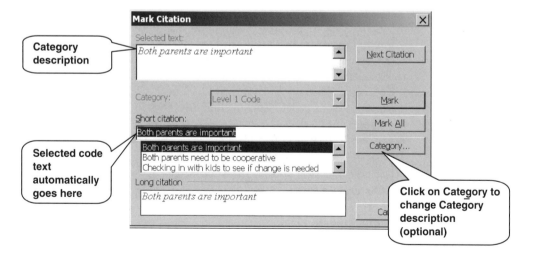

Category description

Selected code text automatically goes here

Click on Category to change Category description (optional)

Step 3

Press *Enter* twice, *or Click on M̲ark, another screen will pop up, Click on M̲ark again.*

Click on Mark in
two successive
screens, or press
Enter twice

Huh?

Step 4

Ctrl+Shift+8

Level 1 Coding
summary

It should be noted that you will do this over and over again, so the process of marking Level 1 codes gets repetitive and very fast. This is why I stress keyboard shortcuts.

After creating the code something weird will happen to your screen, do not worry, the programmers at Microsoft in their kind benevolence thought you might like to see what the behind-the-scenes formatting looks like in *Word*. (Actually, the exposed formatting allows you to make edits if necessary.) The immediate core question for most of us is 'how do you get rid of the *&^!# formatting marks?'

After marking a Level 1 code get in the habit of quickly pressing **Ctrl+Shift+8**. This shortcut key combination eliminates the formatting marks. *If you ever want the formatting marks to reappear so you can edit your citations, press* Ctrl+Shift+8 *again. It is a toggle.*

Marking Level 1 codes gets to be a quick procedure. You may have hundreds of codes to mark. Learn to be fast with the keystrokes that are summarized again below.

Type the code text in the middle column of the code document ▶ Highlight the code text you just typed ▶ Press Alt+Shift+I ▶ Press Enter twice ▶ Press Ctrl+Shift+8

Yes, these commands are a bit out of the mainstream, but the end result is worth it. You will be able to quickly cross reference your codes as you work your way through your code document, and you will have a code map of each transcript when you write your report.

Insert ▶
Reference ▶
Index and Tables
to insert the Table
of Codes
(Authorities)

To insert a Table of Codes in your document, select a location near the beginning of your code document, and then click in the blank row where you want the table to appear. Then select from the menu: Insert ▶ Reference ▶ Index and Tables ▶ select the Table of Authorities tab. *The fonts and other formatting options that make up the Table of Authorities can be modified by clicking on Modify while you are in the setup screen.* When you are ready, press OK.

After creating new entries, update the Table of Codes (Table of Authorities) field by right-clicking on the Table of Codes field, then selecting Update Field.

Writing memos and creating a Table of Contents for the memos

While reading through and coding your code document it is a good idea to write numerous memos. These memos are different than codes. They may include discrete incidents, actions, events (sometimes called *in vivo* codes), and demographic data. They may relate to emerging concepts and themes, but they do not necessarily relate directly to the research questions, or correlate with specific segments of data.

If an idea pops into your head as you are working through the code document write yourself a memo in the center column. The Table of Contents feature allows you to review all of these memos at a glance in chronological sequence.

When finished, the Table of Contents provides a summarized record of the most important non-code items you noted as you coded the document.

Table of Contents - Use for focus on individuals, sections of the transcript, and subject areas. Mark entries by selecting level of Header: *Ctrl+1=Header 1, Ctrl+2=Header 2, Ctrl+3=Header 3.*

Separated 9 yrs divorced 8 3
Married 15 3
Wife initiated 3
Tiffany was 12...3
Sally was 9 3
Wife initiated 4
Mutual agreement to JPC 4
Changed from one week to two week rotations 5
One girl off to college...6
Ex did the paperwork..10
Sometimes visible arguments...12
Nice to have a break on off weeks 24
Not perfect control of anger..25
Got a lawyer involved at a troublesome time 25
Step parent addition to family was hard......................................28
Step parent mediated dispute 28
Ex and current husband tolerate each other 38
Hard to be away from kids when they are sick 43
Kids had two sets of everything 51
Religion discussion..53
Faith traditions stayed more or less intact 53
Mostly in-person communication when younger..........................56
   Now mostly e-mail...56
   Uses e-mail to reinforce memory..57
Communication can swing from friendly to angry 57
   Still talk on phone occasionally..59

Right-click in the table (or Error message) above to update the field after new codes have been created.

Table of Contents illustration.

The Table of Contents (TOC) feature relies on style headings. *For an introduction to Styles see Chapter 10, or use Word's Help to search for 'Format your document with styles.' Press F1 or Help to activate a search.*

Text designated with a 'Heading 1' style becomes a primary TOC entry. Text designated as a 'Heading 2' style becomes a secondary TOC entry. Text designated as a 'Heading 3' style becomes a third level TOC entry, etc.

The following shortcut keys allow you to mark memos as headings: Heading 1 (Alt+Ctrl+1), Heading 2 (Alt+Ctrl+2), or Heading 3 (Alt+Ctrl+3).

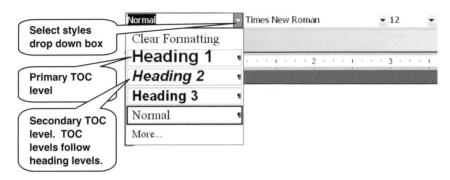

Selecting styles from the Formatting toolbar. Heading levels create the hierarchy that appears in the Table of Contents.

The Heading styles that are reflected in the Table of Contents should be edited so that they appear using smaller font sizes. This allows the headings to fit in the limited column space.

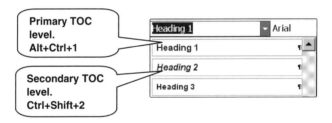

Modify the Heading styles to use smaller fonts.

To modify Styles (to select smaller font sizes) using the menu, click on Format ▶ Styles and Formatting. See Chapter 10 for more details about Style modifications.

Mark all memos and notes (not Level 1 codes) with Heading styles.

171.	Mostly in-person communication when younger *Now mostly e-mail*	P **When the girls were younger, it was more in person or by phone.** *Now, we seem to go mostly with e-mail.* Unless it's something really important that we have to settle quickly, then we'll call.

These memos do not directly help answer the research questions; instead, they help describe the structural environment of the participants.

Refer to the entries in the Table of Contents illustration above on page 101 to see how these headings appear in the Table of Contents. The entries, 'Mostly in-person communication when younger,' and '*Now mostly e-mail*' appear on page 56 of the Table of Contents example.

To insert a Table of Contents in your document, click in a blank line in the document where you want the Table of Contents to appear. This is usually at the beginning of your code document.

Click on Insert ▶ Reference ▶ Index and Tables ▶ select the Table of Contents tab. The fonts and other formatting options that make up the TOC can be modified at this time by clicking on Modify. When you are finished, press OK.

To update the Table of Contents after changes have been made in the document, right-click on the TOC, and then select Update Field.

To change the formatting of the Table of Contents (font size, etc.), select Edit Field instead of Update Field.

Insert ▶
Reference ▶
Index and Tables
to create the TOC

Right-click on the
TOC, and then
select Update
Field to update
the Table of
Contents

Helpful Hint

Return to your last
edit(s) quickly
Shift+F5

It is easy to get lost in a large document. Here are three bookmarking techniques that will help you quickly find your last edit.

1. After you have scrolled away from your last edit to look at another part of the document, use the **Shift+F5** command to quickly jump back to the section of the document you were last editing. **This is a very handy command.**

2. Create temporary table of contents entries when you need to quickly hop back and forth between multiple sections in the document or if you want to create more lasting markers in your document.

    When you prepare to take a break or shift your writing focus, type LAST EDIT (or something similar) in a blank line at the location of your last edit. Then, select the words LAST EDIT and press Alt+Ctrl+1 to make the phrase a Heading 1 style.

    When you want to return to this spot in your code document press Ctrl+Home to move to the top of the document ▶ right-click on the Table of Contents ▶ Update Field ▶ Update entire field.

    You will see the location of your last edit prominently displayed in the TOC. Ctrl+Click on the LAST EDIT entry. This will return you to the location of your last edit. When you get there delete your LAST EDIT bookmark and keep working.

3. The *Word* Insert ▶ Bookmark command is the third technique for jumping to specific parts of a document. Create a bookmark by using Insert ▶ Bookmark from the menu. To go to a bookmark use Edit ▶ Go to ▶ then select the target 'Bookmark' in the 'Go to what:' box. For quicker navigation use Shift+F5 whenever possible.

Creating an Index for your code document

Alt+Shift+X creates an Index entry

As a researcher, you have no doubt learned to rely on indexes in books. A good index lists the topics discussed in a document and the pages on which they appear, and that is exactly the purpose of your code document Index. **Create an Index entry whenever you want to be able to quickly find a word or phrase in your code document**. The word or phrase does not need to be a code or a memo; it can be anything that you want to be able to locate later.

Overview using keyboard shortcuts: Highlight the word or phrase you want to index ▶ Alt+Shift+X ▶ press Enter twice ▶ Ctrl+Shift+8. This is a quick process.

Ctrl+Shift+8 eliminates formatting marks

As with the creation of a Table of Codes you have to deal with those pesky formatting marks. Remember Ctrl+Shift+8!

To mark an Index entry **using menu commands**, select the text to be included in the Index ▶ click on Insert ▶ Reference ▶ Index and Tables ▶ select the Index tab ▶ Mark Entry ▶ Mark ▶ Close.

'Mark All' indexes all words or phrases in the document that match the selection

While you are in the 'Mark Index Entry' box (after clicking Mark) you will notice that advanced things can be done with indexes. Think outside the box; be creative and give the advanced features a try. For example, if you click on Mark All instead of Mark, *Word* will create index entries for *all* words and phrases in your document that match the selected text. Think about that for a minute, and the significance it might have for analyzing your data.

To insert the Index in your document:

You can place the Index anywhere in your document. The traditional end-of-the-document placement may or may not make sense for you in your code document. I prefer placing the Index at the top of the code document after the Table of Contents and Table of Codes. To place the Index in the document, click on a blank row in the desired location then select Insert ▶ Reference ▶ Index and Tables ▶ select the Index tab ▶ OK.

Insert ▶ Reference ▶ Index and Tables ▶ select the Index tab ▶

(Fonts and other formatting options for the Index can be modified by clicking on Modify in the Index tab window. When you are finished, press OK.)

Update the Index field by right-clicking on the field, then selecting Update Field.

Selective audio transcription to create Level 1 codes

Selective audio transcription is a technique of creating Level 1 codes directly from digital audio files without transcribing all of the recorded information. Only the text data that directly contributes to the creation of the Level 1 codes or memos are transcribed; audio data that do not contribute directly to codes or memos are not transcribed.

The codes and memos derived from selective audio transcription, in theory, should be identical to the codes and memos created from a traditionally typed full transcript because the underlying data are identical, albeit in audio rather than typed format. Code documents from selective audio transcription are substantially shorter because they display only the text data directly associated with memos and codes, excluding all data that did not directly relate to codes or memos. The data that do not relate to codes or memos are preserved in the audio file.

For dense and focused audio data I recommend traditional transcription of the entire audio recording because there is much to gain from multi-sensory examination (audio and visual) of all of the data. I do not recommend use of digital coding as a standard practice unless the researcher is visually impaired, or unless the ratio of 'wheat to chaff' is very low. That is, relatively few sections of the audio file contain passages are relevant to the research topic. Digital audio coding should only be done when the researcher can precisely and quickly return to the exact spot in the audio file that contains the data for each memo and code (more on this later).

In addition to significantly reducing the amount of transcript data that must be typed, coding from an audio recording allows the researcher to do his or her Level 1 coding while listening to the nuances, tones of voice, and other subtleties that are not available when coding exclusively from a written transcript.

After any transcription process the researcher must be able to quickly and reliably return to the data for reexamination; therefore, digital coding is possible only with digital audio files that can be precisely examined and transcribed with software like *Express Scribe*.

The location of specific data can be pinpointed, in digital audio files, to one tenth of a second with digital transcription software. By noting the exact location of the data and by creating substantial bookmarks in the transcription software, the researcher can instantly jump to any pre-set location. *Express Scribe* is used in the examples in this section. As noted in Chapter 5, *Express Scribe* is freely available on the Internet.

Before starting the audio coding process, set up a code document in *Word* with three columns that are sequentially numbered as described for full-text transcripts earlier in this chapter.

⇒ The left column is for the sequential numbering of each row
⇒ The middle column is for (a) Level 1 codes, (b) memos and notes that relate to participant demographics, AND (c) the digital audio file time stamp
⇒ The right column is for the verbatim transcribed data related to Level 1 codes, memos, and other pertinent transcript data.

To set up the file, start with a couple of dummy paragraphs in a blank *Word* document and follow the directions above.

Since you will be starting with a blank document you will be adding new rows to the table as new code-related items are added to the digital code document. Rows are added to tables with the following command: Table ▶ Insert ▶ Rows Above, or Table ▶ Insert ▶ Rows Below .

Once the code document is prepared, leave that document open, and then simultaneously open *Express Scribe*.

Listen to the audio file. Headphones can help. When a section is encountered that triggers thoughts about a Level 1 code or a memo, transcribe that section in the right column of the code document, and enter the code or memo in the middle column **with the time stamp from *Express Scribe***.

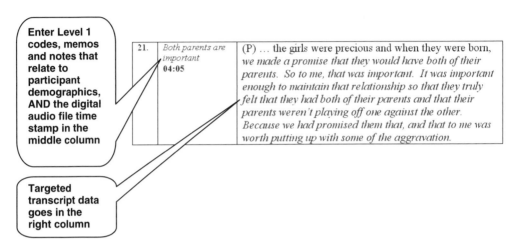

Enter Level 1 codes, memos and notes that relate to participant demographics, AND the digital audio file time stamp in the middle column

| 21. | *Both parents are important* 04:05 | (P) … the girls were precious and when they were born, we made a promise that they would have both of their parents. So to me, that was important. It was important enough to maintain that relationship so that they truly felt that they had both of their parents and that their parents weren't playing off one against the other. Because we had promised them that, and that to me was worth putting up with some of the aggravation. |

Targeted transcript data goes in the right column

Code document with audio time stamp.

Express Scribe uses standard audio buttons for mouse use and also an extensive and highly functional set of shortcut keys. Foot pedals can be purchased as necessary.

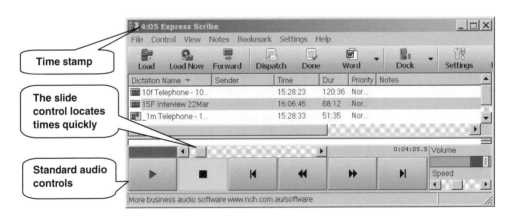

Time stamp

The slide control locates times quickly

Standard audio controls

Express Scribe interface used for digital coding and transcribing.

Important: create a bookmark whenever a new code is created

The bookmark feature of *Express Scribe* makes digital audio coding plausible. The best practice is to write the Level 1 code directly in the 'Enter Bookmark Description' box, and then copy and paste the new Level 1 code into the middle column of your *Word* code document. This will, theoretically, produce identical code and memo phrases in *Express Scribe* and in *Word*.

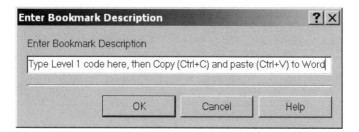

The steps are: Select (highlight) the Level 1 coded text you just typed in *Express Scribe* ► Ctrl+C (copy) ► Click in the middle column of the code document ► Ctrl+V (paste).

By entering your Level 1 codes in the bookmark list it is very easy to locate and instantly go to the code's precise location in the audio file. From *Express Scribe* select Bookmark ► Open bookmark to open the list.

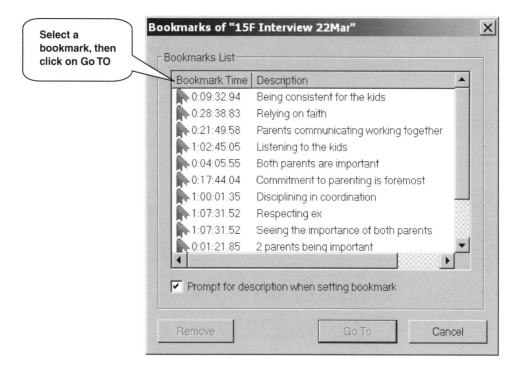

List of time stamps and Level 1 code bookmarks in *Express Scribe*.

After you learn the process and complete your first selective audio code or memo in *Express Scribe* and in *Word*, continue your coding and transcribing progress until you are finished with the audio file. Create a Table of Contents, a Table of Codes, and an Index in your selective audio code document just as you would have in a code document based on traditionally transcribed data.

The process of higher level coding (Levels 2, 3, and 4) is virtually identical for digitally coded documents and for code documents created from traditional full-text transcriptions. The major difference is that instead of going back to sections of the data to re-read a transcript, researchers who digitally coded their documents will return to an audio file to review the context of the original data.

Level 1 coding with Computer Assisted Qualitative Data Analysis Systems

The *Word*, *Access*, and *Excel* templates from this book can be modified to accommodate input from Computer Assisted Qualitative Data Analysis Systems (CAQDAS) and quantitative data from mixed methods studies.

CAQDAS, like NVivo, Atlas.ti, The Ethnograph, and others, broadly speaking, take care of Level 1 coding for researchers. The output from these programs can be very stimulating and interesting, but the ultimate judge is your brain.

CAQDAS programs can be used in different ways. If you use them as the sole source of your Level 1 codes you will make quick progress, but you may be losing an element of richness in your understanding of the data. If you do your own Level 1 coding in *Word* and use CAQDAS programs to supplement your coding, you will stimulate new avenues of thought and quite possibly end up with a better analysis. CAQDAS output can be used instead of, or in addition to, *Word*-based Level 1 codes.

It is certainly not necessary to use CAQDAS programs. They are expensive, they have their own learning curve, and they are no match for a researcher's brain.

Whether or not you use CAQDAS for Level 1 coding, Level 2 coding can proceed with little modification. Use CAQDAS-created Level 1 code equivalents to create your Level 2 database.

Detailed discussions of CAQDAS and quantitative analysis software are not included in the book. More information is available at qrtips.com/chapter6.

Coding at the next level, *Access* or *Excel*?

This is an introduction to Level 2 coding technology. Read it before proceeding to Chapter 7 or 8.

Once you finish Level 1 coding it is time to move to Level 2 coding and beyond. *Access*-based Chapter 7 and *Excel*-based Chapter 8 are two parallel chapters that cover Level 2 coding.

The question is which vehicle suits you the best, *Access* or *Excel*? There are several factors to consider, but I will start with a simple statement: if you are an experienced *Access* user you need go no further in your decision-making process – use *Access*. *Access* is a better tool for the job because of the power of *Access* forms and queries. The dropdown boxes in the Qualitative Research Control Panel form (introduced in Chapter 7) allows a single screen for data entry and high level coding. There is no equivalent Control Panel in *Excel* because *Excel* does not have easily configurable forms.

However, *Excel* is not a lightweight program. It has plenty of power to handle small and medium sized projects. If you are more familiar with *Excel* than *Access* you can get Level 2 and Level 3 coding done just fine in *Excel*. If your research project is not too big, the time you spend learning *Access* may outweigh its superior features.

For those of you who have been looking for an opportunity to learn *Access* this could be your moment. No programming or relational features were used as I developed the tables, queries, and forms that are at the core of the *Access*-related sections of this book. This means that by *Access* standards this is a starter-level project.

If you have not spent much time with either *Access* or *Excel* you have decisions to make. First, consider the size of the project. If you have several hundred pages of transcript data (or more) you will benefit from the power of *Access*, but before choosing *Access* you might want to make sure you have a friend or consultant who can give you some help. Just like the many quantitative researchers who hire statisticians, there is no shame in hiring an *Access* expert.

If you have a smaller project and *Access* seems intimidating then I recommend *Excel*. It is easier to learn, and it is easier to find a friend who knows how to use *Excel*.

As a final word before you move on to *Access* or *Excel*, I recommend that you buy an *Access* or *Excel* manual if you get stuck. To keep things from getting overly complex I keep a narrow focus of the examples in this book, but there is a good chance that you will have creative ideas that take you to new territories. The customization features in *Access* or *Excel* allow you to create qualitative research tools that are made to order for your project. The quality of your analysis will be improved if you delegate the tedious work to *Access* or *Excel*. Then, unshackled by mind-numbing tasks, you can pursue your data more deeply.

As you learn to use *Access* or *Excel* to complete your higher level coding, again, I encourage you to seize the moment to create a system that is truly your own. Tweak it, modify it, and expand it. The high level coding techniques that follow can open new doors of perception for you and leave you with advanced Microsoft *Office* skills that will serve you for years to come.

Chapter summary

After the data are collected, described, and transcribed they are formatted into a code document to facilitate Level 1 coding. The researcher conducts Level 1 coding by carefully reading and reviewing the data in the code document. Every time a passage of text triggers a significant thought that directly relates to the study's research questions, the researcher composes a code phrase to describe the relevance of the data. The code phrases (Level 1 codes) and memos that frame the data are entered into the middle column of the code document, and the accompanying sentences and paragraphs that triggered the thoughts are marked to identify the code-related and memo-related text.

Many research projects have large quantities of text-based data; therefore, research efficiency is enhanced if the researcher can quickly return to codes, memos, and passages. Three types of tables are described that display the most important information in outline form: a Table of Codes, a Table of Contents, and an Index.

Table of Codes

The Table of Codes is an alphabetized list of all Level 1 codes. This list grows every time you create a new code and mark the code description appropriately. To mark Level 1 codes, type the code text in the middle column of the code document ▶ Highlight the code text you just typed ▶ Press Alt+Shift+I ▶ Press Enter twice ▶ Press Ctrl+Shift+8.

Table of Contents

The Table of Contents is a list that contains memo entries that were appropriately marked as they were entered into the middle column of the code document. The Table of Contents lists the memos sequentially as they appear in the code document. Memos must be marked with style headings so they can be compiled into the Table of Contents. Table of Contents entries are displayed in outline form showing a hierarchy of headings and subheadings. Most memo entries are marked with Heading 1 (Alt+Ctrl+1). Memos that are nested under a Heading 1 memo are marked with Heading 2 (Alt+Ctrl+2), or Heading 3 (Alt+Ctrl+3), etc.

Index

Important words and phrases can be marked and compiled into an Index. Index entries do not need to relate to memos or Level 1 codes. To mark a Index entry highlight the word or phrase you want to index ▶ Alt+Shift+X ▶ press Enter twice ▶ Ctrl+Shift+8.

The chapter ends with a discussion that frames the researcher's thinking about the use of *Access* **or** *Excel* for subsequent levels of coding. Both tools allow researchers to complete advanced levels of coding in an efficient manner. Because *Access* is more powerful and has an extensive database-specific toolkit, experienced *Access* users are encouraged to proceed to the *Access*-related instructions in Chapter 7. *Excel* is a powerful tool that may be preferred by researchers already familiar with *Excel*, especially if they are working on small to medium sized projects. If you choose to use *Excel*, proceed to Chapter 8. You are encouraged to spend time researching the differences between *Access* and *Excel*.

CHAPTER 7

Level 2 coding using *Access*

Anything's possible if you've got enough nerve.

J. K. Rowling, *Harry Potter and the Order of the Phoenix*

How can an *Access* database help your research? You will boost your data analysis efficiency because all of your codes, memos, notes, and data highlights will be quickly accessible from a single program; and that program is designed to allow quick data retrieval. *Access* allows you to sort, manipulate, and filter your most important data and thoughts in creative ways without having to fumble through reams of paper, index cards, or disconnected computer files. This system enhances your ability to think analytically.

A generic qualitative research Control Panel form that was designed for this book (downloadable from qrtips.com/chapter7) is used as a tutorial in this chapter. It features numerous dropdown boxes and data input techniques that help in the creation of codes, categories and theories. These form-based controls greatly accelerate and enhance the higher level coding process.

You may be good at *Word* and *Excel*, but totally unfamiliar with *Access* – you are not alone. Despite the trepidation of many, *Access* was designed with the non-geek in mind. The basic tools are within the grasp of everyday computer users even though there is a basic entry-level learning curve to understanding databases.

| Consider *Excel* |

I encourage you to try *Access*, but there may be reasons why *Excel* may work better for your research project than *Access*. If you have a small project and you are not already familiar with *Access* I suggest that you take a look at the end of Chapter 6 and the beginning of Chapter 8 to further explore the pros and cons of *Access* vs. *Excel*.

About the template

Use the template as a finished program or a base for customization

This book is not a general Microsoft *Access* manual. An explanation of all of the fine details of *Access* would be overwhelming, and perhaps frightening, to the novice. To keep things simple, I designed the *Access* template without using any programming or relational tables, making this a great way for first-timers to get going with *Access*.

The techniques illustrated in this book are focused specifically on the use and modification of this book's qualitative research Control Panel template. This may be all you need to complete your project, but enhancements and modifications of the techniques shown herein are strongly encouraged. One of the great strengths of *Access* is the ability of the end user (you) to customize the forms, tables, queries, and reports to reflect the language and logic of your preferred research method.

The next section covers Microsoft *Access* basics. If you are an old pro at *Access* then jump ahead to the section about Level 2 coding.

Microsoft *Access* basics

Many accomplished personal computer users have not attempted to utilize a database program like Microsoft *Access*. In many cases this is understandable because these computer users have not had a clearly perceived reason to use *Access*.

As self-taught computer users find the need to store data in a table, many turn instinctively to *Excel*. It makes sense. *Excel* can store data in easy-to-see rows and columns without much of a learning curve. If the amount of data to be stored is not excessively large, the spreadsheet view (no forms) is acceptable, and there is no need for repetitive data queries, *Excel* is a perfectly good solution.

However, power users who start working with larger data sets find that there are compelling reasons to commit to a database like *Access*. By browsing through the components of *Access* that are described below you will start to see why its use is strongly indicated during the qualitative research coding process.

The Database Window

A Database Window, similar to the one shown below, is always present when *Access* is open, although you may not see it because it is minimized or hidden behind another window. The Database Window allows you to select the type of objects that you want to use: tables, queries, forms, or reports.

The main reason there is more of a learning curve for *Access* than there is for *Word* or *Excel* is that *Access* is not a single-interface program. The objects in *Access* are all separate interfaces to the same data. This gives *Access* powerful dimensions that are not possible with a single-interface program. You get more power. Yes there is more to learn, but the individual interfaces are all quite accessible by users who are willing to invest the time to grasp the concepts.

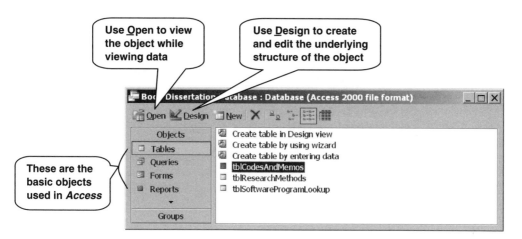

The Database Window allows you to switch between Objects.

Note: I still adhere to a quirky naming tradition that helps in VBA programming (which you will not have to do). I start the name of all tables with tbl, queries with qry, forms with frm, and reports with rpt. For this application there really is no need to use this naming scheme, but I cannot break myself of the habit.

Tables

Tables are the most basic units of a relational database. Tables hold the information you want to store and retrieve.

A database table is best visualized as a grid with rows and columns. On the surface a table might look like an *Excel* worksheet, but there is more than meets the eye. Database tables have special properties that make them especially good at storing information, and then allowing you to selectively and creatively recall the data.

Before we go further it is important that you understand the terms record and field. Suppose you keep the addresses of your research participants in a database. The table might logically be called 'Contacts.' Every contact, along with his or her name and address is stored in a row called a '**record**.' Each column represents a '**field**' that holds the record's elements such as first name, last name, and address.

The introductory illustration below shows five records. Each record is broken down into seven fields: Salutation, First Name, Last Name, Dear, Address, City, and State.

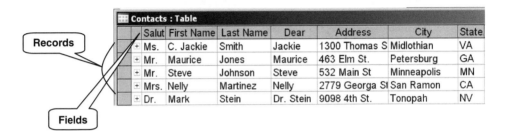

A 'datasheet' view of a table.

Fields are created and edited in the table's Design view.

Database Window toolbar.

Switching from the introductory contact database example above, the fields shown below are from the qualitative research database that is used throughout the book. The table's design window facilitates the easy creation of new fields and the editing of existing fields.

A lot of the power of a database is derived from the unique characteristics assigned to fields. Fields fall into the general categories of text, memo (large amounts of text data), number, date/time, currency, yes/no, hyperlinks that provide access to graphics, web pages, and more. Each of these categories can be fine tuned and refined. Help automatically appears on the screen when you click in the 'data type' field in Design view.

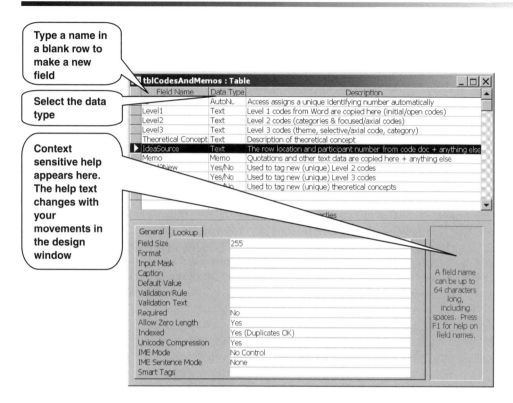

Type a name in a blank row to make a new field

Select the data type

Context sensitive help appears here. The help text changes with your movements in the design window

Field Name	Data Type	Description
	AutoN...	Access assigns a unique identifying number automatically
Level1	Text	Level 1 codes from Word are copied here (initial/open codes)
Level2	Text	Level 2 codes (categories & focused/axial codes)
Level3	Text	Level 3 codes (theme, selective/axial code, category)
Theoretical Concept	Text	Description of theoretical concept
IdeaSource	Text	The row location and participant number from code doc + anything else
Memo	Memo	Quotations and other text data are copied here + anything else
...New	Yes/No	Used to tag new (unique) Level 2 codes
	Yes/No	Used to tag new (unique) Level 3 codes
	N...	Used to tag new (unique) theoretical concepts

tblCodesAndMemos : Table

General | Lookup |

Field Size	255
Format	
Input Mask	
Caption	
Default Value	
Validation Rule	
Validation Text	
Required	No
Allow Zero Length	Yes
Indexed	Yes (Duplicates OK)
Unicode Compression	Yes
IME Mode	No Control
IME Sentence Mode	None
Smart Tags	

A field name can be up to 64 characters long, including spaces. Press F1 for help on field names.

The table in Design view.

Below, is a partial view of a qualitative research database table showing data in the Open view.

tblCodesAndMemos : Table

Level1	Level2	Level3	Theoretical Concept
Monitoring teenagers is difficult	Manipulating by child	Reactions by children	JPC parents try to do what is
Manipulation by kids	Manipulating by child	Reactions by children	JPC parents try to do what is
Not letting the child manipulate the parents	Parents coordinating their	Parental coordination	JPC parents communicate an...
Presenting a united front to the child	Parents working together	Parental coordination	JPC parents communicate an...
Playing consistently different roles in paren...	Parents working together	Parental coordination	JPC parents communicate an...

Record: |◄| ◄ | 355 | ► | ►| | ►* | of 530

The datasheet view appears after clicking on Open.

Tables are the backbone of a database because they store the data in the records and fields that you designate. Tables grow and evolve as you add new records and get more sophisticated with your use of fields. It is perfectly acceptable to add, delete, or modify fields to a table in the course of a project. As you learn more about your topic and data your data storage needs will change. Happily, with *Access*, you can keep tweaking the system as your project and database knowledge grows.

Queries

Queries are used to create smaller/focused sets of data from a single table, and to combine data from multiple tables. With queries you can selectively view, change, and analyze data. Queries are also used as a source of data for forms, reports, and mail merges.

Several types of queries are available in *Access*, but in this book I introduce only the standard type of query called a select query, and I will keep it simple by not using any queries that gather data from multiple tables (relational database features). Our queries gather data from only one table at a time.

In the following example a query is created to extract data from the table 'tblCodesAndMemos.' The database records that the query will display are limited to records that match the phrase 'respecting the ex-spouse' in the field called 'Level 1.'

Shown below, in the design view of the *Access* query tool, are just two fields from the tblCodesAndMemos table: Level2 and Level1. Only these fields will be retrieved by the query. To limit the records returned by the query from the table, 'respecting the ex-spouse' a Level 2 code was entered in the criteria field.

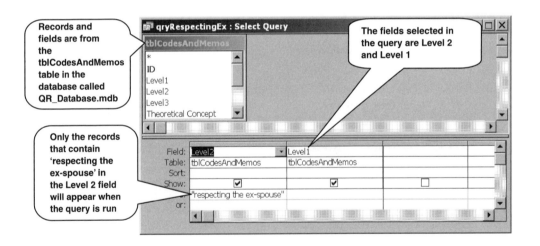

The result of running this query is seen in the datasheet below. Notice in the record bar at the bottom of the datasheet that 31 records appeared as a result of the query even though there are 530 records in the table. This example is provided to help you see that queries allow you to focus on just the information you want to see, count, or use.

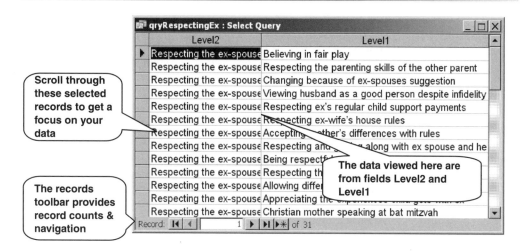

Scroll through these selected records to get a focus on your data

The records toolbar provides record counts & navigation

The data viewed here are from fields Level2 and Level1

More query examples are provided in the advanced data analysis and report writing sections below.

Forms

It is possible to enter data records in the *Access* datasheet view which looks very similar to an *Excel* spreadsheet; however, most significant research projects have sophisticated data storage requirements that make datasheet-view data entry cumbersome and error prone.

One of the worst things about using the datasheet (or *Excel* spreadsheet) as your primary data entry interface is the need to constantly scroll back and forth to get to the field you want to view or edit. The datasheet shown below shows only 5 of the 10 essential fields in this table, and this is a relatively simple table; scrolling is required to access hidden fields.

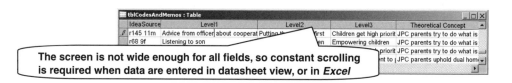

The screen is not wide enough for all fields, so constant scrolling is required when data are entered in datasheet view, or in *Excel*

Access forms provide an interface that is much more flexible and user friendly than datasheets. Forms allow fields to be placed on the page in a manner that makes flows better for the user. The form below displays data from 32 fields. In datasheet view it would be aggravating to scroll back and forth through 32 fields.

A form does a lot more than display data in a manner that allows data entry without scrolling back and forth. By using a form you can enter data with

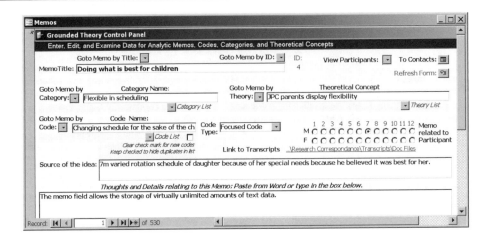

dropdown boxes, build in error checking, filter your data quickly, see all of the fields on the same screen, and much more.

A form is developed and edited in Design view.

Design View

The techniques used to build the form shown above are detailed later in this chapter.

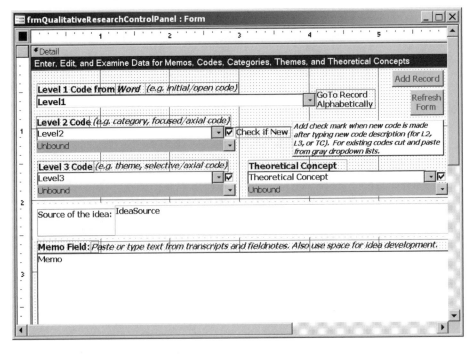

A form shown in Design view.

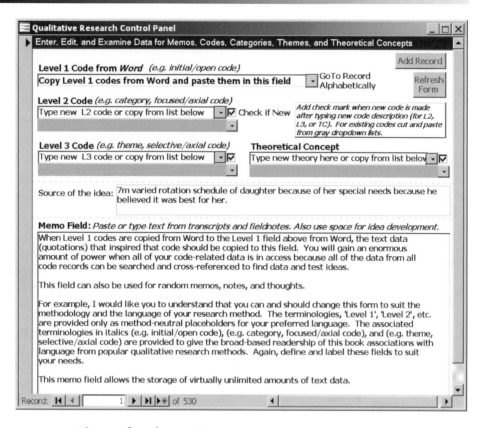

The same form shown in <u>O</u>pen view.

Reports

Access reports can be thought of as an *Access* version of *Word*'s mail merge feature. In fact, you may be able to accomplish all of the report generation you need by joining together data from *Access* with a display design created using in *Word*.

In *Access*, as in *Word*, a report document is created and designed in anticipation of data that will be merged in from a table or query. Reports display your data in the format you need for the printer or screen.

What is a relational database?

Tech Aggressive

> The examples in this book deliberately avoid the use of the relational features of *Access* to keep the technology within reach of *Access* beginners, so feel free to skip this section. But if you see the potential of using relational joins between tables you may choose to learn these techniques on your own.

What are the relational features of *Access*? The simplest answer comes from the root of the word relational – relate. Relational databases allow disparate tables to relate to each other. You can combine and interconnect records from two or more different tables.

For example, suppose there are two tables, Contacts and CodesAndMemos. The Contacts table might hold the names and addresses of participants while the CodesAndMemos table contains the codes and memos that emanated from qualitative interviews with participants. These data can be creatively and selectively combined.

What if you need contact information that is related to a memo? Or conversely, what if you need the memos associated with a contact? Without the ability to use a relational database join you would have to include all contact information with **each** record in the Memos database (all memo information with **each** record in the Contacts database). That would cause tedious data entry, wasted space on your hard drive, and be inefficient.

It is much more efficient to store contact information in the Contacts table and Memos information in the memos table, and then join the information as desired. All you need to do this is to create an equivalent field in each to the database tables.

In the illustration below the equivalent field is called 'ContactID.' The tables are joined using the ContactID field. Records from each table that have the same ContactID can be matched, cross-referenced, and queried. With this type of equivalent field join, *Access* can relate records from both tables when the values in the joined fields are equal.

The easiest way to create this join is with a query. In this example, a query can create a list containing all of the memos that are associated with a single participant. A different query could show all of the contact information associated with specific records from the Memos table.

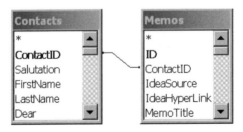

It takes extra front-end work to understand and set up relational joins, but relational features can be much more efficient than flat-file or single-table databases. I encourage you to seek out more information in books, on-line tutorials, Microsoft's Help system, or local training courses.

Level 2 coding using the Control Panel form created in *Access*

The purpose of Level 2 coding is to create categories from groups of Level 1 codes. This means that *multiple* Level 1 codes will be associated with almost every Level 2 code. There are mechanical Level 2 coding steps required to populate the database, but Level 2 coding is primarily a time of contemplation and creativity as you think through the meaning and interconnectedness of each code phrase and its associated data.

Level 2 coding involves the copying of codes and data from your code documents in *Word* to the Qualitative Research Control Panel form in *Access*. You get a big jump start with *Access*-based qualitative research coding if you go to qrtips.com/chapter7 and download the fully functioning database called QR_Database.mdb (.mdb is the extension *Access* uses for its data files). This bare-bones but fully functioning database has an already-created qualitative research database table, the Control Panel form, a report for higher level coding, and some queries.

After you download the QR_Database simply double-click on the file to start the application. *Access* must be installed on your computer before you can run the template, and your computer's security settings may require you to take explicit steps to start the QR_Database.mdb file.

Level 2 coding overview

Again, we start with the goal. We want to bring order to the free-form disorder of the Level 1 codes. We want to find affinities between previously unassociated Level 1 codes. Some of your Level 1 codes will fit together naturally into groups because they are so similar, yet for other codes it will be harder to find affinities.

The goal of Level 2 coding is to create categories by grouping Level 1 codes. This is an iterative process. To help some tangential codes fit into a group you will probably find yourself renaming some newly created Level 2 code groups, but you do not have to try too hard because Level 3 and Level 4 coding offers further chances to refine code groups.

Think of the relationships this way. Very many Level 1 codes are reduced to many Level 2 codes. Many Level 2 codes are reduced to few Level 3 codes. Few Level 3 codes are reduced to very few Level 4 codes (theoretical concepts). The reason for this reduction is to create a tight topic-specific view of the data so your results can be presented in a coherent and focused manner.

The first three steps in Level 2 coding involve the transfer of key data from *Word* to *Access*. These mechanical steps are quick on a per code basis; but, if you have a lot of Level 1 codes the total time required for Level 2 coding could be considerable. For this reason you are encouraged to use keyboard shortcuts during Level 2 coding. They become second nature with practice.

The fourth step is a creative and thoughtful step. This is the time when you create a new Level 2 code or you assign the Level 1 code being reviewed to an existing Level 2 code group.

These coding steps are introduced briefly, and then discussed in much more detail later in this chapter.

Step 1. Copy the Level 1 code phrase from the middle column of the *Word* code document to the Level 1 code field in the *Access* Control Panel form.

Step 2. Copy the text data (verbatim quotation) associated with the code from the right column of the *Word* code document to the Memo field in the *Access* Control Panel form.

Step 3. Create a binomial identifier for the Idea Source field in the *Access* Control Panel form. Enter the row number of the Level 1 code that appears in *Word* and the participant ID (something like, 'r42p4f' or '42-4f' [row 42 participant 4f]). Once you create your system this becomes second nature.

Step 4. (a) If the Level 1 code you are examining does not fit into an existing Level 2 category, think up a good phrase that represents the record you are examining and create a new Level 2 code category. Create a new Level 2 code by typing a code description in the Level 2 field in the *Access* Control Panel (and clicking in the check box next to the field to indicate that this a new code); or, (b) If the Level 1 code under review fits into an existing Level 2 code group, assign the Level 1 code to the existing Level 2 code group.

As you review each Level 1 code for affinities with Level 2 code categories it is helpful to be able to instantly view a list of the ever-growing Level 2 codes. The Control Panel form provides you with a dropdown list of all existing Level 2 codes. If you can match the Level 1 data in the record you are reviewing with an existing Level 2 category, simply assign the Level 2 code to the new record. (This process is presented graphically below.)

The mechanical process is fast. It is harder to explain than it is to do, but this is not a strictly mechanical process. Allow yourself time to think through the assignment or creation of each Level 2 code. **The basic questions are: Does the Level 1 code under examination fit into an existing Level 2 category? or Do the data represent a new Level 2 category? And if a new category is to be created, what should it be called?**

Step 5. Go back to the code document in *Word*, select the next Level 1 code and repeat the process on a new record in *Access*.

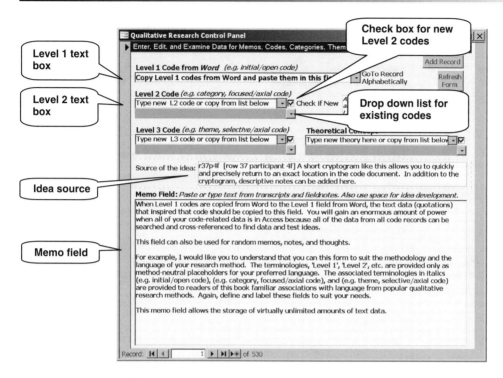

The Qualitative Research Control Panel.

Level 2 coding – Step 1, copy the Level 1 code from Word

Copy the Level 1 code from *Word*.

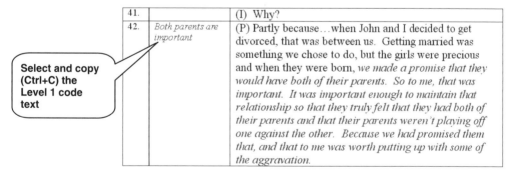

This is a section of a code document in *Word*.

Paste the code to the Level 1 code field in the Access Control Panel.

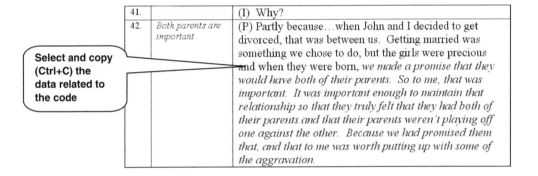

Level 2 coding – Step 2, copy text data from Word

Copy the text data (verbatim quotation) associated with the code from *Word*.

41.		(I) Why?
42.	*Both parents are important*	(P) Partly because…when John and I decided to get divorced, that was between us. Getting married was something we chose to do, but the girls were precious and when they were born, *we made a promise that they would have both of their parents. So to me, that was important. It was important enough to maintain that relationship so that they truly felt that they had both of their parents and that their parents weren't playing off one against the other. Because we had promised them that, and that to me was worth putting up with some of the aggravation.*

Select and copy (Ctrl+C) the data related to the code

Paste into the Memo field in the *Access* Control Panel.

Memo Field: *Paste or type text from transcripts and fieldnotes. Also use space for idea development.*
we made a promise that they would have both of their parents. So to me, that was important. It was important enough to maintain that relationship so that they truly felt that they had both of their parents and that their parents weren't playing off one against the other. Because we had promised them that, and that to me was worth putting up with some of the aggravation.

Paste the full text here (ctrl+V)

Level 2 coding – Step 3, identify the data source

Create a binomial cryptogram (identifying label) for the Idea Source field that allows the identification of the specific code document and the location in the code document of each Level 1 code. The precise location of each code is important because it allows subsequent visits to the raw data. (The Idea Source cryptogram also allows you to focus filters on individual participants, a technique that is described later in the chapter.)

For your cryptogram I recommend the combination of an identifier for the code document (participant event, focus group, field site, object, or transcript) and the row number where the Level 1 data is stored.

First, you need an efficient way to identify your code document. I encourage you to create this code using at least one letter to facilitate efficient record filtering.

In this example, the code document contains the transcript of a participant who was the 4th female interviewed, so the participant and the code document are labeled '4F.' Since we know that the code document is associated with participant 4F and that the Level 1 data are in row 42 (see illustration above) the cryptogram identifier could be something like 'r42p4f,' or '42-4f,' or 'r424f' [row 42 participant 4F]). Type the cryptogram in the Idea Source field in the Access Control Panel.

Source of the idea: r424f

Be creative but also be consistent in the construction and use of your idea source cryptograms.

Level 2 coding – Step 4, create the Level 2 code

Creating new
Level 2 codes

There is no pre-existing list of Level 2 codes at the very beginning of the Level 2 coding process, but there should already be a good foundation for the creation of Level 2 codes. By the time you get to Level 2 coding you have almost certainly started to recognize patterns and affinities in your data. These cognitive associations in your mind are the foundation for your category development during Level 2 coding. Use your observations, ideas, and perceptions as your guide.

To create a new Level 2 code, first think about the possible phrasing of that Level 2 code. There is no need to be obsessive about perfection at this point, because the codes and the code language can be edited as your thoughts coalesce during the analytic process, and they will be further refined in Level 3 coding.

Once you get the code phrase organized in your mind, the mechanical process of creating a Level 2 code is easy – type the new code in the Level 2 field in the *Access* Control Panel, and then click in the check box next to the field (to indicate that this a new code).

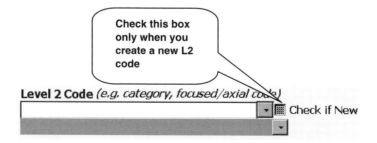

Check this box only when you create a new L2 code

Level 2 Code *(e.g. category, focused/axial code)*

Check if New

Simply type in a new code, and check the box to create a new code.

Selecting a Level 2 code from a list

Each new Level 1 code record copied into the Control Panel from *Word* requires contemplation. Is there an existing Level 2 code group that fits this newly transferred Level 1 code record? Whenever a Level 2 category exists that 'fits' the new record, then that Level 2 category should be associated with the incoming Level 1 data. The purpose of Level 2 coding is to create categories from groups of Level 1 codes. This means that *multiple* Level 1 codes are eventually associated with almost every Level 2 code.

Every time you create a new Level 2 code the list of existing Level 2 codes grows by one. In a large project the Level 2 code list can grow rapidly, making it hard to remember exactly what codes you have already created.

But how do you view all of the Level 2 codes to help with your decision making? How do you assign an existing Level 2 code to a new record? The Control Panel form makes this easy.

Review the illustration below in a clockwise direction, starting with the number 1 on the right side of the illustration.

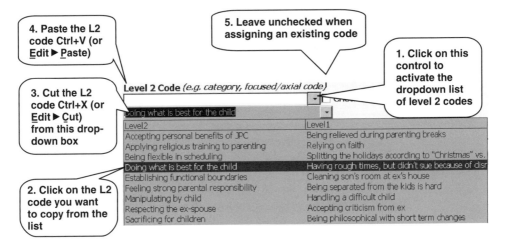

Assigning an existing Level 2 code to a new record.

Technical note: When you 'cut' the code from the dropdown box rather than 'copy,' the box is cleared. This reduces clutter on the screen after you finish assigning the new code.

As this template was created I used the cut and paste method, shown above, for the Control Panel rather than a programmatic solution that automatically pastes the Level 2 code into the text box. This keeps the Control Panel simpler and easier to modify by new *Access* users.

Database operations with the Control Panel form

To manipulate the ever-growing database as you proceed with coding, *Access* offers a number of tools for entering, filtering, and searching records directly from within a form. This makes the Control Panel form a direct conduit to a lot of valuable information.

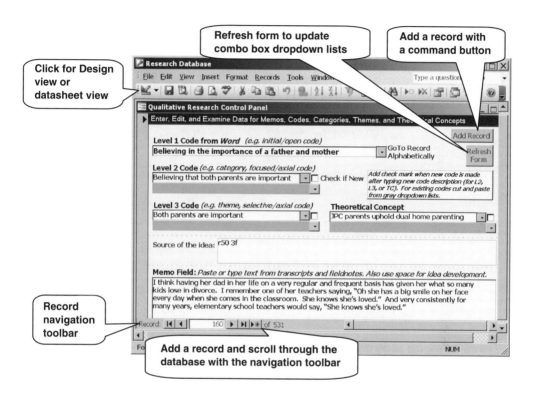

Access offers powerful commands that are quick and helpful – with no programming required. If you are not familiar with the commands on the toolbar, take a look.

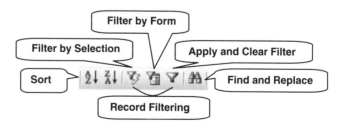

Sort

Access forms allow easy record-to-record scrolling with the record navigation toolbar at the bottom of the form. Scrolling through the records in your database allows you to find records you need and review your data one record at a time. However, scrolling is inefficient if the records are not properly sorted. The good news is that all of the records viewable in the form can be sorted with just a couple of clicks.

To sort all of the records viewable by a form:

1. Click in the field in the form that you want to be the focus of the sort command. For example, if you want to sort all of the records by Level 2 codes, click in the Level 2 text box in the form.

2. Click on the 'A to Z' or the 'Z to A' toolbar icon ![icon]. That is all it takes, your records are sorted.

To sort by a different field, click in that field and click on one of the sort icons.

Find and Replace (edit your codes)

The little binoculars ![icon] are extremely helpful because they help you find specific records.

1. Click in the field on the form that you want to be the focus of the find command. For this example I clicked in the Theoretical Concepts text box.

2. Click on the Find icon ![icon] (Ctrl+F). The Find and Replace window will appear.

3. Type or paste the text you want to find

4. Select the settings for your search

5. Click on the 'Find Next' button as often as necessary to scroll through the records that match the search criteria.

Suppose you created a Level 2 code early in the Level 2 coding process. You have assigned this code to many records, but now you have decided that the phrase originally chosen for the code needs to be fine tuned. This is far from a hypothetical situation. As your ideas mature, so too will your description of those ideas.

Replace
A quick way to change the language of a code group

It would be painfully slow to manually change each record, but with Find and Replace it is quick. Click on the Replace tab of the Find and Replace window shown below, type the old text that you want replace in the 'Find What:' field, and type the new text in the 'Replace With:' field. Make sure all of the settings are correct, and then click on Replace to view one record at a time, or click on Replace All to replace all records with one click.

Find all entries with 'JPC' in any part of the field and replace with 'Joint Physical Custody'

Filter by selection (count your codes, focus on one participant at a time, and more)

To filter by selection, click on

, or use the *Access* Records menu, or right-click in any field on a form

The records viewable in a form can be overwhelmingly numerous. They might include many disparate records in a gigantic table, but the good news is that they can be quickly focused by form-based filters. By limiting the records available to the form it is possible to scroll through the form to examine data in a meaningful way.

The *Access* filter-by-selection command is the simplest way to apply a filter. The command can be executed by using the *Access* Records menu, the

icon, or by right-clicking in any field on a form. To keep it simple, the following examples feature the icon.

To filter by selection: (a) click in a field that already contains the data you want to use as the filter, and (b) click on the filter-by-selection icon. That is it.

Now for a more detailed explanation:

1. Go to a record that matches your search criterion. For example, you may want to limit the records to those that have 'Doing what is best for the child' in the

Level 2 code text box field. First, use the find command, or scroll to a record with 'Doing what is best for the child' in the Level 2 text box. Click in the Level 2 text

box to make sure it has the focus. Click on the Filter-by-selection icon . Your records are now filtered.

Example 1: Filter-by-selection operations can be based on all or part of the field

When you filter-by-selection you can click anywhere in a field and *Access* will search for the entire text string in that field, such as, Doing what is best for the child . An additional feature of filter-by-selection (but not filter-by-form) allows searches on any part of the data in a field. Highlight the word 'child' ('Doing what is best for the child') in the Level 2 code field, and then click on

filter-by-selection . This shows all of the records with 'child' anywhere in the field, not just records with the entire text string 'Doing what is best for the child.'

2. When you are done and you want to remove the filter, click on the funnel icon

.

How do you know it worked? Scroll through the results, or keep track of the number of records listed in the record navigation toolbar at the bottom of the form. The filter should reduce the number of records available to the form.

Note: If you prefer seeing the filtered records in a list instead of in a form, use the filter-by-selection procedure with a table, a query, or the form in datasheet view. A form can be switched to datasheet view from the dropdown list on the left–most icon on the Form View toolbar.

> When you filter-by-selection the number of records that match your search criterion (Level 2 codes = 'Doing what is best for the child') are listed at the bottom of the form in the record navigation toolbar. To find out how many records match each code, run the filter-by-selection command for each of the codes.

A quick way to count your codes

If you want to save the results of these code-counting filters, record the results on paper or in a computer file because filter-by-selection actions cannot be saved.

Example 2: Focus on the records from a single participant

In a large database it can be hard to focus on a single participant (or focus group, or field observation site, etc.). There may be hundreds of data records from many sources. This example will show you how to see only the records of a single participant using the binomial data in the Idea Source field.

Earlier in this chapter in 'Level 2 Coding – Step 3' the entry of data in the Idea Source field was introduced. When a Level 2 code is created, an identifier is provided for each participant, event, field site, focus group, or transcript. To facilitate efficient searches I encouraged you to use this identifier in a binomial cryptogram. For example, the participant who was the fourth female interviewed was assigned the participant code of '4F.'

This participant identifier was combined with the row in the Word code document that was the source of the data (row 42) to create a complete 'source of the idea' cryptogram of 'r424f' (row 42 participant 4F).

Source of the idea: r424f

Continuing the example, in the Control Panel form go to any of the records from participant 4F (not case sensitive), highlight '4F,' and then click on the

filter-by-selection icon . The filtering takes place with this single click. You can now scroll through the records with an exclusive focus on only this participant. You can also see how many records in your database are related to participant 4F.

This technique can be used to filter any part of any field. Use it creatively.

Remove the filter by clicking on the funnel icon 　.

Tech Aggressive

More advanced filter-by-selection options are available by right-clicking in a field, on a form, or by using the Records menu. The most noteworthy of these options is the **Filter Excluding Selection** command. This filters the record set to allow everything *except* the selected text.

Filter-by-form (sophisticated data views)

The filter-by-form command is a lot like the filter-by-selection, but it is multi-dimensional. It allows the user to simultaneously filter on multiple fields, and to save the filtering criteria as a query.

Filter-by-form can be done from the Control Panel form in form view or datasheet view. Unlike filter-by-selection, you do not need to start with a selected field in a form.

From the menu, select Records ▸ Filter ▸ Filter By Form. The filter-by-form

window will appear. You can also click on the icon.

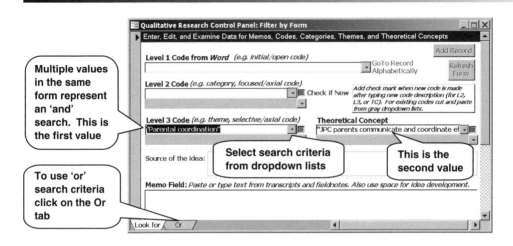

Specify your filtering criteria in the filter-by-form window by selecting from field-based dropdown lists. Click the first field that has a value you want to use in your filter. Enter the value you want to use by selecting from the list that appears after you click in the field. Add values in other fields as necessary to create a multi-field filter.

To find records in which a particular field is empty or not empty, type 'Is Null' or 'Is Not Null' into the field.

Once your filter criteria are established, click Records ▶ Apply Filter to view the filter results, or click on the filter apply/remove icon.

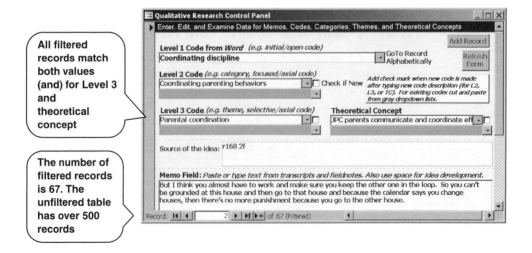

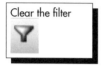

Clear the filter

To clear the filter, click on the filter apply/remove icon   .

If you want to reuse the same filter settings in the future, save the filter as a query. With the filter-by-form in design mode and populated with the values you want, select from the menu File ▸ Save As Query.

To run queries, select Queries from the Database Window.

More details about the design and operation of the database

The QR_Database is a fully functioning software application. The database objects used in the QR_Database.mdb template are deliberately held to a minimum, but they are robust enough to allow you to do complete Level 2 coding, Level 3 coding, and theoretical concept development. There is also a built-in report that facilitates higher level coding.

This section of the book is partly a QR_Database user's manual, partly an *Access* tutorial, and partly an *Access* user guide. Even if you are an experienced *Access* user you will benefit from the qualitative research coding logic associated with the Control Panel form ('frmQualitativeResearchControlPanel'), and you will be introduced to every object on the form. If you are a beginner and have not already done so, I encourage you to review the *Access* basics that are presented earlier in this chapter. In the tutorial that follows I will be using terms and explaining procedures based on the expectation that you are at least somewhat familiar with the basics.

It is possible to complete full research projects by using the QR_Database as-is – without modifying the tables or forms in the QR_Database. However, the QR_Database is not intended to solve all research problems; it is designed to get you started, pique your curiosity, and stimulate you to create the research system that is perfect for your needs.

The fields in the QR_Database

Before fields can be added to a form they must be created in a table. The QR_Database has one primary table called tblCodesAndMemos. This table has only 10 fields. These 10 fields use only 4 data types.

The first field in the Design view illustration shown below is the ID field. This is a special '**autonumber**' field that assigns a unique identifier to each record that is created. Unique identifiers are important in queries and other objects that need to look up and go to specific records.

Level1, Level2, Level3, TheoreticalConcept, and IdeaSource are all '**text**' fields. They can hold up to 255 alphanumeric characters.

The creatively-named Memo field uses the '**memo**' data type; it can hold up to 65,535 characters.

Level1New, Level2New, Level3New, and TCNew are all 'yes/no' fields. These fields are used in check boxes in the Control Panel form to provide data that queries will use to limit the contents of combo boxes (dropdown lists).

No **numeric** fields, **date/time** fields, **currency** fields, **hyperlink** fields, or **OLE object** fields are included in tblCodesAndMemos. There may be very good reasons for adding these specialized fields to your qualitative research application. The Microsoft help system does a good job of explaining these field types.

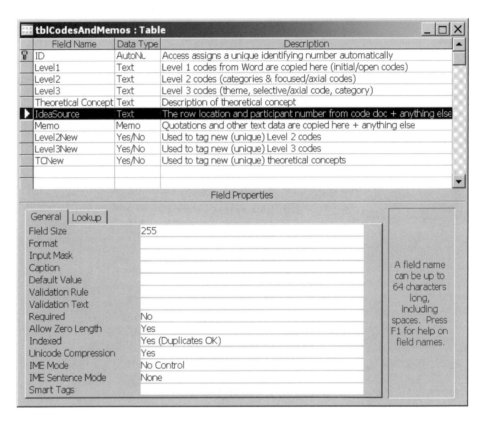

The Design view of QR_Database.mdb.

Database fields can be readily edited, and there are good reasons to do this from time to time. For example, the IdeaSource field, as shown, has a 'text' data type. For most users, the 'text' limitation of 255 characters is adequate; however, for users choosing to be more verbose about identifying the record's source, the data type can be changed from 'text' to 'memo.'

Field Name	Data Type
ID	AutoNumber
Level1	Text
Level2	Text
Level3	Text
Theoretical Concept	Text
IdeaSource	Text
Memo	Text
Level2New	Memo
Level3New	Number
TCNew	Date/Time
	Currency
	AutoNumber
	Yes/No
	OLE Object
	Hyperlink
	Lookup Wizard...

The dropdown list makes establishing data types easy. Press F1 for help

Be careful about changing field names since the fields are used to populate data in forms and queries. If you change a field name, the form or query will not know about your handiwork; therefore, the form or query will display an error message. (This is not an insurmountable obstacle because forms and queries can also be edited.)

Adding new fields to a table

New fields can be added to a table by clicking in the blank row below the existing fields shown in Design view. Type the new field name, select the appropriate data type, and add a description (optional). That is all there is to it. If you need to make changes to the field later, you can. A database table is a dynamic object, so it can be edited in the course of a project as necessary.

Once the fields are created and edited it is time to put them to work. When the table is opened (click on <u>O</u>pen), the table will switch from Design view to Datasheet view. In Datasheet view records can be added to the table, and data can be edited.

Generally, I recommend adding data through forms instead of in Datasheet view, but the occasional use of datasheets is useful for adding, editing, finding, and filtering records. Techniques for doing this are described later in this chapter

The Control Panel form design

The Control Panel form is the workhorse of the QR_Database system. As described earlier, Level 1 codes and their accompanying data are copied into this form from the *Word* code document. At the time each Level 1 code record is created, a Level 2 code should be selected by the researcher that has an affinity with the Level 1 code. If no Level 2 code exists that matches the Level 1 code a new Level 2 code is created. After this very quick review of the form's operation we will take a look at its design.

The form below, which I decided to call frmQualitativeResearchControl-Panel (again, apologies for my naming scheme), is shown in Design view.

The properties, colors, sizes, and locations of every object on the page are subject to editing.

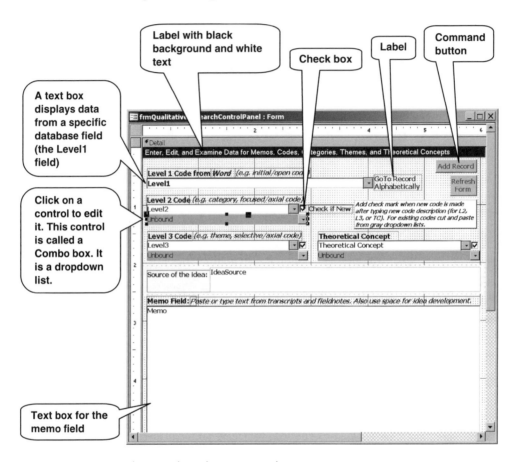

The Control Panel in Design mode.

By right-clicking on any of the objects on a form, the menu to the right will appear. Many of the most common editing tasks are shown on the menu, but an extremely detailed set of editing properties appear when you click on the bottom menu choice, "Properties".

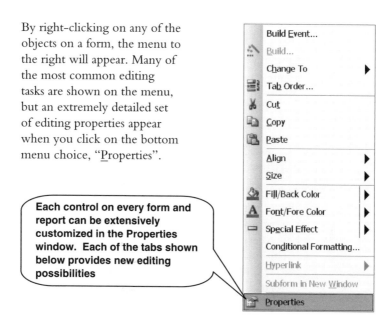

Each control on every form and report can be extensively customized in the Properties window. Each of the tabs shown below provides new editing possibilities

A *lot* of customization is possible for each control on all forms. Use the tabs at the top of the Properties window to narrow the type of changes you want to make.

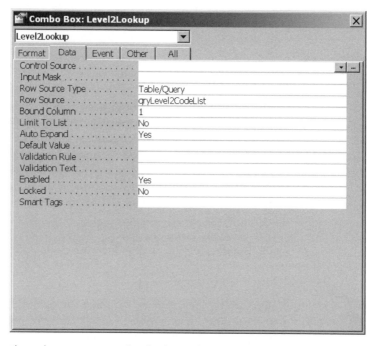

This is the Properties window for the Level2Lookup Combo Box control on the form called frmQualitativeResearchControlPanel. This Combo Box control is shown on the left side of the illustration on page 136.

As stated earlier, this book is not a broad-based *Access* users' guide. It is my hope that you have been able to get a sense of the basic flow of designing and using *Access* by examining some of the elements of the template. I encourage you to create your own research system and to seek help with *Access* if you get stuck.

Higher level analysis

As the analysis of your data gets more focused and sophisticated you will gain efficiency as your *Access*-related skills improve. The 'what if' games you can play with your database records are virtually endless, but you need to know how to use the tools.

Curiosity about your data should be the driving force behind the tools you use. You may wonder about relatively simple things, such as the number of codes that are contained in your study. (The joint physical custody study that provides the examples used in this book had 520 Level 1 codes, 32 Level 2 codes, 19 Level 3 codes, and just 6 theoretical concepts.) Or you may want to take a closer look at the data using creatively filtered views.

The sections that follow focus on creative, perhaps critically important, ways to view and display your data. If you get stuck with *Access* basics go back to the beginning of this chapter, reexamine the sections below, use the Microsoft help system, buy an *Access* user guide, hire a consultant, but do not give up without trying. The results can be very rewarding.

Analytic queries

Queries allow users of *Access* to sort and filter records in a table by specific fields and according to specific criteria. A query allows the user to view the records in a database with precision and to save the query for future use. For example, a large contacts database (names, addresses, etc.) might be queried to display only males between the age of 35 and 45 who attended Yale University or Oxford University, and whose last names start with the letter P. For introductory concepts see 'Microsoft *Access* basics' at the beginning of this chapter.

Queries often serve as data sources for forms, reports, and individual objects on forms and reports such as dropdown lists (technically called combo boxes).

Tech Aggressive

Access queries can combine data from multiple tables using *Access*' relational features, but relational examples are not provided in this book. Refer to 'What is a relational database?' earlier in this chapter, and search the Microsoft *Access* help system for 'join tables and queries' to learn more.

Design view of a query

The following query example is provided to help tie together some *Access* concepts. The query, qryLevel2CodeList, is used in the downloadable template as the row source for a dropdown list in the Control Panel. Specifically, the query provides the list of currently available Level 2 codes shown in the 'Level 2 Coding – Step 4' illustration.

This is what the query looks like in Design view.

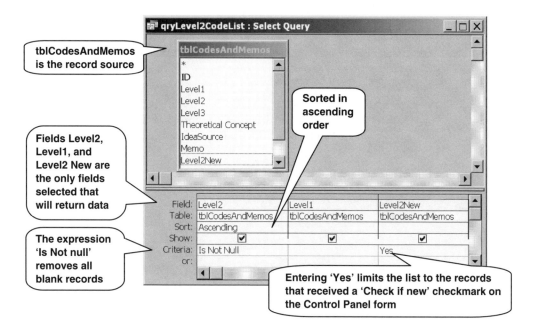

tblCodesAndMemos is the record source

Fields Level2, Level1, and Level2 New are the only fields selected that will return data

The expression 'Is Not null' removes all blank records

Sorted in ascending order

Entering 'Yes' limits the list to the records that received a 'Check if new' checkmark on the Control Panel form

Running the query

To switch from the Design view so you can see the results of the query, select from the menu, Query ▶ Run or click on the red exclamation point on the toolbar . Toggling between the query in Design view and the query Datasheet view allows you to fine tune the query during the development process.

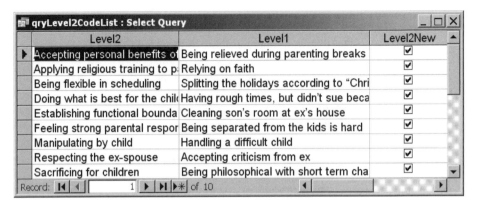

qryLevel2CodeList : Select Query		
Level2	**Level1**	**Level2New**
Accepting personal benefits o	Being relieved during parenting breaks	☑
Applying religious training to p	Relying on faith	☑
Being flexible in scheduling	Splitting the holidays according to "Chri	☑
Doing what is best for the chil	Having rough times, but didn't sue beca	☑
Establishing functional bounda	Cleaning son's room at ex's house	☑
Feeling strong parental respor	Being separated from the kids is hard	☑
Manipulating by child	Handling a difficult child	☑
Respecting the ex-spouse	Accepting criticism from ex	☑
Sacrificing for children	Being philosophical with short term cha	☑

Record: ⏮ ◀ 1 ▶ ⏭ ▶* of 10

Datasheet view of the query.

Notice that this query in datasheet view displays the same records as the dropdown list combo box from frmQualitativeResearchControlPanel.

Level 2 Code *(e.g. category, focused/axial code)*

☐ Check if New

Doing what is best for the child	
Level2	Level1
Accepting personal benefits of JPC	Being relieved during parenting breaks
Applying religious training to parenting	Relying on faith
Being flexible in scheduling	Splitting the holidays according to "Christmas" vs.
Doing what is best for the child	Having rough times, but didn't sue because of disr
Establishing functional boundaries	Cleaning son's room at ex's house
Feeling strong parental responsibility	Being separated from the kids is hard
Manipulating by child	Handling a difficult child
Respecting the ex-spouse	Accepting criticism from ex
Sacrificing for children	Being philosophical with short term changes

The list above is the row source for the Level2Lookup Combo Box. Combo boxes create dropdown lists.

In the 'Control Panel Form' the query 'qryLevel2CodeList' is used as the Row Source for the 'Level2Lookup' combo box. The illustration below shows a view of the Properties Data tab for the Level2Lookup Combo Box control.

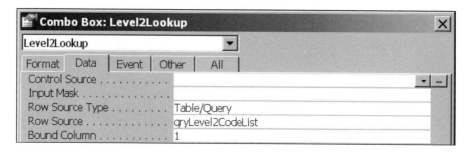

Level2Lookup Combo Box.

The datasheet toolbar for tables and queries

Even though datasheets look like *Excel* spreadsheets, the Datasheet view of tables, queries, and forms is a powerful database tool for the examination of *Access* data, and much of its power is accessible from the toolbar. The toolbar has icons for filtering, sorting, finding, and replacing records.

> The Datasheet toolbar

The most noteworthy toolbar commands are pointed out in the illustration below. Some of the commands are straightforward but a few deserve extra explanation. To see the toolbar, <u>O</u>pen the table or query from the database window, as shown on page 113.

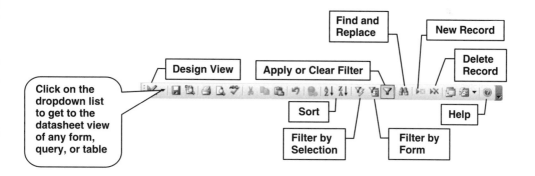

The toolbar above controls the output to the Datasheet view shown below.

IdeaSource	Level1	Level2	Level3	Theoretical Concept
r145 11m	Advice from officer about cooperat	Putting the children first	Children get high priorit	JPC parents try to do what is
r68 9f	Listening to son	Respecting the children	Empowering children	JPC parents try to do what is
r214 4m	Setting boundaries with ex without	Doing what is best for the	Children get high priorit	JPC parents try to do what is
r81 9f	Seeing son and Dan's kids every d	Feeling strong parental re	Strong commitment to	JPC parents uphold dual hom

Record: 458 of 530

A table in Datasheet view.

Sort

Sorting is easy in datasheets. Click in the column (field) that is to control the sorting procedure, and then click on the 'A to Z' or the 'Z to A' toolbar icon

.

Filter by selection (quickly create lists)

> To filter by selection use the *Access* <u>R</u>ecords menu, right-click in any field on the datasheet, or
>
> click on

A detailed description of the filter-by-selection process is included earlier in this chapter. The filter-by-selection procedures are virtually identical for forms and for datasheets. Refer to the earlier discussion for the intricacies of the process.

In Datasheet view, find and select the record and field that has the data that you want to use as the base of your filter. For example, this might be 'Respecting the Children' in the Level 2 column (field). Click on that record in the proper field, and then activate the filtering process by using the <u>R</u>ecords

menu, or right-click in the field on the datasheet, or click on .

To remove the filter click on the apply/remove icon .

Filter by form (create very targeted lists)

The filter-by-form command for datasheets is almost that same as it is for forms (as discussed earlier in this chapter). Refer to that section for more details.

The advantage of the filter-by-form command over the filter-by-selection command is that it allows the user to simultaneously filter on multiple fields, and to save the filtering criteria as a query.

From the menu select Records ▶ Filter ▶ Filter By Form . The filter-by-form

window will appear. You can also click on the 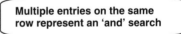 icon.

> **Multiple entries on the same row represent an 'and' search**

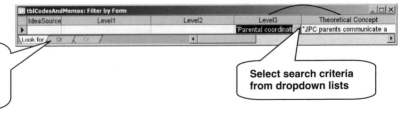

> **To use 'or' search criteria click on the Or tab**

> **Select search criteria from dropdown lists**

From the filter-by-form window, specify criteria for the form. Click the field(s) you want to use to specify the values to be matched. Enter the values by clicking on the dropdown list that is available in each field.

Once your filter criteria are set, click to view the

filter results. Click on the funnel (filter apply/remove) icon .

Find and Replace for datasheets

This is a command that you have likely used in *Word*, but there is one extra step in *Access* – before you click on the find or replace command click on the datasheet column (field) that contains the data you want to find or replace. Then from the menu select `Edit ▶ Find` or `Edit ▶ Replace`, or from the toolbar

click on the binocular icon ⬚ .

The datasheet find and replace functionality is very similar to the form-based find and replace described in the section on navigating with the Control Panel form. Refer to that section for more details.

Reports

Access reports are powerful, they can list your data in comprehensive ways, and they can drive you crazy. For the most part, I do not recommend that early-stage *Access* users with a low tolerance for frustration spend much time with *Access* reports.

In the Level 3 and Theoretical Concepts section I provide a pre-formatted report template that is important in the advanced coding process. When we get there, instructions are provided for using this report. If you are ambitious, feel free to study this report so you can modify it or use it as an example as you create your own reports.

The *Word* mail merge function provides a somewhat easier interface for merging *Access* data to a report. An introduction to mail merge in *Word* is provided in Chapter 3.

Report Hint 1: If you want to print lists that include your research data using *Word*'s mail merge feature, first create a *Word* table with columns for each of the data fields you want to display, then put your mail merge fields from the *Access* table or query in the *Word* table's columns using the mail merge feature. The *Word* table (mail merge form) needs only one row if you can fit all of the fields across a single page. When you run the report, all of the records will appear in the columns. Fields with a lot of data will word wrap.

Report Hint 2: Another alternative to using the *Access* report generator is to create and then print a query that displays the data you need to show.

You can display the query in a *Word* document by 'printing' the query to an Adobe PDF file, and then inserting that object (Insert ▸ Object) into your *Word* document.

A similar way to get an image of your query into a *Word* document is to display the query on your screen, capture a screenshot, and then save the screenshot as a graphic file (.jpg, .gif, .tif, etc.). That picture can then be embedded in your document using *Word*'s Insert ▸ Picture feature. Screen capture techniques are discussed in Chapter 10.

Report Hint 3: You can use the *Access* File ▸ Save As feature to save a query or table as an *Access* report. This is a way to learn about the *Access* report system. Once you study what is going on you can modify the report to suit your needs.

Report Hint 4: If you want to create an *Access* report from scratch, use the *Access* report wizard. From the Database Window select 'Reports,' and then 'Create reports by using wizard.' You will almost certainly have to modify the report that the wizard creates, but this is achievable if you diligently study the layout of the report generated by the wizard.

Persistence

If you have not yet finished Level 2 coding, keep at it.

Energy and persistence conquer all things. (Benjamin Franklin)

You have been dedicated to your research project for quite a while by the time you become actively involved with Level 2 coding. It can seem like there is no end in sight. Completing Level 2 coding can be exhausting, but there is no substitute for the qualitative researcher's personal immersion in the research process and the data. This immersion takes time.

This is the time for a good pep talk. If you have a friend, advisor, mentor, or other encouraging person in your life, let him or her know you need encouragement. Build short breaks into your coding time to get some exercise, or just to let your mind rest. But do not give up hope.

Persistence pays off. If you keep at it you will finish. Hopefully the following information will help – the coding steps and report writing that follows will be *much* easier because of the hard work you are expending during the Level 2 coding process.

1. Level 3 coding and Theoretical Concept development (Level 4 coding) are low-tech and like a breath of fresh air after seemingly endless time previously spent at the computer. These steps are fun.
2. The hard work you put into all stages of coding will make it relatively easy for you to write the results and conclusions sections of your final report. **All of your data, all of your codes, and the hierarchy of all of your codes will be at your fingertips.**

3. The Level 4 > Level 3 > Level 2 code hierarchy serves as a natural structure for headings and subheadings in the conclusions section of the report, making the final section of your paper relatively easy to write.

Chapter summary

Level 1 codes and the data immediately associated with those codes are drawn into a central data depository during Level 2 coding. The consolidation of these data makes further analysis much more efficient and effective. Microsoft *Access* allows the researcher to collect, store, and analyze qualitative research data using a robust database tool.

The qualitative research system introduced in this chapter features a single-table repository for all of the project's refined data. The data are entered into a specially designed qualitative research Control Panel form using convenient dropdown boxes and data entry fields.

The basic steps to Level 2 coding are:

Step 1. Copy the Level 1 code phrase from the middle column of the *Word* code document (Ctrl+C) to the Level 1 code field in the *Access* Control Panel form (Ctrl+V).

Step 2. Copy the data associated with the Level 1 code from the right column of the *Word* code document (Ctrl+C) to the Memo field in the *Access* Control Panel form (Ctrl+V).

Step 3. Create a binomial identifier that relates the new *Access* record to a specific code document and row number in that document. The identifier is entered in the Idea Source field in the *Access* Control Panel form.

Step 4. (a) If the Level 1 code you are examining does not fit into an existing Level 2 category, compose a descriptive phrase for a new Level 2 code category. Create the new Level 2 code by typing code description in the Level 2 field in the *Access* Control Panel (and clicking in the check box next to the field to indicate that this is a new code).

or

(b) If the Level 1 code under review does fit into an existing Level 2 code group, assign the existing Level 2 code to the new Level 1 code record.

Step 5. Repeat the process of copying Level 1 codes from *Word* to *Access* until all Level 1 codes are stored in *Access*.

The data in *Access* can be manipulated in many ways using *Access* database tools that allow database records to be sorted, filtered by form, filtered by selection, and queried. Additionally, the find and replace command allows the researcher to quickly and globally refine code descriptions.

Qualitative research data in *Access* can be presented on the screen, via e-mail, and on the printed page using *Word*'s mail merge feature, the *Access* report generation module, or *Access* queries.

CHAPTER 8

Level 2 coding using *Excel*

Civilization is the process of reducing the infinite to the finite.

Oliver Wendell Holmes

Introduction

Microsoft *Excel* is mostly known as a powerful program for crunching numbers, but it is often used as a database. The use of *Excel* as a database during Level 2 qualitative research coding is especially attractive to those investigators who are already proficient at *Excel*.

Excel may not be the best tool for the job

Now for an odd start to a chapter featuring *Excel* – *Access* may be a better tool for your Level 2 coding. *Excel* is an excellent and capable software program, but its primary design is not to serve as a database. Data entry in *Excel* often requires frustrating scrolling back and forth because *Excel* lacks easily customizable data entry forms. Note: *Excel* does offer a form for data entry that I do not recommend because the form is small and inflexible. If you want to try this form with the *Excel* template, delete the top row of the downloadable worksheet then select Data ▶ Form.

Other advantages of *Access* are its database-specific reports and the many tools that accompany a program that is designed specifically to be a database. I bring up these advantages of *Access* at the beginning of this chapter to encourage you to take a close look at *Access* in Chapter 7 (a) if you have a large research project with a lot of data, (b) if you will be using the services of relatively untrained data entry personnel who would benefit from a data entry form, (c) if you do not like busy spreadsheet screens with small fonts, and/or (d) if you envision your project growing over time.

… but *Excel* can get the job done admirably for many users

Now that I have made these disclaimers, the rest of the chapter will show you how *Excel* can do a remarkable job of Level 2 coding. The simplified *Excel* template provided at qrtips.com/chapter8 will be used for all of the examples in this chapter. This template can serve as a turn-key application for small projects, but you are encouraged to customize it to meet your specific needs.

It is important that you understand the fundamentals of *Excel*. If you are an *Excel* beginner, please review the *Excel* basics section in the Appendix before proceeding. No formulas or equations are used in the template so there is no need to spend time studying these functions.

Overview

Excel allows you to consolidate all of your codes and all of the data that relates to the codes into a single *Excel* workbook. Getting all of your data into *Excel* carries significant benefits because of *Excel*'s data management capabilities.

Excel allows you to sort, manipulate, and filter your most important data and memos in creative ways without having to fumble through reams of paper, index cards, or disconnected computer files.

Excel stores data in easy-to-see rows and columns. For beginners this interface is relatively intuitive. For the most part *Excel* is a what-you-see-is-what-you-get program. The basic tools are well within the grasp of everyday computer users.

The illustration below shows an annotated view of the Level 2 Control Panel workbook. Most *Excel* users will be technically comfortable with the Control Panel workbook, QR_ExcelControlPanel.xls, but even experienced *Excel* users will need to read through the coding procedures.

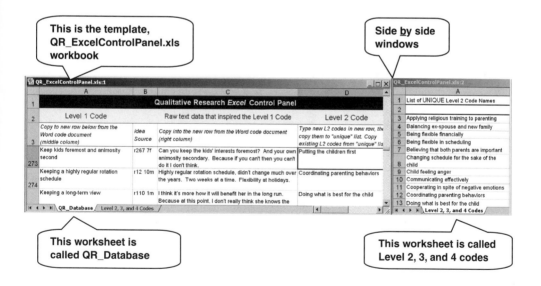

The techniques shown in this chapter are focused specifically on the use of the generic qualitative research *Excel* Control Panel. Enhancements and modifications of the techniques shown here are strongly encouraged, but not necessary.

The Excel *settings used in the template*

We all work on different computers, and I am not even talking about my friends who are steadfast and loyal Mac users. A file that looks great on one screen is virtually unreadable on another. The setup defaults that one user likes might be annoying to someone else.

The following sections explain the changes that were made to customize the Control Panel workbook. Use these changes as examples of how you can change the settings to suit your needs. Some of the settings below are already built into the template, while others must be completed locally on your computer.

Font size

The cells in a new blank *Excel* workbook are usually populated with a 10 point Arial font size. Since I knew that a lot of data was going to have to be displayed on the screen, the font size was reduced to 9 point Arial.

To make a change, select the cells that you want to change then, Format ▶ Cells (Ctrl+1) ▶ Select the Font tab and change the font size.

Wrap text

The large amount of text data that will be placed in the columns virtually guarantees that your data will be too big for some cells. These data will be truncated on the screen unless you allow the text to wrap to the next line in the cell.

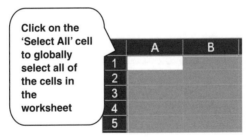

Click on the 'Select All' cell to globally select all of the cells in the worksheet

Apply 'wrap text' to every cell in the workbook by clicking on the Select All cell in the upper left corner of the worksheet. Once all of the cells in the worksheet are selected, use the shortcut keys (Ctrl+1) or the menu Format ▶ Cells ▶ Select the Alignment tab ▶ check Wrap text.

Helpful Hint

Select an entire row or column

To select an entire row for formatting, click on the number (1, 2, 3, etc.) on the left border of the worksheet.

To select an entire column, click on the letter (A, B, C, etc.) on the top border of the worksheet.

Vertical cell alignment

In rows 273 and 274 in the Control Panel illustration earlier in this chapter, the text is vertically aligned to the top of the cells. *Excel*'s default setting is to vertically align the text at the bottom of each cell. The default setting works fine in most circumstances, but extensive word wrapping in some cells creates a lot of blank space in other cells. I find it easier to read the worksheet if the relatively empty cells are vertically aligned to the top.

Click in the Select All cell in the top left corner of the worksheet ▶ Format ▶ Cells (Ctrl+1) ▶ Select the Alignment tab ▶ Select Top from the Vertical dropdown list.

Formatting toolbar

The default *Excel* worksheet opens with only the standard and the task pane toolbars showing. Because the *Excel* Control Panel involves a significant amount of text manipulation I find it handy to put the formatting toolbar on the top of the *Excel* window.

View ▶ Toolbars ▶ click Formatting.

Freeze panes

Take a close look at the far left column of the *Excel* Control Panel worksheet illustration at the beginning of this chapter. You will notice that the row numbering goes 1, 2, 3, 273, 274. Now that is a big discontinuity! How can such a thing happen? I used the freeze pane command to lock the top rows in place. Give it a try in the template, scroll as far as you like down the worksheet, the top three 'header' rows always appear at the top of the window.

Select the entire row *below* (or right of) the row(s) you want to freeze ▶ Window ▶ Freeze Panes.

Variation: If you click on a single cell, then execute the freeze panes command, all of the cells to the left of *and* above the selected cell will be frozen.

Establish side-by-side windows

In the Control Panel illustration below the 'Qualitative Research *Excel* Control Panel' window is shown on the left, and the 'List of UNIQUE Level 2 Codes' window is shown on the right. This configuration significantly improves the Level 2 coding process.

A few steps are required to create this configuration. First select Window ▶ New Window ▶ Compare Side by Side.

These commands result in a confusing jumble if you are starting from scratch. You must resize and move the windows to suit your needs. Notice the details pointed out below.

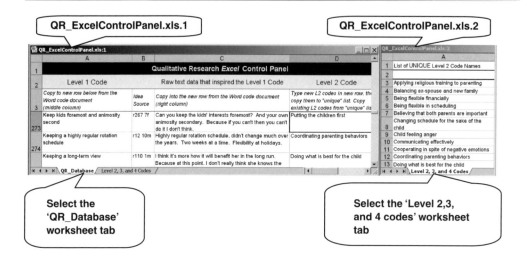

Select the 'QR_Database' worksheet tab

Select the 'Level 2,3, and 4 codes' worksheet tab

QR_ExcelControlPanel.xls.1 and QR_ExcelControlPanel.xls.2 are separate instances (windows) of the same workbook. In the small screen on the right, the 'Level 2, 3, and 4 Codes' worksheet is active. In the bigger screen to the left, the QR_Database worksheet is active.

When you set up the new side-by-side window configuration, make sure that Synchronous Scrolling is turned off. This control is on the Task Pane toolbar that pops up when you are working in the Compare Side by Side mode.

Level 2 coding using *Excel*

Open the template in *Excel*

The purpose of Level 2 coding is to create categories from groups of Level 1 codes. This means that *multiple* Level 1 codes will be associated with almost every Level 2 code. There are mechanical steps with Level 2 coding, but there are also times of contemplation and creativity as you think through the meaning and interconnectedness of each code phrase and its associated data.

If you have not done so already, go to qrtips.com/chapter8 and download the fully functioning database called QR_ExcelControlPanel.xls. Start *Excel* and open this file. *Excel* basics are provided in the Appendix.

Level 2 coding overview

Again, we start with the goal. We want to bring order to the relatively free-form chaos of the Level 1 codes. Some of your Level 1 codes will fit together naturally into groups because they are so similar, yet for other codes it will be harder to find affinities.

The goal of Level 2 coding is to create categories by grouping Level 1 codes. To help some tangential codes fit into a group you will probably find yourself renaming some Level 2 code groups, but you do not have to try too hard because you can use *Excel*'s Find and Replace feature, and Level 3 coding offers further chances to refine code groups.

Think of the relationships this way. Very many Level 1 codes are reduced to many Level 2 codes. Many Level 2 codes are reduced to few Level 3 codes. Few Level 3 codes are reduced to very few Level 4 codes (theoretical concepts). The reason for this reduction is to create a tight topic-specific view of the data so your results can be presented in a coherent and focused manner.

Level 2 coding involves copying codes and data from your code documents in *Word* to the 'Qualitative Research *Excel* Control Panel' in *Excel*. The mechanical steps involved with this data transfer are quick on a per-code basis, but if you have a lot of Level 1 codes (and you probably do) the total time required for Level 2 coding could be considerable. For this reason you are encouraged to use keyboard shortcuts during Level 2 coding. They become second nature.

The overview of the Level 2 coding steps will be followed by more detailed explanations of each step.

Step 1. Copy a Level 1 code phrase from the middle column of the *Word* code document to a blank row in the Level 1 column in *Excel*.

Step 2. Copy the text data (verbatim quotation) associated with the code from the right column of the *Word* code document to the 'Raw text data that inspired the Level 1 Code' column in *Excel*. This text should be copied to the same row that holds the Level 1 code that was copied in Step 1.

Step 3. Create a binomial identifier for the Idea Source column in the *Excel* Control Panel worksheet. Enter the row number of the Level 1 code that appears in *Word* and a code document ID (something like, 'r42cd4f' or '42-4f' [row 42 code document 4f]).

Step 4a. For *new Level 2 codes,* create a Level 2 code by typing the new code name in a new row in the Level 2 column. After typing the new code, Copy (Ctrl+C) and then paste (Ctrl+V) the new Level 2 code from the Level 2 Column to a new row in the 'List of UNIQUE Level 1 code names' in the 'Level 2, 3, and 4 Codes' worksheet (see the tabs at the bottom of the workbook).

Step 4b. When a newly copied (from *Word*) Level 1 code fits into an existing Level 2 code group, Copy (Ctrl+C) from the 'List of UNIQUE Level 2 code names' to the 'Level 2 Code' column in the new row (Ctrl+V). The 'List of UNIQUE Level 1 code names' appears in the right pane of the side-by-side window display, and the 'Level 2, 3, and 4 Codes' worksheet (see the tabs at the bottom of the workbook).

Discussion

It is not a problem if the Level 1 code you are examining does not fit into an existing Level 2 category. New Level 2 codes are often necessary.

Compose a good phrase that represents the idea in the record you are examining. This phrase will be the new Level 2 code category.

The mechanical process is fast. It is harder to explain than it is to do, but this is not a strictly mechanical process. Allow yourself time to think through the assignment or creation of each Level 2 code. The basic questions are: Do the data fit into an existing Level 2 category or do the data represent a new Level 2 category? And if a new category is to be created, what should it be called?

Step 5. When you have completed copying and processing one Level 1 record from *Access* to *Excel*, go back to the code document in *Word*, select the next Level 1 code and repeat the process in a new row in *Excel*.

Level 2 coding details – Step 1, copy the Level 1 code from **Word**

Copy the Level 1 code from *Word*.

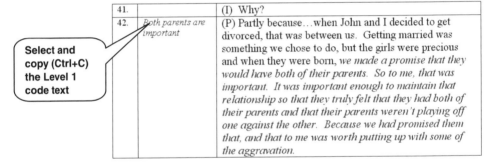

Select and copy (Ctrl+C) the Level 1 code text

This is a section of a code document in *Word*.

Paste the code to a new row in the Level 1 column in the Excel Control Panel. To create a new row, click in the row that will be moved down and then select Insert ► Rows .

Paste the Level 1 code text in new row here

Click on 'Paste options,' select Match Destination

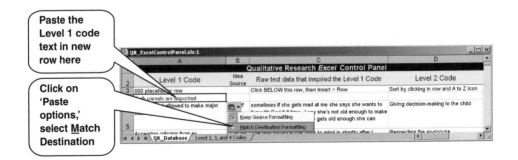

Each time data are pasted into *Excel* from *Word* it is important to notice and click on the Paste Options dropdown box that appears. Select M̲atch Destination Formatting. If you allow *Excel* to keep the formatting used in *Word* the data will not wrap in the cells, and the data will align at the bottom of the cells.

The illustrations below provide a visual overview of steps 2, 3, and 4.

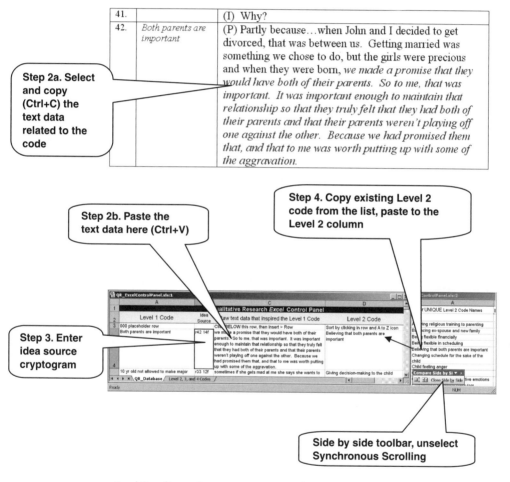

41.		(I) Why?
42.	*Both parents are important*	(P) Partly because…when John and I decided to get divorced, that was between us. Getting married was something we chose to do, but the girls were precious and when they were born, *we made a promise that they would have both of their parents. So to me, that was important. It was important enough to maintain that relationship so that they truly felt that they had both of their parents and that their parents weren't playing off one against the other. Because we had promised them that, and that to me was worth putting up with some of the aggravation.*

Step 2a. Select and copy (Ctrl+C) the text data related to the code

Step 2b. Paste the text data here (Ctrl+V)

Step 4. Copy existing Level 2 code from the list, paste to the Level 2 column

Step 3. Enter idea source cryptogram

Side by side toolbar, unselect Synchronous Scrolling

Level 2 coding – showing steps 2, 3, and 4.

Level 2 coding details – Step 2, copy text data from *Word*

   a. Copy the data (verbatim quotations) associated with the code from the right column in the *Word* code document (Ctrl+C)|, then

   b. Paste the data in the 'Raw text data that inspired the Level 1 code' column in *Excel* (Ctrl+V)|.

Level 2 coding details – Step 3, identify the data source

Notice the Idea Source column in the illustration above. This is a cryptogram (identifying label) that allows you to identify a precise location in a specific code document so you can readily return to the raw data. This binomial identifier also allows you to filter the worksheet to focus on individual participants, focus groups, ethnographic sites, etc.

I recommend the combination of an identifier for the participant (event, focus group, field site, or transcript) and the row number where the Level 1 data are stored in the *Word* code document.

I encourage you to create codes using at least one letter for the participant, site, group, etc. (This will facilitate efficient searches later in the process.) Create a labeling system that suits your project.

For this example, the participant was the 14th female interviewed, so the participant and the code document are labeled '14F.' Since we know that the code document is associated with participant 14F and that the Level 1 data are in row 42 (see illustration above) the cryptogram identifier could be something like 'r42cd14f,' or '42-14f,' or 'r4214f' [row 42 code document 14F]. Type the cryptogram in the Idea Source column.

Be consistent in the construction and use of your Idea Source cryptograms.

Level 2 coding details – Step 4, create the Level 2 code

| Creating new Level 2 codes |

There is no pre-existing list of Level 2 codes at the very beginning of the Level 2 coding process. It is up to you to create the first one, but there should already be a good foundation for the creation of Level 2 codes. The researcher's brain works diligently on multiple levels throughout the research process. Starting during data collection and continuing during Level 1 coding, the researcher's mind should be active in building cognitive associations that might eventually build into categories and themes.

Even though formal Level 2 coding does not take place at the time of Level 1 coding, most researchers perceive emerging patterns during the Level 1 coding process. Use these observations, ideas, and perceptions to guide you as you create your Level 2 codes.

The purpose of Level 2 coding is to create categories from groups of Level 1 codes. This means that *multiple* Level 1 codes are associated with almost every Level 2 code.

To create a new code, first think about the phrasing. What do you want your Level 2 code to communicate? There is no need to be obsessive about perfection at this point, because the codes and the code language can be easily edited as a group (find and replace). You may fine tune a single code several times.

Once you get the code name (phrase) organized in your mind, the mechanical process of creating a Level 2 code is easy: type the new code in the Level 2 column, and then copy and paste it to a blank row in the 'List of UNIQUE Code 2 Names' window.

Selecting an existing Level 2 code from the list

Every time you create a new Level 2 code the list of existing Level 2 codes grows by one. The Level 2 code list can grow rapidly, making it hard to remember exactly what codes you have already created. This is why the maintenance of the 'List of UNIQUE Code 2 Names' is so important.

Whenever a Level 2 category exists that 'fits' a new record (Level 1 code just copied from *Word*), that Level 2 category should be assigned to the new record. Without having to retype and risk a typo, copy (Ctrl+C) from the 'List of UNIQUE Code 2 Names,' then paste (Ctrl+V) to the Level 2 column.

Navigating the *Excel* workbook

Excel offers a number of tools for entering, filtering, and searching worksheets. Because the primary use of *Excel* is not as a database it takes a little digging to get to some of the commands and icons. The good news is that you do not have to dig too deep. Some valuable research-related tools are waiting to be put to good use.

The Excel *toolbar*

Excel includes solid tools for filtering, sorting, finding, and replacing records. Unfortunately, the default configuration of *Excel* needs modification. This is a one-time setup operation and it is not hard to do.

Some of the most important commands that relate to database operations have clumsy keyboard shortcut commands and their icons are missing from the toolbar. The modified toolbar that I recommend is shown below. The command icons that I added to the toolbar are marked with an asterisk (★).

The modified *Excel* toolbar

You may also find it helpful to add the formatting toolbar to the top of the screen. Instructions for adding the formatting toolbar and new icons to the standard toolbar follow.

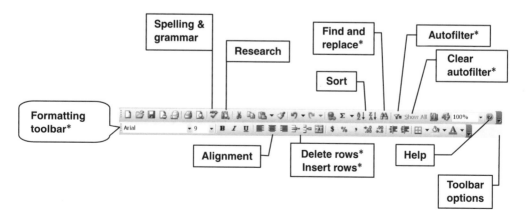

* This feature is not part of the default *Excel* configuration.

Adding the Formatting toolbar and moving toolbars

Select View ▶ Toolbars ▶ click on Formatting . The Formatting toolbar will be added near the top of the *Excel* screen.

Toolbars can be moved around to optimize the way you like to view them, and to maximize the space available for your data. To move a toolbar or menu, hover your mouse over the vertical dots at the left side of any toolbar or menu. When the cursor turns into a four-way arrow, hold down the left mouse button and drag the toolbar to the location you prefer. Toolbars can be placed on the top, bottom, left, right, or center of the screen.

Adding icon buttons to toolbars

Before adding items to the toolbar, note the menu group (File, Edit, View, etc.) that contains the command you want to add. For example, the Delete Rows and Find commands are under the Edit menu, the AutoFilter and Show All commands are under the Data menu, and the insert Rows command is under the Insert menu.

With the memory of the menu group in your head, right-click on any toolbar ▶ click on Customize (at the bottom of the list) ▶ select the Commands tab ▶ select the menu category that contains the command you want to add ▶ scroll down until you see the command ▶ depress the left mouse button and drag the icon to your preferred location in any toolbar (use a toolbar that makes sense to you) ▶ release the mouse button .

To delete a toolbar icon, click on Toolbar Options at the right side of the toolbar you want to adjust ▶ Add or Remove Buttons ▶ Check or uncheck the buttons you want to add or remove .

Repeat the process until your toolbars are optimized for the way you work.

Sorting rows

Level 1 codes, as they are copied into *Excel*, are substantially unsorted. Even if you started with a nicely sorted list in *Excel*, that list will become unsorted every time out-of-sequence data are added to the worksheet.

The good news is that sorting *Excel* worksheets can be done with two clicks. For a simple sort of the whole worksheet based on the data in a single column (e.g., Level I codes), click on a cell *in* that column (do not select the whole column), and then click on the 'A to Z' or the 'Z to A' toolbar icon

↓ ↓ .

Excel is smart enough to know that it is not supposed to sort the header row (unless you changed the default settings) so you do not need to do anything special to tell *Excel* how much of the row to sort. Simply click in a cell in the row that is to control the sort and *Excel* will know it is supposed to sort all of the non-blank and non–header rows.

More advanced searches are available by selecting Data ▶ Sort from the menu. These searches allow searches by a primary row, a secondary row, and a tertiary row. Advanced searches are discussed as a part of Level 3 coding in Chapter 9.

Find your data in Excel

This is a command that you have likely used in *Word*, but there is one extra step in *Excel*. Before you click on the Find or the Find and Replace command you need to tell *Excel* where to search. You can search rows, columns, a selected range of cells, or the whole worksheet.

The default search order when you select Data ▶ Sort (Ctrl+F), or click on the binoculars icon starts at the location of the active cell in the worksheet and works its way down to the bottom of that column, one 'find' at a time. After the search reaches the bottom of the column it moves on to neighboring columns until the entire worksheet has been searched. In other words, the default 'find' searches the entire worksheet.

If you want to search only a selected part of the worksheet, highlight that range of cells before initiating the search.

The Options command button in the Find and Replace window allows you to search by row instead of column, search the entire workbook instead of just the active worksheet, and more.

Find and Replace (edit your codes quickly)

The Find and Replace command works just like the simpler Find command, but adds the ability to globally, or one cell at a time, replace one data string (code) with another data string (a revised code). For example, to change a Level 2 code from 'Having a strong commitment to parenting' to 'Being committed to parenting', enter those phrases in the Find and Replace window as shown below.

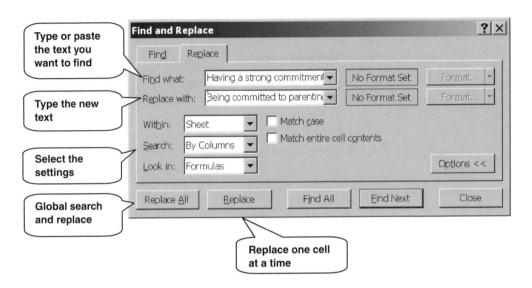

Type or paste the text you want to find

Type the new text

Select the settings

Global search and replace

Replace one cell at a time

A quick way to change the language of a code group

Edit your codes as necessary. When you created a Level 2 code early in the Level 2 coding process your analytic thinking about that category was still in a formative stage. You made up a code name and you assigned this code to many records, but now you have decided that the phrase originally chosen for the code needs to be changed. This is far from a hypothetical situation.

I encourage you to be proactive with your codes and to fine tune them until they are phrased just right. Do not let inertia stop you from improving code names and making other emerging refinements, especially when it is so quick and easy to make 'Replace All' changes.

Hint

To make sure do not mistakenly replace unwanted parts of your data, use the Replace, not the Replace All command, or highlight a limited range of cells before invoking the Replace All command.

AutoFilter (count your codes)

Group your records (rows) with the AutoFilter command. There are multiple reasons why you might want to view and analyze subsets of your data. By limiting the records available to the worksheet it is easier to scroll through the worksheet to examine data in a focused and meaningful way. Later in the research process, during the report-writing phase, the AutoFilter technique of *Excel* can become integral to the development of your analytic thoughts.

The following example of the AutoFilter command shows you how the command works, and as a side benefit you will see how to get a tally of how many records match each of the Level 2 codes.

To activate AutoFilter, select Data ► Filter ► AutoFilter or click on the AutoFilter icon ▼=. With AutoFilter activated dropdown buttons appear ▼ on the right side of all the column headers.

Click on a dropdown button and a list will appear showing all of the available values in that column.

In the following example, the filter was activated when 'Respecting the Children' was selected in the Level 2 column (field). At that point the list of rows was reduced from 530 to 31. This tally appears in the bottom left corner of the screen after the filter is applied. (If you want to record this number, write it down because the numbers disappear when further work is done in the worksheet.)

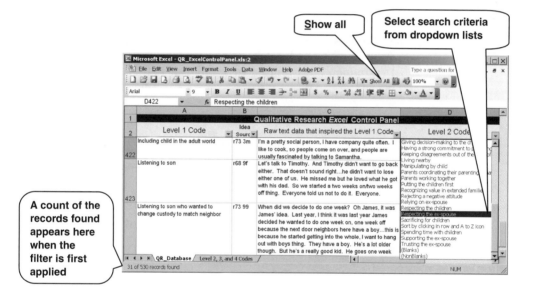

To remove the filter, click on Data ► Filter ► Show All , or click on the Show All button on the toolbar.

AutoFilter ► Custom (focus on one participant, and other sophisticated data views)

Focus on the records from a single participant

With a large database it can be hard to focus on a single participant (or focus group, or field observation site, etc.) when there are hundreds of data records from many sources. This example shows you how to isolate all of the records from a single participant using the Idea Source field. In the process you will learn how to use the AutoFilter ► Custom feature .

As discussed earlier in this chapter, a cryptogram identifier for each participant is entered in the Idea Source column at the time of Level 2 coding.

Searching and filtering works efficiently if the cryptogram includes a unique letter/number identifier for each participant. For example, a participant who was the fourth female interviewed might get a participant code of '4F.'

This participant identifier is combined with the data's location in the code document (row 42) to create a complete 'source of the idea' cryptogram: 'r424f' (row 42 participant 4F).

After all, Level 2 coding is completed the codes related to participant 4F will be scattered throughout the Excel document (depending on the currently active sort criteria). What if you want to focus exclusively on one participant? How do you isolate the records just from one source? The answer is to use a custom AutoFilter.

First, put *Excel* into AutoFilter mode: Data ▶ Filter ▶ AutoFilter or click on the AutoFilter icon ![Y=]. After starting with either of the two methods, click on the dropdown button ![▼] in the column that holds the data that will be the object of the filter.

At the top of each AutoFilter dropdown list are a few special commands. Select Custom, which will appear near the top of the list.

After the Custom AutoFilter box appears type '*4f*' or '*4F*' into the input field shown below. The use of the * asterisk wildcard character is important.

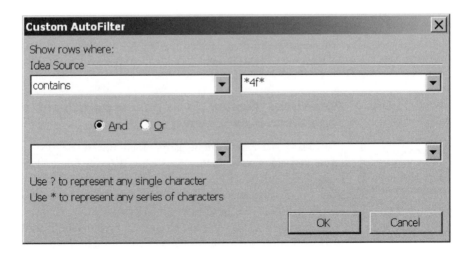

Study the illustration above to see how multi-field filters can be applied with the 'and' or the 'or' operators. After your filter criteria are established, click on OK to complete the filtering process. This technique can be used to filter any part of any field. Use it creatively.

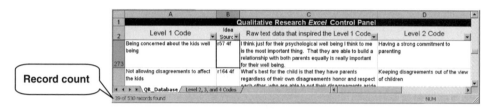

Results from the sample filter.

To remove the filter, click on Data ▶ Filter ▶ Show All, or click on the Show All button on the toolbar.

About wildcard characters

In filters and searches it is sometimes essential to use wildcard characters. The two most important of these characters are the asterisk (★) and the question mark (?).

Asterisk (*)

Asterisks screen out any number of characters before and/or after the asterisks by turning these unwanted characters into wildcards. For example, ★4f★ finds and includes in the filter 'r1004f,' or '4fr100,' or 'Jane Doe, r1004F on 6 June.' Asterisk wildcards work well in the Idea Source column.

Question mark (?)

Question marks turn any single character in to a wildcard. Question mark wildcards are most helpful when there is a variable character within a character string.

For example, suppose your cryptogram system identifies participants by focus group (FG) and by location (New York). Participants FG4aNew York, FG4bNew York, FG4cNew York, FG4dNew York, and FG4eNew York are all part of the same focus group. What if you want to create a filter to find all members of focus group 4?

The filter ★FG4?New York★ creates a filtered list of all rows with members from focus group 4 who are from New York.

Suppose focus group 4 had members in Boston, New York, and Atlanta and you want to create a filter to include group members from all cities. Change the filter to ★FG4?★, or better yet, ★FG4★.

The filter feature can significantly help you scroll through focused records as you are analyzing results, developing conclusions, and writing the report. Use AutoFilter creatively and often.

Persistence

Energy and persistence conquer all things.

Benjamin Franklin

Completing Level 2 coding can be exhausting; especially after everything that preceded Level 2 coding is considered. There is no substitute for the qualitative researcher's personal immersion in the research process and data. This immersion takes time and energy. It helps to have an organized system like the one described in this book, but detailed coding can be mind-numbing work no matter how well you create your system.

You have been committed to your research project for quite a while by the time you become actively involved with Level 2 coding. Every step you took to get to this point has probably taken a lot of time, especially if you have a lot of data. It can seem like there is no end in sight.

This is the time for a pep talk. If you have a friend, advisor, mentor, or other encouraging person in your life let him or her know you need encouragement. Also, build short breaks into your coding time to get some exercise or just to let your mind rest. But do not give up hope.

Hopefully the following information will help – the steps that follow will be *much* easier because of the hard work and good organization you are completing during the Level 2 coding process.

1. Level 3 coding and Theoretical Concept development (Level 4 coding) are low-tech and like a breath of fresh air after seemingly endless time previously spent at the computer.
2. The hard work you put into all stages of coding will make it remarkably easy for you to write the results and conclusions sections of your final report because all of your data, all of your codes, and the hierarchy of all of your codes will be at your fingertips.
3. The Level 4, Level 3, and Level 2 code hierarchy serves as a natural outline for the headings and subheadings in the conclusions section of your final report, making the final section of your report relatively easy to write.

Chapter summary

Level 1 codes and the data immediately associated with those codes are drawn into a central data depository during Level 2 coding. The consolidation of these data makes further examination of the data much more efficient and effective. Microsoft *Excel* allows the researcher to collect, store, and analyze qualitative research data using a software program that is widely used and understood.

The qualitative research system introduced in this chapter features a single workbook repository for all of the project's refined data. This workbook is formatted to take advantage of *Excel*'s database features. No calculations or arithmetic formulas are used.

The basic steps to Level 2 coding are:

Step 1. Copy a Level 1 code phrase from the middle column of the *Word* code document to a blank row in the Level 1 column in *Excel*. This new row is the equivalent of a database record.

Step 2. Copy the text data associated with the Level 1 code from the right column of the *Word* code document to the 'Raw text data that inspired the Level 1 Code' column in *Excel*.

Step 3. Create a binomial identifier that relates the record to a specific code document and row number in that document. The identifier is entered in the idea source column.

Step 4a. For *new Level 2 codes*, create a Level 2 code by typing the new code name in a new row in the Level 2 column of the worksheet. After typing the new code, Copy (Ctrl+C) and then paste (Ctrl+V) the new Level 2 code from the Level 2 column to a new row in the 'List of UNIQUE Level 1 code names' in the 'Level 2, 3, and 4 Codes' worksheet.

Step 4b. When a newly copied (from *Word*) Level 1 code fits into an existing Level 2 code, copy the existing code (Ctrl+C) from the 'List of UNIQUE Level 2 code names' to the 'Level 2 Code' column in the new record (Ctrl+V).

Step 5. Repeat the process of copying Level 1 codes from *Word* to *Excel* until all Level 1 codes are stored in *Excel*.

The data in *Excel* can be manipulated in many ways using existing *Excel* commands that allow database records to be sorted and filtered. Additionally, the Find and Replace command allows the researcher to quickly and globally refine code descriptions. Qualitative research data in *Excel* can be presented on the screen, via e-mail, and on the printed page using *Word*'s mail merge feature.

Level 3 and Level 4 (theoretical concepts) coding

Genius is one per cent inspiration, ninety-nine per cent perspiration.

Thomas A. Edison

Higher level coding is refreshing. Up until now you have been mechanically, laboriously, and thoughtfully coding your data. You paid your dues to develop an amazing set of building blocks – your own Level 1 and Level 2 codes. It is finally time for computer-free cognition.

Access-based Chapter 7 and *Excel*-based Chapter 8 were two parallel chapters that covered Level 2 coding. In Chapter 9 the parallel paths rejoin because the core processes for higher level coding are done away from the computer. Before proceeding with higher level coding, your Level 2 coding should be substantially finished. Level 2 codes are the base for higher level coding.

While much of the time during higher level coding is done away from the computer, be prepared to go back into the data in *Word, Access,* or *Excel* to reexamine the roots of your thinking. When your thoughts are unclear there is no substitute for the original data.

Overview of Level 3 and theoretical concept (Level 4) coding

Higher level coding is old school. It is done with pieces of paper, scissors, a large table, and paper clips! Even though the Level 3 technology is different than the Level 2 technology the idea is similar – examine lower level codes until you create affinity groups. The labels that you give these groupings are your Level 3 codes. The goal is to continue focusing your codes. By the time you finish your last level of coding you want to have your data distilled down to a few highly significant points that concisely answer your research questions.

An overview of the Level 3 coding process follows.

1. **Print the 'code sheet' summary report**. The *Access* template from qrtips.com provides a pre-made report. *Excel* code sheets are cut from a specially formatted worksheet (details follow). These reports list your Level 2 codes alphabetically. Grouped with each Level 2 code is an alphabetical subgrouping of associated Level 1 codes.
2. **Create code sheets from the reports.** Cut the printed reports from *Access* or *Excel* to keep the Level 2 Code groupings intact. With *Access* that simply involves cutting on all of the dotted lines.

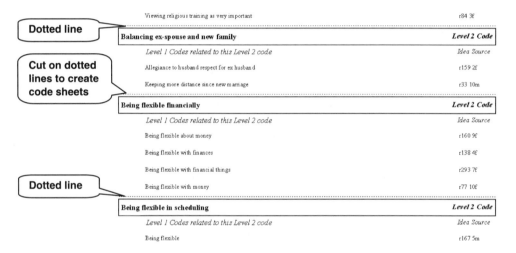

This *Access* report is provided with the template.

The content of the *Excel* report is identical, but it looks significantly different.

This *Excel* printout must be set up by the user (instructions below).

Whether you print from *Access* or *Excel*, cut the printed sheets so that Level 2 code groups are preserved. Paperclip or staple together any Level 2 code groups that span multiple pages.

3. Place all of these Level 2 code sheets on a large table (or on the floor). The goal is to find multiple Level 2 codes that group together to support coherent themes. Those themes will be your Level 3 codes.

    You are looking for a relationship of many (Level 2 codes) to few (Level 3 codes). Keep working and reworking the emerging Level 3 code groupings to create thematic affinities. These Level 3 groupings take shape (literally) as small piles of Level 2 code sheets. After you feel that you have created some viable Level 3 code groups, take pieces of scrap paper and write down names for the Level 3 code groups. Place the tentative names on top of each pile and leave them on the table. Go away for a while and let your mind do other things.

4. Go back to the table after you are refreshed – review Step 3 and the tentative Level 3 code groupings. Sort the piles again, add or subtract code groupings, and revise Level 3 code names. Return to your data in *Access*, *Excel*, and *Word* to clarify your thinking. Reprint the code sheets if you make substantial revisions.

    Sort the piles again. Go away for a while and let your mind do other things. Keep looping through the Level 3 coding process until you are confident that you have created the best possible Level 3 codes.

Level 4 (Theoretical concept development)

This is a big step that can be described with few words.

1. If you need to further focus your data to create Theoretical Concepts or more concentrated Level 4 codes, paperclip and label the piles of paper that represent the Level 3 code groups. Shuffle each of these Level 3 piles to create Level 4 grouping using the procedures described in Steps 3 and 4 above.

2. If necessary create Level 5 codes.

    These steps are far too important to rush. Give your thoughts time to develop. You worked hard to make your data easily accessible in *Access*, *Excel*, and *Word*, so go back to your data often. Have fun with your unfettered thinking process but take it seriously. You are shaping the 'Analysis and Results' and 'Conclusion' sections of your report.

Details of printing the code sheet in Access

Paper and
scissors

Open *Access*, minimize any forms that may appear so the underlying database window is visible, then click on Reports. Preview (open) the report called rptCodeSheets_ForHighLevelCoding. If you did not change field names and have completely populated the Level 1 and Level 2 fields the report should look fine. If the Preview looks right, print it. *The report was created for the European A4 paper size. If you are living in a part of the world where the larger 8.5 × 11 paper size is common, and if you need larger field sizes you might find it advantageous to adjust the paper size in the report.*

After you print the report, cut the pages along the dotted lines to create individual Level 2 code sheets.

Viewing religious training as very important	r84 3f

Balancing ex-spouse and new family	*Level 2 Code*
Level 1 Codes related to this Level 2 code	*Idea Source*
Allegiance to husband respect for ex husband	r159 2f
Keeping more distance since new marriage	r33 10m

Being flexible financially	*Level 2 Code*
Level 1 Codes related to this Level 2 code	*Idea Source*
Being flexible about money	r160 9f
Being flexible with finances	r138 4f
Being flexible with financial things	r293 7f
Being flexible with money	r77 10f

Being flexible in scheduling	*Level 2 Code*
Level 1 Codes related to this Level 2 code	*Idea Source*
Being flexible	r167 5m

Troubleshooting

If the report does not look right, you will have to switch to the design view of the report to make adjustments to the layout or the record source.

Problem 1: The report cuts off part of the text. A common problem is that text is truncated in some report fields. This is usually because the data in the field are too large for the allotted size of the report field. This problem can be remedied by increasing the space available for the text as described below. The Level 1 field is used as an example. The procedure works with any field.

1. Open the report in design view, then hover the mouse over the interface between the Detail and Page Footer sections of the form until the mouse pointer turns to a double arrow, then hold down the left mouse button and drag down the margin to make the detail section bigger.
2. Click on the Level 1 text box to give it the focus.
3. Hover the mouse over the small black square at the bottom of the Level 1 text box until the mouse pointer turns to a double arrow, then hold down the left mouse button and drag down the bottom of the field to make more space available for more text data. The text will wrap to use multiple lines if there is available space. Repeat Steps 2 and 3 for the Idea Source field if necessary. Note: The fields' width and height can also be expanded.
4. Click on Layout Preview on the left side of the toolbar to see if the text now fits. Keep tweaking until all of the text is visible.

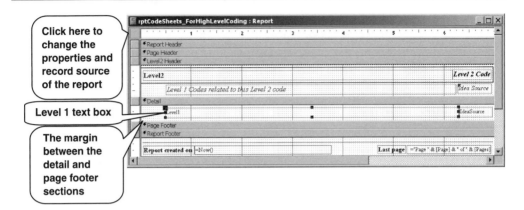

Click here to change the properties and record source of the report

Level 1 text box

The margin between the detail and page footer sections

Design View of the Code Sheet Report.

Problem 2: The report has missing data or no data. The record source of the template report is a query named 'qryForCodeSheetRpt.' This query includes all of the records from the main table in the template called 'tblCodesAndMemos.' The query design looks like this:

Code sheet query design.

I used a query for the record source of the report because I wanted to control the sorting of the records, and also because I wanted to eliminate records that had no data in the Level 2 field (Is Not Null).

If you added fields or changed field names in the table, the report will not recognize your data. To fix this you may need to change the record source of the entire report. Open the report in Design view ▶ right-click on the square in the upper left corner of the report ▶ click on Properties ▶ select the Data tab and change the Record Source of the table to reflect the data source and field names that you are using.

In a similar way you can change properties of each object in a report or form. Right-click on the text box or other object ▶ click on Properties ▶ change the property or properties that will make the report better.

Other problems: If the report still does not work properly, continue troubleshooting with the Microsoft *Access* help system, refer to third party books that focus on *Access,* or perhaps enlist the help of a friend or consultant who is proficient with *Access.* This report is important.

Details of setting up Excel to print the code sheet report

Paper and scissors

Excel allows you to print code sheets, but it does not have an *Access*-style report generator. This means that you will have to reformat your *Excel* worksheet one step at a time so it can print your data in code sheet style. Follow the ten steps below carefully. Even though the code sheet setup is tedious it is a one-time procedure. The template available at qrtips.com includes page settings that eliminate a few steps including narrowing the margins, creating an out of the way page footer, and changing the print settings so *Excel* will print row and column headings.

Keep in mind that the goal of the report is to create printed groups of Level 2 codes that are associated Level 1 codes and idea source cryptograms.

To create a worksheet with this formatting you will need to decimate the original workbook that contains your data. Since you need your original workbook in the future, the report formatting will be in a workbook saved with a new name.

Note: Since this is a one-time procedure I am including only one set of commands, e.g., Ctrl+X for cut, instead of also including tool bar icons and menu command. Use the style of commands that you like the best.

Step 1 – Copy the workbook so the report can be created in a new file. Open the original workbook called QR_ExcelControlPanel.xls ▶ select File ▶ Save As ▶ type in a new filename. I suggest QR_ExcelControlPanel-Report.xls.

A window will appear with a Save button, but before you click on Save take a look at the 'Save in:' field at the top of the window. Note the name of the folder where the file will be saved. Change the Save in: destination if necessary. Click on the Save button to finish the process.

This procedure automatically closes the primary workbook, yet the newly created file remains open and active. Check to make sure the new file is active (not the primary file) by looking at the filename in the title bar at the very top of the *Excel* program. The filename is listed next to the words Microsoft *Excel.*

Step 2 – Clear all filters. Data ▸ Filter ▸ ShowAll . If the ShowAll selection is light gray and not accessible there is no filter active. That is what you want.

Step 3 – Eliminate the Side-by-Side windows. Window ▸ Arrange ▸ click on Tiled ▸ OK .

Now you will be able to see both windows. Delete either window (it does not matter which one) by clicking on the X in the top right corner of either window. Maximize the remaining window by clicking on the maximize button. This button is located left of the X in the top right corner of the remaining window ▬ ▢ ✕ .

Step 4 – Delete the title row. Click on the number 1 in the row heading (the gray cell) at the left side of row 1. This will select the entire row including the text 'Qualitative Research *Excel* Control Panel.' Select Edit ▸ Delete (Delete Row) to delete this row. (This step is necessary because the merged cells in this title row make it difficult to move columns.)

Step 5 – Create a blank column 'A.' Click anywhere in column A, which now contains Level 2 data. Select Insert ▸ Columns . This creates a new column that is necessary for the next step.

Step 6 – Move the Level 2 column to the left. Click on the gray column heading above the Level 2 Code label (Column E) to select the whole column ▸ Cut the column (Ctrl+X) ▸ Click on the gray column heading at the top of Column A to select that column ▸ Paste the Level 2 Code column by pressing Ctrl+V .

Step 7 – Sort the data. Click anywhere in Column A (Level 2) ▸ Data ▸ Sort . The box below will appear.

Once the Sort box is set up as shown, click on OK.

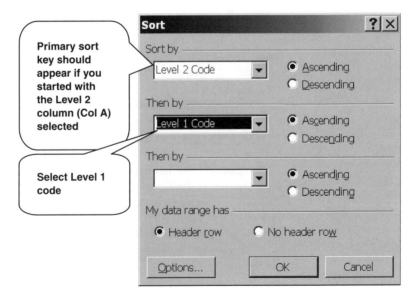

Step 8 – Adjust column widths. To suit the length of your codes, widen or narrow the worksheet columns as necessary. In the gray column heading area hover the mouse in the boundary between columns. When the mouse pointer changes to a double arrow, hold down the left mouse button and then drag the mouse to the left or right to adjust the column widths. Make sure the combined width of the three columns is not wider than the width of a printed page.

Step 9 – Set the print area. In the column heading area in Column A left-click and hold down the mouse button ▶ while the mouse button is depressed, drag the mouse to the right until Columns A, B, and C are highlighted ▶ Release the mouse button ▶ select File ▶ Print Area ▶ Set Print Area.

Step 10 – Print Preview. File ▶ Print Preview. Review the print preview pages. If all is well, then print. If not, adjust, preview again, and when all is well print the page (Ctrl+P).

After you print the worksheet, cut the pages so all of the Level 2 codes are grouped together to create individual Level 2 code sheets.

Cut between Level 2 code breaks	12	Balancing ex-spouse and new family	Allegiance to husband respect for ex husband	r159 2f
	13	Balancing ex-spouse and new family	Keeping more distance since new marriage	r33 10m
	14	Being flexible financially	Being flexible about money	r160 9f
	15	Being flexible financially	Being flexible with finances	r138 4f
	16	Being flexible financially	Being flexible with financial things	r293 7f
	17	Being flexible financially	Being flexible with money	r77 10f
Cut between Level 2 codes	18	Being flexible in scheduling	Being flexible	r134 2f
	19	Being flexible in scheduling	Being flexible	r167 5m
	20	Being flexible in scheduling	Being flexible at holidays	r12 10m
	21	Being flexible in scheduling	Being flexible is important over time	r52 8m
	22	Being flexible in scheduling	Being flexible to take child at unscheduled times	r40 3m

This *Excel* printout must be set up by the user (instructions below).

Paperclip or staple together any Level 2 code groupings (code sheets) that span multiple pages. For the sake of visibility you may want to use a felt pen to write the Level 2 code prominently on each code sheet.

Level 3 coding in detail

A large table, scrap paper, and a dark pen

At this stage the results, literally, come together.

As with Level 2 coding, Level 3 coding focuses on a many to few relationship. The goal is to find multiple Level 2 codes for almost every Level 3 code group. This means that the Level 3 code descriptions must be broad enough to encompass multiple Level 2 codes.

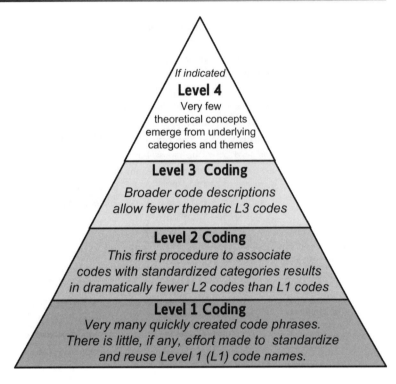

Hundreds (or more) Level 1 codes are reduced to very few Level 4 codes.

The Level 3 coding process is accomplished away from the computer. If you have completed the report printing process in *Access* or *Excel* and cut the reports into code sheets you are ready to proceed.

With your code sheets in hand move to a big empty table. Randomly spread out all of the code sheets, and immediately start focusing on patterns and affinities. Think about which of the Level 2 categories can be combined to create Level 3 themes. Shuffle the code sheets freely and creatively.

Create piles of the code sheets that form around axes and themes. When you have a rough idea of what to call these themes, write tentative Level 3 names on pieces of scrap paper and put the labels on top of the piles. Keep pondering the piles; rework them freely.

Once you are fairly happy with the piles and the Level 3 code names give yourself a break. Do whatever it is that you do that facilitates background thinking so you can come back to the piles with a fresh perspective.

After your break go back to the table. Reexamine the piles and your tentative Level 3 code names. Make changes. Go back to your data in *Access*, *Excel*, and *Word*. Mix it up. Make radical changes. Write new code names on more pieces of scrap paper.

Repeat … again.

When you feel that you finally have it right, paperclip the piles with the final Level 3 code names on top. You now have your Level 3 codes. Make sure you write down this precious list and back it up. You do not want a sudden gust of wind to undo your good work.

Theoretical concept development (Level 4 coding)

Add some paper clips

Before continuing with Level 4 coding think about your finished product. It may be a thesis, dissertation, journal article, or other report. Your conclusion section will need focus. This focus should be directly related to the data. This means that the final number of codes must be reduced to a very small number. Your conclusion will appear scattered if you have too many codes after your final stage of coding.

How are you doing? How much more concentrated order do you need to bring to the original chaos of your data? If you feel that your data are reduced enough to fit nicely into your report's conclusion section after Level 3 coding, stop here; there is no need to proceed to Level 4 coding.

Large projects with a lot of data frequently require at least four levels of coding. The number of codes must be logically and incrementally reduced with each progressive coding level. You must persevere with your coding efforts until you distill your data into focused results that are as clear and simple as possible.

Level 4 coding starts with all of the Level 3 codes. Your Level 4 focus is to combine the Level 3 themes into even more concentrated groupings. Because these concentrated groupings combine several related themes, the grouping descriptions (Level 4 code names) must be broad enough to fairly represent all of the component themes.

Use the same process described for Level 3 coding to further reduce your Level 3 data into theoretical concepts. The difference is that in Level 3 coding you started with Level 2 codes as your components, in Level 4 coding you start with Level 3 codes as your components.

A note to phenomenologists and others not developing theory. At this point I feel that it is important to repeat a statement from the Introduction in case you missed it. Throughout the book I refer to Level 4 coding as theoretical concept development. This was done to provide a mental end game for the many qualitative researchers who are interested in developing theory.

I know that many other qualitative researchers are more interested in the exploration of phenomena than the development of theory. My apologies to all of you who fit into this category. Please substitute 'Level 4' for 'theoretical concept' as you progress through the iterative stages of data exploration.

When you are finished with Level 4 coding, proceed to Level 5 coding if your codes are not appropriately reduced after the Level 4 coding process. However, if you believe that you have the focus you need, you are finished with coding. **Place each stack of Level 3 codes that now represents a Level 4 code group into its own file folder. Label the folder with the Level 4 code name. Write down the Level 4 code list, and make sure the list is backed up.**

Congratulations, this is a big step. Enjoy the answers you now have to your research questions.

You have your results, now prepare for report writing

Now that you have your coded results, it is good practice to go back to *Access* or *Excel* to enter the results of your Level 3 (and higher) coding in the blank Level 3 and Level 4 columns. Because higher level coding is done on a physical table not in a computer program the Level 3 and Level 4 (Theoretical Concepts) columns in your datasheets are still empty at the end of these procedures.

The views and tools available to your report writing will be more robust if you can manipulate a database or worksheet that is fully populated with your results. This is a somewhat tedious step, but the copy and paste command in datasheet view makes it go quickly.

Go back to Access or Excel to fill in the blanks

The sample tables shown below are datasheet views of a very simplified *Access* table. You can easily see the similarities between the datasheet view of *Access* and the *Excel* worksheet. Even though the following discussion uses *Access* language and illustrations, the procedures described below work equally well in *Access* and *Excel*.

The first sample datasheet on the next page shows the database before Level 3 and Level 4 codes are entered. The second table shows a fully populated datasheet.

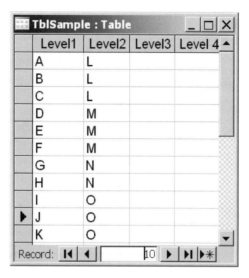

Many Level 1 codes and few Level 2 codes.

After higher level coding, many Level 2 codes, fewer Level 3 codes, and fewest Level 4 codes.

Instructions for quickly populating Level 3 and Level 4 columns in a datasheet or worksheet follow.

Step 1. The quickest way for *Access* users to populate the Level 3 and Theoretical Concept (Level 4) fields is in datasheet view, so open tblCodesAndMemos in datasheet view. *Excel* users open your worksheet.

Step 2. Click in the Level 2 column and sort on that column by clicking on the 'A to Z' icon on the toolbar. Now all of your Level 2 codes will be grouped together as shown in the illustration above. It is not necessary to do a secondary sort on the Level 1 column.

Step 3. With your Level 4 file folders at your side, your job is to dig into the folders to get the information that allows you to fill in the blanks in the database table. One pile at a time, leaf through the Level 3 (paper clipped) groupings so you can correlate the Level 2 codes shown on the datasheet with Level 3 code names. In the example above all of the Level 2 codes 'L' and 'M' are grouped together to correlate with the Level 3 code 'P.'

Step 4. 'Many' Level 2 codes will correspond with each individual Level 3 code. **You only need to type a Level 3 code into the datasheet once.** After it is typed, copy the Level 3 code once (Ctrl+C) and repeatedly paste it (Ctrl+V) next to all of the Level 2 cells that are associated with that Level 3 code.

In the example shown above, type then copy 'P' once, and then paste it five times.

Repeat until all Level 3 codes are entered in the database table.

Step 5. After completing Step 4, fill in the Level 4 column/Theoretical Concept using the same technique. Before you start filling in the Level 4 column remember to sort the datasheet by the Level 3 column. Click in the Level 3 column, and sort on that column by clicking on the 'A to Z' icon on the datasheet toolbar.

Step 6. Repeat for all higher levels of codes.

At the completion of this 'fill in the blanks' procedure you will have a database that will help significantly during the report-writing phase. Proceed to Chapter 10.

Chapter summary

The goal of higher level coding is to distill the data until a very small number of codes concisely summarize the results of the study. Level 3 and Level 4 codes facilitate the final stages of analysis and form the backbone of the 'Analysis and Results' and 'Conclusions' sections of your report.

During Levels 3 and 4 coding you will work with Level 2 code sheets printed from *Access* or *Excel*, scissors, and paper clips.

1. Print the "code sheet" summary reports from either *Access* or *Excel*.
2. Create individual Level 2 code sheets from the reports by cutting the reports so each Level 2 code is on a separate sheet. The Level 1 codes that are associated with the Level 2 code will also be visible.
3. Physically shuffle the Level 2 code sheets on a large table. Create groupings with thematic affinities. When completed, these groupings will be summarized and labeled to become Level 3 codes.
4. Take a break after your first session of Level 3 coding. Go back to the table after you are refreshed and sort the piles again. Return to your data in *Access*,

Excel, and *Word* to clarify your thinking. Keep looping through the Level 3 coding process until you are confident that you have created the best possible Level 3 codes.

5. If you need to further focus after Level 3 coding to create Theoretical Concepts or more concentrated Level 4 codes, paperclip the labeled piles of paper that represent the Level 3 code groups. Shuffle each of these Level 3 piles to create Level 4 groupings using the procedures described in Steps 3 and 4 above.

6. If necessary create Level 5 codes.

After you have completed Level 3 and Level 4 coding (if necessary) return to *Access* or *Excel* to enter the results of your Level 3 and Level 4 coding. All records in the database should include data for all completed levels of coding. A fully populated database will help you significantly during the writing of the 'Analysis and Results' and 'Conclusions and Recommendations' sections of your report.

CHAPTER 10

Writing the report – The final draft

What is written without effort is in general read without pleasure.

Samuel Johnson

After all of the coding is done it is finally time to write the thesis, dissertation, academic journal article, or intra-organizational report. The writing phase of research is more efficient and productive because of the hard work that you put into the collection, organization, and coding of your data.

Specific report formats vary widely, but there is a common structure in most academic publications. The sections that follow present a model of a typical five-chapter dissertation. A template of this dissertation model, including embedded formatting, may be downloaded from qrtips.com/chapter10.

The five-chapter dissertation template is presented as an example only. Most universities, journals, corporations, and government agencies provide very specific publication guidelines. In all cases it is easier to follow editorial style guidelines if you use the style-oriented tools of *Word* in conjunction with an integrated bibliographic reference manager.

The Styles and Formatting feature of *Word* can save you time and frustration. It takes initiative to set up styles to match your editorial requirements, but this one-time effort eliminates inefficient repetitive formatting motions when you are writing the paper. **With Styles a shortcut key combination or a click of the mouse will format each *section* and *section heading* with the correct font size, font style, and font weight; the proper line spacing, indents and margins; page headers, page footers, and page numbers. The use of Styles also allows the automatic creation of a table of contents, a list of tables, a list of figures, and more.**

The section-by-section examples in this chapter introduce you to many of the style and formatting features of *Word*, but the examples are not a style guide. There are hundreds of different editorial styles required by different organizations. The good news is that you can customize *Word* to match the editorial style guide that is required for your research output.

If you followed the suggestions in Chapter 3 and have kept all of your bibliographic references in a reference management program (EndNote, Biblioscape, Reference Works, etc.) you are prepared to efficiently create citations in your report. If you are not yet using a reference management program with cite-while-you-write features I suggest that you acquire one of these programs before you proceed.

Styles and Formatting

Writing a significant paper or report without using the 'Styles and Formatting' feature of a word processor would be like trying to travel between London and Glasgow on a bicycle. Most of us would make it eventually, but we would have to suffer through many exhausting rainy days. Planes and trains have long-since been invented for travel; likewise, full-featured word processing programs have Styles and Formatting features. It is in the best interest of most of us to use these modern conveniences.

Styles are the lead component of *Word*'s Styles and Formatting feature. Two commonly used terms, 'writing style' and 'publisher editorial style' both use the word style, so to avoid confusion the word Styles is capitalized when I specifically refer to the *Word* feature.

The Styles feature allows you to make precise and extensive changes to the appearance of specific parts of a *Word* document with a single keystroke. Styles save sets of formatting characteristics such as font sizes, margins, font faces, line spacing, and more. When you apply a Style, you apply all of the formatting characteristics with one command.

For example, instead of taking several separate steps every time you format your block quotations, you can save all of the exacting settings as a Style. With Styles it becomes a fast one-keystroke (or click) command to change the font and paragraph settings to 12 pt, Courier New, left-aligned, paragraph indent of 0.5 inches (1.3 cm) from the left margin, left margin 1 inch, right margin 1 inch, and no first line indent. Click on the Block Quotation Style and you are done.

In addition to formatting text, **Styles control Table of Contents entries.** The Table of Contents (TOC) is a critically important feature to a large paper or report, and Heading Styles are the key to the table of contents entries. Text designated as a 'Heading 1' Style becomes a primary TOC entry. Text designated as a 'Heading 2' Style becomes a secondary TOC entry. Text designated as a 'Heading 3' Style becomes a third level TOC entry, etc.

If you do not take the time to mark the headings in your report, a table of contents cannot be easily compiled.

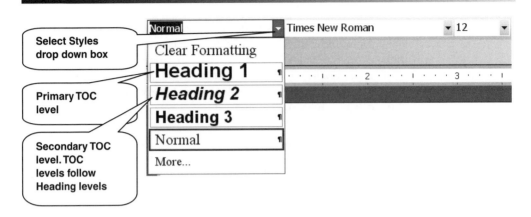

To apply Styles to headings or sections of text, the first step is always to designate the text that is to be formatted. This can be done by highlighting the entire block to be formatted, or by clicking anywhere in a discrete paragraph.

The simplest way to apply a Style after designating the text is with the dropdown list on the left side of the Formatting toolbar as shown in the illustration above. Once the target text is designated, click on the Style that you want to apply from the list.

A second way to apply Styles is to use the keyboard shortcuts after designating the text to be formatted. The shortcuts are:

Heading 1	Alt+Ctrl+1
Heading 2	Alt+Ctrl+2
Heading 3	Alt+Ctrl+3
Normal Style	Ctrl+Shift+N

To edit the settings for a Style click on the Styles and Formatting icon on the left side of the formatting toolbar ▯, or from the menu select Format ▶ Styles and Formatting. This will cause the Styles and Formatting task pane to appear on the right side of the *Word* window. With the task pane in place, right-click on the appropriate Style in the task pane.

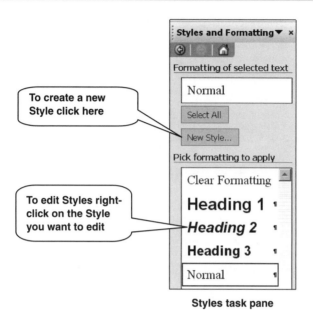

To create a new Style click here

To edit Styles right-click on the Style you want to edit

Styles task pane

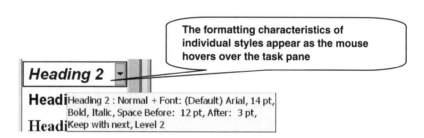

The formatting characteristics of individual styles appear as the mouse hovers over the task pane

Style editing is done in the Modify Style window shown below. The Format button in the bottom left corner of the Modify Style window allows you to access settings for fonts, paragraphs, tabs, borders, language, frames, numbering, and shortcut commands that will be compiled into the Style.

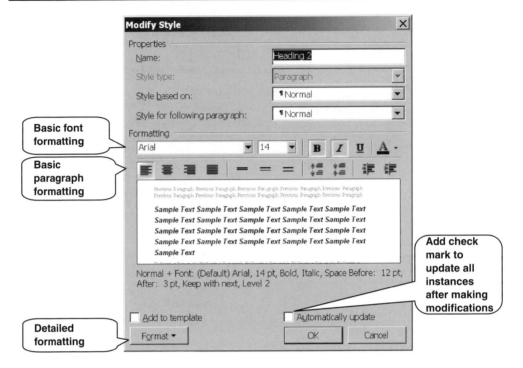

Basic font formatting

Basic paragraph formatting

Add check mark to update all instances after making modifications

Detailed formatting

This is the Style editing interface.

Styles can be modified to match the precise specifications of the editorial style guide that you are required to use for your report or paper. The key to success in using Styles is to use them consistently throughout your publication. *Every heading must have a Style assigned or the table of contents will not display entries for all sections.* Even the normal or body text should be assigned the Normal Style or the Body Text Style (use one or the other – be consistent), all block quotations should be assigned a Block Quotation Style (you may have to make a new Style for this), and all numbered and bulleted lists should have their own Styles.

Word's Styles can save you a lot of time and frustration, especially when you have to adhere to a rigid editorial style guide. The use of Styles insures rigid compliance without the tedious frustration of ultra-precise typing.

You may want to know what happens if you make a mistake when you first create or edit a style? Suppose you have assigned 64 Heading 2 Styles to headings and now you realize that your editorial style guide specifies *italics* for the second level of headings and you used **bold**.

You will be happy with the answer to this dilemma. After fixing your mistake by modifying the Heading 2 Style, select 'Automatically Update' (immediately above the OK button), and all of the Level 2 Style selections will be automatically fixed.

Formatting sections of your report

How do you integrate your coded data into your report? An editorial style guide tells you how to format the Style elements, but it does not help with the basic structure of the report or the content that you choose to enter into the report. If you followed the instructions earlier in this book for coding your data, you are in good shape. The coding levels that you created serve as logical section headings in the Results and the Conclusions sections of your report, and the data associated with your database's code records are readily available for inclusion into the body of the report (copy and paste). But what of the organizational structure of your report – the introduction, body, and conclusion?

A dissertation is one of the most formal and structured reports that most researchers are likely to write; therefore, it is likely to contain most of the components that are required in smaller reports. Because of this the organization of the rest of this chapter uses the example of a typical five-chapter dissertation model.

The techniques discussed in one section may apply to multiple sections.

The report's preliminary pages

Prior to the paper's Introduction section there may be several pages of 'front matter' including a title page, copyright page, approval signature page, abstract, dedication, acknowledgements, table of contents, a list of tables, and/or a list of figures.

Most of these pages are one-time-only entries that are most efficiently formatted manually without extensive use of *Word*'s Style and Formatting features. However, three of the front matter items, the Table of Contents, List of Tables, and List of Figures are much easier to produce with the use of Styles, so they are presented in this section.

Table of Contents

Word's pre-programmed Table of Contents capabilities allow you to create a specially formatted 'field' in *Word* that dynamically updates the Table of Contents entries and associated page numbers. This remarkable field keeps track of additions and edits to the report as they are made. **The Table of Contents feature is not hard to use, but it requires the use of Heading Styles throughout the *Word* document.** If you do not know how to use Styles and you skipped the section earlier in this chapter, go back to review Styles and Formatting.

To make sure that *Word* can create a reliable Table of Contents, always use Heading Styles at the beginning of each section and subsection. The Table of Contents sequentially lists all headings and subheadings.

Table of Contents

Table of Contents illustration.

Insert ▶
Reference ▶ Index
and Tables to
create the TOC

To insert a Table of Contents in your document, click in a blank line in your document where the Table of Contents should appear, as specified by your editorial style guide. This is generally near the beginning of your document.

Select Insert ▶ Reference ▶ Index and Tables ▶ select the Table of Contents tab. The fonts and other formatting options that make up the TOC can be modified now or at a later time. When you are finished with any modifications, click on OK.

Right-click on the
TOC, and then
select Update
Field to refresh
the TOC

To update or edit the format of the Table of Contents after changes have been made in the document, right-click on the TOC. To update the page numbers and section headings select Update Field. To change the formatting of the Table of Contents (font size, etc.) select Edit Field.

The Field editing window might surprise you the first time you see it because it includes a list of all of the special fields in *Word*. Scroll down the list to find 'TOC.' That is the table of contents field. Click on it, then on the Table of Contents button that appears in the right pane of the window.

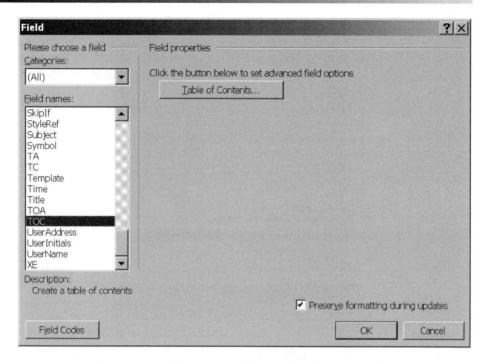

Field Editing Window – select TOC for the Table of Contents field.

Once in the Table of Contents editing window, most of the heading-by-heading formatting options are accessed through the Modify button. One at a time, make changes to each of the Heading levels. All font, spacing, margin, and paragraph settings can be modified on a heading-by-heading basis. While in the Table of Contents editing window, notice the other changes that can be made through the Options button and the controls in the window.

Reminder: mark all new headings and subheadings with Heading Styles as follows: Heading 1 (Alt+Ctrl+1), Heading 2 (Alt+Ctrl+2), or Heading 3 (Alt+Ctrl+3), etc. It is also possible to mark heading levels by clicking on the Select Styles dropdown box on the Formatting toolbar. These Heading Styles are the essential building blocks for your Table of Contents.

> Heading Styles will be compiled into the table of Contents – Heading 1 (Alt+Ctrl+1), Heading 2 (Alt+Ctrl+2), Heading 3 (Alt+Ctrl+3), etc.

List of Figures and List of Tables

Figures and tables used in most large reports are separately itemized in a List of Figures and a List of Tables. Tables consist of rows and columns of exact numeric data. Quantitative studies often contain many tables, but qualitative reports are a different story. Because much of the data used in qualitative studies are non-tabular, non-numeric, and not quantified, qualitative studies contain far fewer tables than quantitative studies. If you have no tables in your report, then you will not need a List of Tables.

Qualitative studies are rich in textual data, and they sometimes include visual imagery. Illustrations that depict these data enhance the ability of readers to grasp the concepts being described in the study. Illustrations that are do not consist of numbers presented in rows and columns are called figures, and these are normally presented in a List of Figures.

In *Word* the List of Figures and List of Tables are created using the same table-of-contents-like field called a Table of Figures. Even though both lists are generated from the same interface, separate lists are made for tables and figures. Caption labels are the building blocks for these lists.

Captions (above or below) tables and figures control Lists of Tables and Lists of Figures. There can be no Lists of Tables or Figures without properly created Captions.

To create a Caption, first select (click on) the figure or table that needs to be captioned, then Insert ▶ Reference ▶ Caption.

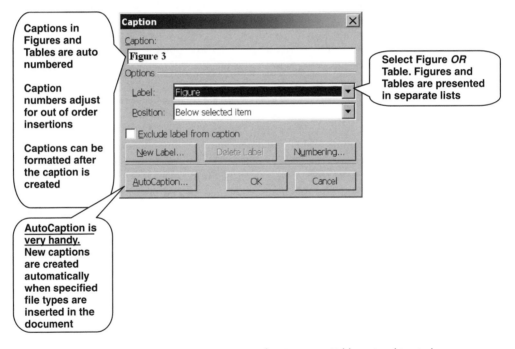

Figure 3. Captions are assigned to Figures or Tables using this window.

If you have a lot of figures or tables, I recommend the use of the AutoCaption feature. AutoCaption allows you to associate file types with tables and with figures. For example, every time an *Excel* worksheet (.xls) is inserted into *Word* the AutoCaption feature can be configured to automatically insert a *table* caption. In a parallel manner, every time a graphic file (.gif, .tif, .jpg, etc.) is inserted into the *Word* file the AutoCaption feature can be configured to automatically create a *figure* caption.

At the time of their creation, the List of Tables and the List of Figures are inserted independently, generally on separate pages. To create the lists (one at a time), click in a blank line in the appropriate location of your report. This location is specified in most editorial style guides. Insert the specialized *Word* fields by selecting Insert ▶ Reference ▶ Index and Tables ▶ select the Table of Figures tab. The following window will appear.

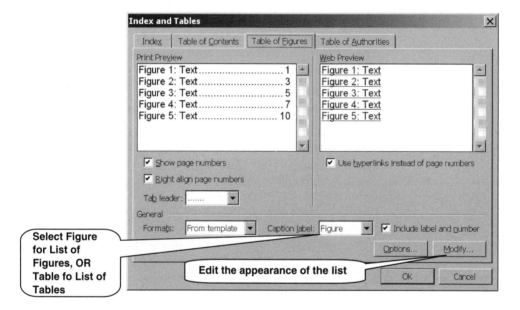

Insert List of Figures or List of Tables with this window.

When you insert a List of Tables **or** List of Figures, *Word* searches for all related captions, filters them by the type of caption, and numbers them sequentially.

If you make changes in your report that might change the captions' page numbers or the number of captions, you will need to update the List of Figures and the List of Tables. To update the List of Figures or the List of Tables, right-click on the list and select Update Field.

Note: Lists of Figures and Lists of Tables are edited by clicking on the Modify button after selecting Insert ▶ Reference ▶ Index and Tables ▶ select the Table of Figures tab. Unlike Tables of Contents, these lists cannot be edited directly by right-clicking on the List, and then clicking on Edit field.

Chapter 1: Introduction/Statement of the Problem

The report Introduction, sometimes called the Statement of the Problem, introduces the research question, the purpose of the research, its scope, and its relevance to the field or discipline.

Apply the Heading 1 style to the chapter title

The Introduction/Statement of the Problem heading is the first formatting task for you to accomplish when you start the chapter. Most chapter headings use the Heading 1 style. To apply this style, type the name of the chapter on its own line, leave the cursor anywhere in the title, and then press `Ctrl+Alt+1`, or select Heading 1 from the Formatting toolbar as described in the Styles and Formatting section above.

Apply a heading style every time you make a new heading. This applies to chapters and sections at all levels.

Create a Normal style that matches your style guide

This is the first section where you will be typing standard sentences and paragraphs that must be formatted according to the specifications of your editorial style guide. Your efficiency improves when *Word* automatically applies the correct formatting every time you start typing in the body of your report document.

Word's standard paragraph Style that is the default in all blank documents is the 'Normal' style. Because this is the style that *Word* uses, I recommend that you modify the Normal style in your report document to reflect the specifications of your editorial style guide. This procedure is described in more detail at the beginning of this chapter. A quick summary: `Format ▶ Styles and Formatting` (causes the task pane to appear on the right side of the *Word* window). Then, from the list, right-click on `Normal ▶ click on Modify ▶ make the changes necessary ▶ click OK`.

Quick tip: Every time you paste a selection into your document, or do anything that causes your standard paragraphs to be incorrectly formatted, press `Shift+Ctrl+N` (the Normal Style shortcut command). The errant text will quickly snap back to its Normal format.

Reminder: Apply heading styles when you start a new chapter, section, or subsection.

Chapter 2: Literature review

The literature review section identifies your research project's position within the framework of previous research on the research topic. The literature review is more than a list of books, articles, and Internet sites related to the topic. It is also an organized and coherent synthesis of the best and most relevant research related to your research project.

Use a bibliographic reference manager

During your review of the literature (often presented in Chapter 2) you will identify, review, and write about many references that relate to your research topic. Keeping track of references, inserting properly formatted citations, and precisely preparing the final reference/bibliography section is mind-numbing and a painfully tedious task.

It is worth mentioning, again, that bibliographic reference managers like EndNote, Biblioscape, and Reference Works, can liberate you from wasting hours of time consuming and painfully precise typing. Review these packages, and if you do not yet have one, take action, acquire one, and use it.

EndNote is the most popular program in the academic world and it contains many features. Biblioscape is less expensive than EndNote, but it lacks all of the high-powered features of EndNote. These features may not matter for many students. Reference Works is ideal for networks. It uses a client/server architecture so team members in larger projects have simultaneous use of the same bibliographic database.

Chapter 3: Methodology

The methodology section of a report explains in detail how the study was conducted based on the explanation of methods that you used. It also allows interested researchers to follow the methods you used in order to replicate the research procedures to verify the findings. This section must be detailed and exact.

In the methodology section you should refer readers to the source of your ideas about the research methods you used. If you developed innovative new techniques, present these techniques so others can build upon your innovative concepts.

The methodology section is the place to describe your research philosophy, your study's theoretical framework, the research design strategy, how you collected your data, how you analyzed and coded your data, how you verified your data's accuracy, and ethical issues.

Also, I am interested in hearing about creative research techniques that you associated with the concepts presented in this book.

Reminder: *Apply heading styles when you start a new chapter, section, or subsection.*

Chapter 4: Data Analysis and Results

The Data Analysis and Results section is frequently called 'Measures' in quantitative reports. This section presents the non-evaluative reporting of the data, supported by illustrations, pictures, figures, charts, and tables where applicable.

As you start writing about data analysis and the results of that analysis, keep in mind the assets at your disposal. Use these assets creatively to present the data that supports your results.

⇒ The database that stores your codes (*Access* or *Excel*) provides virtually instantaneous access to all of your codes on every level, the raw data that inspired the codes, and the location of the raw data in the original code document.

⇒ The Level 1, Level 2, Level 3, and Level 4 coding techniques provide a logical framework for the description of analytic framework/outline for the project.

⇒ More help from *Access* or *Excel* database filters and data sorting of your code records allows you to create meaningful views of your data that are ideal for report figures and illustrations.

⇒ While writing your report you will undoubtedly describe the individual participants, field settings, objects, and constituent groups that contributed raw data to the code documents in your study. Providing details about your data sources and the manner in which their unique characteristics influenced your analysis adds richness to the report. Database filters and data sorting of your code records allows you to quickly focus on any code document.

⇒ The Table of Contents entry in each *Word* code document provides an excellent summary of the structure and demographics of each data collection session. When you are pondering a certain discussion or observation, a review of the code document's table of contents helps you quickly identify the memos and data you need.

The quality of your report and the speed of your writing are greatly enhanced by your access to the organized tools you created.

Making figures and illustrations from screen shots

The data analysis and results section of a scientific paper traditionally includes the frequent use of figures, illustrations, and/or tables. Filters, sorts, and (in *Access*) reports can isolate ideal views on your screen that are perfect for your report. But how do you get those great images that you see on your screen into your report? The answer is to capture the image from your screen and save it as a graphics file.

Using the Paint software already on your computer it is possible to capture and edit information on your screen. I do not recommend the following procedure unless you are desperate or you are only going to capture one or two screen images. The procedure works, but it involves a ridiculous number of steps.

Here is how you can capture a screen image with Windows operating system software. First, make sure the image you want to capture is completely visible on the screen ▶ press the Print Screen key (this captures an image of *everything* on your screen) ▶ open Paint *(Start ▶ Programs ▶ Accessories ▶ Paint)* ▶ from the Paint menu select *Edit ▶ Paste,* this will paste the screen shot image of your entire screen shot into Paint. You will obviously need to cut away all of the unwanted parts of this screen shot. ▶ Click on the Select tool from the toolbar ▶ use the scrollbars in Paint to isolate the section of the screen shot you want to use in your report ▶ use the Select tool to highlight only the area you want to use in your report ▶ copy this selection to the clipboard (Ctrl+C) ▶ close Paint without saving it ▶ open Paint again ▶ press (Ctrl+V) to paste your selection into Paint ▶ save the file. And, with tongue in cheek, that is all there is to it.

Far preferable to the Print Screen/Paint techniques are the inexpensive or free software utilities designed explicitly for capturing areas and objects on your screen. I suggest that you do an Internet search for 'screen capture software.' Download and use free screen capture software, or pay a modest fee for software with more features.

These screen capture programs allow you to efficiently capture specific areas, objects, menus, or windows from the screen so you can avoid the tedious step of cropping the image.

What is the best file format for saving your screen shot?

⇒ If you are writing your report in the Windows version of *Word* and the images will not be used elsewhere, I recommend that you save your screen shots in Windows' native image Windows Metafile Format (.wmf or .emf). If your screen capture program (like Paint) does not save .wmf files, .bmp files are another good choice.

⇒ If the pictures might eventually be used in a Web page then the .jpg format is recommended. All Web browsers know how to read .jpg files. The problem with .jpg files is resolution. If you have to resize .jpg files in *Word* you may end up with unsatisfactory picture quality.

⇒ If you are preparing a report that must be printed in high resolution and you are not worried about relatively large graphics files, I recommend the .tif format. These files produce high quality images for typesetters and others who may not be using Windows programs.

Experiment with different file formats to see what works best for your system.

Reminder: Apply heading styles when you start a new chapter, section, or subsection.

Chapter 5: Conclusions and recommendations

The final section of the report can be challenging yet exciting to write because it requires you to evaluate your own work and provide personal insight into and interpretation of the study's results. The conclusions section should assess whether, and how well, the study addressed the problems and questions that preceded the study. This final section usually provides recommendations for further research that can build upon your study.

The discussion of your results should be structured in a manner that best outlines the conclusions that you have drawn from your extensive examination, coding, and analysis of the data. The 'very few' codes from the highest level of coding that you completed (Level 3, Level 4, or beyond) provide a logical presentation structure for the 'discussion of the results' section of the Conclusion.

For example, the study that provided many examples used in this book focused on the parents who maintained successful long-term joint physical custodies. Over 500 Level 1 codes reduced down to just six theoretical concepts (Level 4). **These Level 4 codes told the story remarkably well and served as headings in the Conclusions section**. The parents in the study (a) were committed to parenting and saw the importance of both parents, (b) cooperated in spite of negative feelings, (c) adequately coordinated parental activities, (d) tried to do the best for their children, (e) were flexible, and (f) made sacrifices but also felt rewarded. These behaviors and attitudes were pervasive and they were sustained despite serious life challenges.

Level 3 codes are also valuable as you write the conclusion. Level 3 codes contain valuable and concentrated thematic ideas that add significant depth as you answer your original research questions.

Level 3 codes were the building blocks for Level 4 codes; therefore, **Level 3 concepts are used as subsections in the Conclusions section to fully explain the rich dimensions of your Level 4 codes**. Try to include a representative quotation (verbatim data section) in your final report from every Level 3 code. **It is quick and easy to find the perfect quotation to represent each Level 3 code** because the focused raw data you need is readily available in your *Access* or *Excel* code database.

To see the data for any individual Level 3 code, apply a filter in *Access* or *Excel* to isolate only the records (rows) from that Level 3 code. The filter allows you to scroll exclusively through the records associated with that Level 3 code. You will be able to efficiently scan the records for the best data to include in the report. When you see a text passage you like, copy and paste it into your report.

Writing your final report can be efficient and fast since your ideas are organized and you do not have to fumble around looking for data. By using your Level 4 codes as section headings and organizing your points of discussion in Level 3 code subsections, you can start writing the 'Conclusions and Recommendations' section with a readily established structure.

Reminder: Apply heading styles when you start a new chapter, section, or subsection.

Bibliographic references

Bibliographic reference manager software programs include many different automatic bibliography output styles that 'match' the editorial style guides of publication manuals. Automatic bibliographies are produced by these programs using *Word* fields that are programmatically similar to the fields that display the Table of Contents and the List of Figures.

The format of the bibliography field created is controlled uniquely by each brand of reference manager software and the bibliography and reference sections created by these programs are not always perfect. It is up to you to closely examine the automatically-generated bibliography to make sure it complies with your editorial style guide. To correct the mistakes of your reference manager you have two choices:

1. Use the editing features of your reference manager to fine tune the layout that is produced by that software program. This is the best way to produce perfect bibliographies every time. The problem is that the tools that reference managers provide for fine tuning their output can be hard to use.
2. If you cannot figure out how to use your reference manager's editing tools, you can use *Word*'s formatting features to override mistakes made by your reference manager. The main problem with this approach is that when you update the bibliography field all of the overriding corrections you made with *Word*'s formatting features are erased. This is because of the cite-as-you-write feature of most reference managers. To avoid this frustrating problem, create a *Word* Style that properly formats your bibliography. (The creation of Styles is discussed at the beginning of this chapter.) This way, every time your reference manager updates the bibliography field and messes up the formatting you can correct the style mistakes by applying the *Word* Style you created for the bibliographic section.

Chapter summary

The research project's report tells the story of your topic, methodology and conclusions. Most scholarly and professional reports (theses, dissertations, academic journal articles, and intra-organizational papers) follow a similar structure. They start with preliminary pages like the title page, abstract, and the table of contents. These pages are followed by the introduction/ statement of the problem, literature review, description of methodology, data analysis/results section, and finally the conclusions and recommendations section.

These report sections have unique formatting requirements that can be tedious and exacting. *Word*'s Styles feature significantly eases the burden of the researcher because Styles can be customized to match the exact editorial style required for your report.

Heading Styles should be applied to all chapter, section, and subsection headings because they are required for the automatic compilation of the Table of Contents. Headings can be marked using keyboard shortcuts for heading 1 (Alt+Ctrl+1), heading 2 (Alt+Ctrl+2), and heading 3 (Alt+Ctrl+3).

The List of Figures and List of Tables are compiled based on the creation of captions above or below the tables and figures included in the report. To create a caption, first select the figure or table that needs to be captioned, and then click on Insert ▶ Reference ▶ Caption.

References to existing literature placed in the body of the report and in the Bibliography/Reference section at the end of the report are best handled by a third party bibliographic reference software program. This software automatically handles the tedious formatting that accompanies references and bibliographies.

APPENDIX

Microsoft *Office* basics

If I have the belief that I can do it, I shall surely acquire the capacity to do it even if I may not have it at the beginning.

Mohandas Gandhi

Gandhi **had to learn** many things as he developed his strategy of nonviolent protest that eventually led to the independent nation of India. His efforts paid off dramatically because he had the confidence to get started and to learn.

If you are a Microsoft *Office* beginner do not give up on developing new skills before you diligently try. Persevere when you get confused. Software can be frustrating for everyone. You are not the only one who has had your computer crash for no apparent reason. We have all searched for 'impossible to find' commands endlessly. Even though I am the author of this book, which includes many technology tips, I have often been perplexed and frustrated by computers and software. One of my secrets of success is-don't give up – keep trying.

If you get so frustrated that you want to throw your computer out of the window you are not alone. Computer horror stories are abundant, but that is no excuse to ignore the amazing power of computers and computer software. I believe that for any big research project a cost vs. benefit analysis will massively favor the use of computers. Why? Because **computers and current-generation software will save you time and increase the quality of your work.**

But you might say, 'I am a social scientist, I work with people not machines.' Well, yes, that may be true. However, as a social scientist researcher you cannot possibly keep everything in your head. For any sizable project you will generate an enormous amount of data. If you pass up the power of computers and software in favor of piles of paper you are ignoring tremendous efficiencies.

What about the learning curve? I acknowledge that it takes time to learn to use computer programs, but it is time well spent. If you master only a few of the ideas contained in this book you will have improved your research efficiencies and you will have learned a lot about the most common business and educational software in use today – Microsoft *Office*.

This is *not* an exhaustive training guide for Microsoft *Office* products. The tips presented here are intended to be a catalyst to get you started with the basic functions of Microsoft *Office* that are most important to qualitative researchers. It is up to you to uncover the features that are most important to your projects. Be aggressive and determined with the Microsoft *Office* software tools; it will pay off for years to come.

Be like Gandhi; believe in yourself even if you are not starting with a lot of experience. If you believe that you will benefit from more basic software training then you are encouraged to enroll in local courses, participate in on-line tutorials, and/or buy some reference books.

What is Microsoft *Office*?

Office is a suite of individual software programs that have been designed to share data and look similar. The full *Office* range of products includes programs that are beyond the scope of this book. This book focuses on products that come with the *Office Professional Edition Suite: Word, Excel, Access*, and *Outlook*.

Word is a word processor; *Excel* is a spreadsheet that can be used as a giant data table and to do calculations; *Access* is a database program that allows sophisticated data storage and manipulation; and *Outlook* handles e-mail, calendars, and tasks. Data can be shared between all of these programs.

The menus and toolbars in *Word* look very similar to those in *Access, Outlook,* or *Excel*. Because of this you are learning to navigate all programs when you learn your first *Office* application.

The ability to share data between *Office* programs is a keystone feature that is used extensively in the data analysis section of this book. You will learn that data sharing is remarkably easy and productive.

We are lucky to live in an era when software programs like *Office* are mature and relatively bug free. In the early days of personal computing, programs were famously hard to use and prone to rude and unannounced crashes. If you were soured by earlier experiences with software I suggest that you do not give up. Yes, programs might still lock up occasionally, but the improvements, even in the last five years, have been dramatic.

Things that all *Office* programs have in common

Love it or hate it, Microsoft brought a common interface to its programs. Because of Microsoft's dominant position in the industry, software programs by other companies have almost universally adopted the look and feel of Microsoft's current programs. This means that many of the basic things you learn in one program, say *Excel*, will also be applicable to many other programs.

The menu commands

At the top of all *Office* programs is the menu bar. For *Excel, Word,* and *Access* the top line menu choices all start with 'File,' 'Edit,' 'View,' 'Insert' ... You are probably comfortable and familiar with clicking on these menu choices to proceed with your work so I won't belabor this section, but I do want to point out a detail about the menus that you may have overlooked.

Notice the underlined letter in each of the following commands: 'File,' 'Edit,' 'View,' and 'Insert.' These underlined letters have a purpose; they allow you to execute commands with your keyboard instead of your mouse. The menu commands associated with the underlined letters can be activated by holding down the Alt key, and then pressing the letter associated with the menu command you want to invoke.

> Commands can be executed by (a) clicking on the menu, (b) clicking on the toolbar icon, (c) using the Ctrl hotkeys, or (d) the Alt quick key sequences

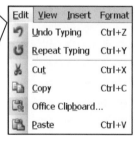

For example, holding down the Alt key and then pressing 'E' (Alt+E) will result in the appearance of the Edit menu. Taking this one step further, Alt+E followed by ► Alt+U will execute the 'Undo Typing' command.

To keep going with this example, menu commands can also be executed by (a) clicking on the successive menu commands with the mouse, (b) clicking on the toolbar icon associated with the command , (c) using the hot key combination of Ctrl+Z, or (d) using the 'Alt' quick key sequence of Alt+E ► Alt+U. All of these methods execute the 'Undo Typing' command.

This example illustrates the multiple ways in which Microsoft often lets you execute commands. Use the technique that works the best for you.

Toolbars

As described above, commands can be executed in *Office* programs by clicking on toolbar icons. At their most basic level toolbars are very easy to understand; simply click on the icon that represents the command that you want to execute. If you are not sure what command an icon represents, hover your mouse over that icon. A 'tool tip' will appear that describes the command.

What is not as obvious is how you can change which toolbars appear on your screen and how to change the contents of toolbars.

If you are not seeing a toolbar that you want, you can add that toolbar to your screen; or conversely, if you have too many toolbars cluttering the top of your screen you can remove unwanted toolbars.

Right-click on any toolbar to view a dropdown list of all available toolbars. The toolbars that are currently visible in the program on your screen are identified by the check mark that appears next to the entry on the list. In this illustration the checkmark indicates that the Formatting toolbar is activated ✔ Formatting.

To add a toolbar that is not currently active on your screen, click on the desired toolbar from the dropdown list. The checkmark will appear in the dropdown menu and the toolbar will appear on the top of the screen.

To remove a toolbar, activate the View ▶ Toolbars list, and then click to uncheck toolbar selection you want to remove.

To add a command to a toolbar, first make sure that toolbar is currently active on your screen, then right-click on that toolbar, and then click on Customize. A small window will appear that gives you access to the toolbar icons for countless commands. Your job is to find the icon you want and drag it to the toolbar on your screen. To find the toolbar icon you want you will have to scroll through the available commands that are grouped by categories (File, Edit, View, etc.). Once you find the command icon you want, click and hold down your left mouse button over the command icon, and then drag it to the desired location in your target toolbar.

Right-click on a toolbar to add, remove, or edit the toolbar

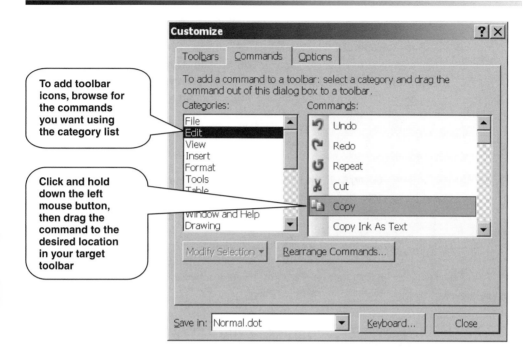

To add toolbar icons, browse for the commands you want using the category list

Click and hold down the left mouse button, then drag the command to the desired location in your target toolbar

Copy/Cut and Paste

If you are not a pro at *quickly* copying and pasting data, now is the time to learn. The following techniques are critical to efficiently copying data from one file to another and from one program to another, a technique used frequently during coding.

What is copy and paste? It is a way to **copy** text, pictures, numbers, and other data from one place to another within Windows. It can be within a single file or between files, and the best part is that the data can be copied between different programs, e.g. *Word* to *Excel*.

What is cut and paste? It is a way to **move** text, pictures, numbers, and other data from one place to another within Windows. It is just like copy and paste, but it starts with the Edit ▶ Cut command instead of the Edit ▶ Copy command.

How does it work? After either the Copy or the Cut command the selected data are instantly stored in Windows' clipboard (your computer's memory). The data are stored in the clipboard until the computer is turned off or until different data are copied to the clipboard to replace the original data.

As long as your computer remains on, you have as much time as you need to locate the place you want to insert the data. Put the cursor in the insertion point in the receiving program or file, and then paste the data from the clipboard. At the simplest level this is done with the Edit ▶ Paste command.

If you followed this explanation you now know that you can copy data to the clipboard with the `Edit ▶ Cut` command or the `Edit ▶ Copy` command, and you can paste it to your insertion point with the `Edit ▶ Paste` command.

Now I want you to forget these commands! They are much too slow when you get into big copying projects. Even the toolbar icons of copy 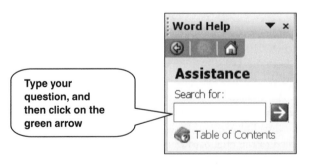, cut, and paste on the Standard toolbar are too slow.

For high-speed copying and pasting you have two good choices:

1. **Copy/Cut and Paste using Right-click**. `Select the data you want to copy or cut ▶ right-click ▶ click on Copy or Cut ▶ go to the insertion point (where you want to paste the data), and then right-click ▶ Paste`. This method is acceptably fast.

2. **Use the hot keys!** This is my preferred method, for me it is the fastest. I use it all the time every day in virtually every program I use. Since I am a terrible typist I do everything possible to avoid entering data by typing. I copy and paste even the simplest things.

> Copy and Paste with Ctrl+C ▶ Ctrl+V
> Cut and Paste with Ctrl+X ▶ Ctrl+V

To copy/cut and paste, **select the data you want to copy or cut ▶ press Ctrl+C for copy (or Ctrl+X for Cut) ▶ go to the insertion point (where you want to paste the data) and press Ctrl+V**.

Why is it fast? Because it is ergonomic. The X, C, and V keys are next to each other within easy reach of the Ctrl key with your left hand. Give it a try; you will see what I mean.

With a little practice you will be copying and pasting like a pro.

Help

> Press F1 in any *Office* program to get Help

When you are perplexed, try Help. Microsoft's help system is powerful. Use Help from the menu, or press the F1 key to get into the help system. The quickest way to get an answer is to type your question into the 'Search for:' field in the help box. After clicking on the green arrow or pressing Enter, a list of help articles will appear. Click on the article that seems to best answer your question. If you do not get an article that appropriately answers your question go back to the 'Search for:' field to enter a rephrased question.

> Type your question, and then click on the green arrow

Word Help ▼ ✕

Assistance

Search for:

→

Table of Contents

If you get too many responses, then narrow your search phrase.

Microsoft *Word* basics

Researchers must use the written word to communicate their findings. Students present their papers, theses, and dissertations; and post-grad researchers present their findings in journals, books, and at conferences. All researchers want to present typo-free and grammatically correct documents. *Word* can help.

Word has grown from a buggy second-best program to the overwhelmingly dominant word processor in the world. Even though it drives some Apple and open source aficionados crazy, a *Word* document attached to an e-mail message is standard fare. It is assumed that the receiver of the message will be able to open and read the attached *Word* document.

Since your success as a researcher depends, in part, on your final written product it behooves you to become an accomplished *Word* user.

Spell checking, grammar checking, and the thesaurus

Spell and grammar checking happens 'automatically' as long as the appropriate options are turned on in *Word*. Unless you, or someone else, deliberately turned off the default settings in *Word* you will see red underlines under misspelled words and green underlines under grammatical errors.

Usually I agree with (and appreciate) Microsoft's recognition of my typos, spelling goofs, and grammar faux pas. However, sometimes I have the temerity to think that Microsoft's programmers are fallible and I ignore Microsoft's corrections. Yes, your human brain should have the confidence to ignore or override Microsoft's suggestions when they are wrong.

Red and green wavy underlines bring potential errors to your attention. Right-click to accept, reject, or further explore the spelling and grammar issues that Microsoft has flagged.

Right-click to correct or reject spelling and grammar issues flagged by red or green wavy underlines

When you right-click on a red underlined word a box will pop up that suggests alternatives to the 'misspelled' word that is not in Microsoft's dictionary. The example illustrated here offers several possible words that match the word (spel) that was misspelled. Click on the properly spelled word (spell) to have it replace the misspelled word.

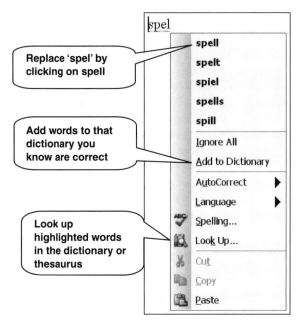

Replace 'spel' by clicking on spell

Add words to that dictionary you know are correct

Look up highlighted words in the dictionary or thesaurus

If Microsoft's dictionary does not recognize a word that you know is spelled correctly, click on 'Add to Dictionary.' This will halt the appearance of the red underline every time you type the word and it will become a possible spelling correction if you misspell the word sometime in the future.

The lookup feature is especially handy while writing reports and other manuscripts. If you are searching for a similar word or want the definition of a word, right-click on the target word, and then click on Look Up. Dictionary and Thesaurus entries will appear when they are available.

The wavy green underline represents a possible grammar error. Right-click to see what Microsoft thinks is wrong. A menu will pop up that explains the problem and (sometimes) suggests a solution. Again, use your own judgement. Microsoft is not always right.

Using tables

Tables in *Word* are used to organize text and other data into grids of rows and columns. Only a cursory mention of tables is made here because a detailed explanation of task-specific table usage is presented in Chapter 6.

The easiest way to create a table is to use the Insert Table wizard. Click your mouse in the location in the document in which you want the table to appear, then from the menu click on Table ▶ Insert ▶ Table. A dialog box will appear that allows you to select the number of rows and columns you need.

Don't worry about creating a perfect table through the wizard. The Table menu offers you numerous choices for formatting, adding rows, deleting rows, adding columns, and deleting columns.

This is a table with three rows and three columns. This row features merged cells, a black background, and a white font color.		
Label for row 1	1	11
Label for row 2	2	22

Table borders and fill colors are customized using the Format menu. Select Format ▶ Borders and Shading to gain access to many possibilities for changing the appearance of your table. Once you get into the Borders and Shading pane, notice the three tabs at the top of the window: Border, Page Border, and Shading. These tabs give you access to the different formatting options. A little experimentation will allow you to do some creative things with tables.

If you are familiar with Microsoft *Excel* you know that *Excel* is a giant and very sophisticated table. *Excel* can help you create tables in *Word* because selected cells in *Excel* can be inserted into *Word* documents using the copy and paste command. If you are more comfortable with *Excel* than you are with *Word*'s table features, go ahead and create your tables for *Word* in *Excel*. After getting things the way you want them in *Excel*, select the *Excel* range of cells you want, and then use the Copy and Paste features of *Excel* and *Word* to transfer your handiwork from *Excel* to *Word*.

Formatting of font type, font attributes, and paragraph settings can be done manually or combined and saved as a Style. Style allows the quick and easy formatting of *word* documents

Styles

Styles are often overlooked and under-used even by relatively experienced *Word* users. Why should they bother? After all, they can create the look (style) they want by manually formatting the font style, font size, font weight, and paragraph settings using toolbars and menus. While manual formatting works fine in small documents, manual formatting is slow, tedious, and error prone in large reports, theses, and dissertations. Speed and accuracy are important reasons to use styles.

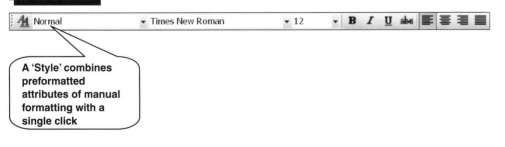

A 'Style' combines preformatted attributes of manual formatting with a single click

The levels of tables of contents are built from Heading styles that are assigned throughout the document.

Customize Styles
using the Format
▶ Styles and
Formatting menu
selections

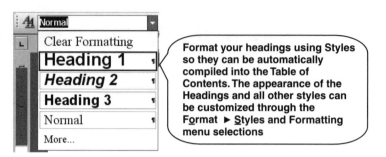

Format your headings using Styles so they can be automatically compiled into the Table of Contents. The appearance of the Headings and all other styles can be customized through the Format ▶ Styles and Formatting menu selections

In summary, use Styles to:

⇒ Save a lot of time formatting large documents and reports
⇒ Produce internally consistent documents
⇒ Quickly review the structure of large documents
⇒ Automatically create Tables of Contents.

Chapter 10 goes into detail about the techniques used to customize Styles to accommodate the requirements of the editorial style guide (APA, Chicago, Oxford, Cambridge, etc.) that is appropriate for your report, thesis, or dissertation.

Microsoft *Outlook* basics

Even though Microsoft *Outlook* is often thought of primarily as an e-mail program, it will do a lot more than e-mail. *Outlook* is a personal information manager – a collection of programs that helps you manage your schedule (calendar), your tasks, your address book (contacts), tasks, and it features a computerized version of yellow Post-it-style notes.

Opening *Outlook*

Start ▶ Programs
▶ Outlook

Start ▶ Run ▶
Outlook

This discussion touches on only a few of the most basic features of *Outlook*.

If you don't have an *Outlook* icon on your desktop, two alternative methods of starting *Outlook* are shown below.

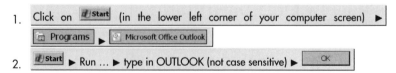

1. Click on ⊞ Start (in the lower left corner of your computer screen) ▶ 🗀 Programs ▶ 🗐 Microsoft Office Outlook

2. ⊞ Start ▶ Run ... ▶ type in OUTLOOK (not case sensitive) ▶ [OK]

Using Outlook *for your e-mail*

It is important to understand the difference between an e-mail account and the software program that you use to read and send your e-mail. Most e-mail accounts like Yahoo Mail and Gmail can be accessed through Internet browsers like Internet Explorer or Firefox, but they can also be accessed through client programs like *Outlook*, *Outlook Express*, and *Eudora*.

Perhaps you have an e-mail account with your company or university, and you also have an e-mail account with Yahoo, Hotmail (Windows Live), or Google (Gmail). The incoming and outgoing mail for all of these services is processed through mail servers hosted by the organization that manages your account. These mail servers can be independent of the program that you choose to read and write your e-mail.

Yahoo, Google, and other Web-based e-mail accounts are usually accessed through Web browsers. Many people do not understand that many of these accounts can also be accessed from *Outlook*.

Today's Web browser e-mail interfaces from Yahoo, Google, Hotmail, and other similar companies are quite usable and they are often integrated with address books, calendars, and notepads, but they are designed to be used only while connected to the Internet. All of your data are stored on their host servers. If you do not have an Internet connection you have temporarily lost contact with your data.

Outlook is not a Web browser program. Yes, it sends and receives e-mails and other data through the Internet, but it works through a sophisticated customized program that is installed on your computer. Web browsers are less customizable than client programs like *Outlook*; therefore, the user interface of *Outlook* is more robust, sophisticated, and faster than it can be in one-size-fits-all Web browser programs.

In addition to a better user interface, another reason to use *Outlook* for your e-mail is that **the data you receive through *Outlook* is stored locally on your computer and you can use it even if you do not have Internet access.**

Technical note: If you are using *Outlook* through an organization's Exchange server the collaborative teamwork functionality of *Outlook* is achieved only if you are connected to your organization's network.

Connect your Yahoo, Gmail, or other account to *Outlook*

To connect your e-mail account(s) from companies like Yahoo, Google, and Hotmail to *Outlook* you will need to get some information from the company that provides you with your e-mail service. *Outlook* needs to know your e-mail address and details about the address of your e-mail provider's mail server. The good news is that all major e-mail service providers make this information readily available in easy-to-follow step-by-step instructions.

To find your e-mail service provider's step-by-step instructions use their Help system. Usually the 'Help' link is in the upper right corner of the Web-based mail home page. After clicking on Help look for a search box that allows you to enter a question. In Gmail the search box is titled 'Search Help Center,' in Yahoo the search box is called 'Ask Yahoo Help.' If you have a different service the Help interface will differ, but you will probably get your questions answered by following the same logical path.

Once you find the Help search box type in 'Outlook POP' to find the step-by-step instructions for configuring *Outlook* to use your current e-mail account. Once you find and follow the instructions **you will be able to use** *Outlook* **to send and receive your e-mail and you will still be able to use the Web browser interface from your e-mail provider.** POP stands for Post Office Protocol. This is the industry standard protocol that allows e-mail programs like *Outlook* to retrieve and send information from remote mail servers.

Multiple e-mail accounts can be managed with a single copy of *Outlook*. For example, if you have e-mail accounts with both Gmail and Yahoo you can set up POP accounts for both of these services in *Outlook*. When *Outlook* checks for new e-mail messages it can check both accounts. Incoming messages for both accounts will appear together in the same Inbox.

Some 'free' e-mail providers like Yahoo and Hotmail charge a nominal fee for an upgraded level of service that allows POP access. The choice is yours, but my suggestion is that the efficiency you gain from *Outlook* will make your investment well worth it.

> Manage multiple e-mail accounts in *Outlook*

Sending an e-mail message and attaching files

Since you may be using *Outlook* for the first time I will get you started on the most basic level – sending e-mail. This introduction will be brief because it is assumed that you have used other e-mail programs in the past.

If you need more help, I suggest that you get more training from a book, a class, or from the free resources available through the *Outlook* Help menu (Help ▶ Microsoft Office Outlook Help F1 ▶ look for 'Training' in the *Outlook* Help pane that appears).

To get started in e-mail, first make sure you are in the correct section in *Outlook*. Look for 'Inbox' near the top of the *Outlook* window. If you do not see 'Inbox' click on the Mail button in the Navigation pane on the left side of the screen.

To start a new e-mail message, click on File ▶ New ▶ Mail Message (Ctrl+N), or click on the New ▼ button on the toolbar.

To attach a file to an e-mail message, click on the paper clip 'Attach' icon on the toolbar. An 'Insert File' pane will appear. To find the file you want to attach to the message, browse through the folders on your computer. Once the file has been located, double-click on that file, or select the file and click on the Insert button to attach the file to the e-mail message.

> Click on the paper clip icon or Insert ▶ File to insert a file

Configuring **Outlook**

> Navigation pane

Outlook can be configured in many ways to suit your working style.

The navigation pane on the left side of the *Outlook* screen allows you to switch between Mail, the Calendar, Contacts, Tasks (the small red checkmark

Sort columns by clicking on the column headings

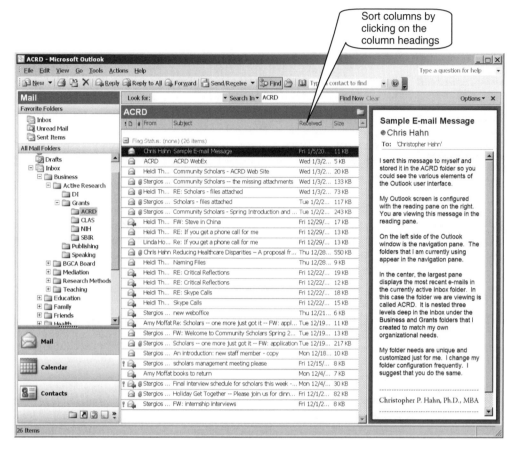

Navigation pane

List of messages in a folder – sort by clicking on the column headings

Reading pane

below Contacts), and more. The navigation pane also allows you to quickly view the contents of your folders.

The center column of the *Outlook* screen allows you to view the messages that are contained in your inbox, or any other folder. Open any message by double-clicking the message.

Resize columns

The size of the columns in the center pane (From, Subject, Received, etc.) can be customized by carefully placing your mouse pointer between column headings. After the cursor changes from the mouse arrow to the double-arrow, hold down the left mouse button. While the mouse button is depressed, move the mouse to the left or to the right to make the column smaller or larger. This technique works in many other situations within Microsoft *Office* applications.

Add or delete columns

Reading pane

Configuring *Outlook* and the panes

To add or delete columns, right-click on any of the column headings. Select 'Remove this column' to delete a column, select 'Field Chooser' to add columns. The right-click menu also provides other formatting options.

The reading pane is shown on the right side of the *Outlook* window in the illustration above. This pane is provided as a preview pane. Double-click on the message to read the message in its own window.

The default appearance of *Outlook* is functional and you may be happy with it, but if there is an appearance or behavior you want to change you will find that *Outlook* is configurable. Detailed instructions for changing the appearance and behavior of *Outlook* are beyond the scope of this book, but I will provide a few rules to get you started.

⇒ The configuration technique to try first is to put the mouse pointer in the area you want to change and **right-click**. Microsoft has programmed the right mouse button to do a lot of powerful things; remember to use it when you can. From the menu:

⇒ Tools ▶ Customize allows you to change the toolbars

⇒ Tools ▶ Options is your gateway to changing the settings of E-mail, Calendar, Tasks, Contacts, and Notes

⇒ View ▶ Reading Pane allows you to change the location and appearance of the reading pane.

Creating e-mail folders

Wasting time can be wonderful if it involves sipping a cool drink on the shores of a tropical island. But when you are trying to get something done quickly it is good to be efficient. The last thing you want to do is to look for lost communiqués.

E-mail is a primary communication pathway in everyday life and in work settings. It is often valuable to be able to retrieve earlier e-mail exchanges, and that means you need to employ an effective system of keeping your e-mail in order.

If you use *Outlook* for all of the e-mail related to your research project you are off to a good start. If you followed the instructions earlier in this Appendix you know that you can handle e-mail from several accounts in a single copy of *Outlook*. This is an efficient way to handle e-mail, but the job does not end in a single Inbox folder.

What happens after you read your e-mail messages? Frequently messages contain valuable archival information that you know you will want to read again later. How are you going to find that e-mail message again?

If you save all of your messages in the Inbox you will create an impossibly long list of old e-mail messages. Scrolling through these messages in search of an important old message can be a tedious waste of time. So how can you efficiently store your messages? Use folders.

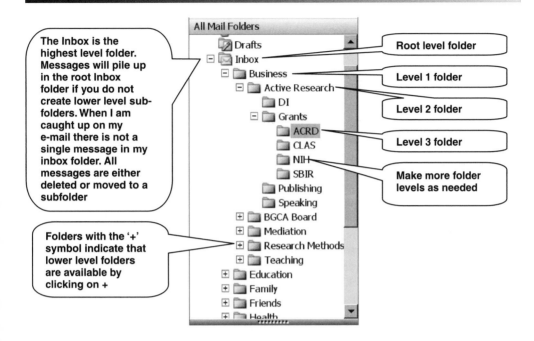

You should create new folders when a parent folder starts to become too cluttered. Break down the messages into subcategories. Each of the subcategories becomes a new subfolder.

In the illustration above notice that the 'ACRD' Level 4 folder is selected. The following example shows you how to create new folders, one for the first half of the year and the other for the second half of the year. In the process I will make a Level 5 folder.

Step 1: Select the ACRD folder by clicking on it.

Step 2: From the menu, select File ▶ New ▶ Folder (Ctrl+Shift+E).

Step 3: Type in the name of the new folder. In this case, 'First Half of Year,' then click on OK.

To create a folder for the second half of the year, repeat the process, again starting at the ACRD folder, but name the second new folder 'Second Half of Year.'

Once you have created your new folder you can populate it with e-mail messages you want to store by dragging messages from the Inbox (or any other mail directory) to the new directory.

The organization of folders is also addressed in Chapter 3 in the section about *My Documents*.

Contacts

For a discussion of the Contacts feature of *Outlook* refer to Chapter 3, beginning on page 48.

Microsoft *Excel* basics

Excel is one of the cornerstone programs of Microsoft *Office*. *Excel* is generally thought of as *Office*'s number cruncher program, but its versatility allows the use of *Excel* in many different ways. If you are familiar with *Excel* or a similar product, you know that a spreadsheet is a great tool for what-if thinking. Rows and columns can be easily moved, changed, and inserted to explore developing ideas.

This book often offers multiple methods of approaching tasks. When Microsoft *Excel* is mentioned in the book it is always as an optional method of accomplishing a goal. For this reason, it is not imperative that you learn *Excel* to work with the ideas presented in the book. However, many *Excel* users are quickly hooked by its ease and power.

This is a simplified worksheet.

Each *Excel* file is collection of worksheets called a workbook. The specific use of workbooks to store and organize qualitative data is discussed in detail in Chapter 8.

Excel is best known for its ability to perform calculations and to do statistical analysis, but that is just a beginning. *Excel* spreadsheets can be used as databases, calendars, budgets, lists, project planners, expense reports, schedules, time sheets and more. Go to http://office.microsoft.com/en-us/templates/ to select from many templates if you want to get started with sample workbooks. If you get stumped by a procedural 'how-to' problem that is not illustrated in this book it is recommended that you find a reference book and other training resources. As always, remember to use F1 for <u>H</u>elp.

Entering text, formulas, and numbers

Enter text, formulas, and numbers in the function bar

Text and numbers can also be entered directly in cells

Formulas offer countless powerful calculations. The formula in this cell calculates the number of days between the start date and end date

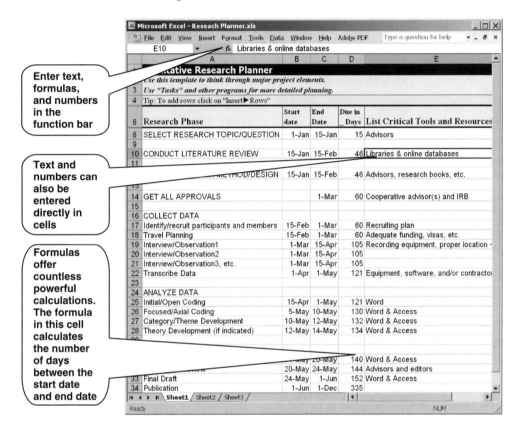

This *Excel*-based Research Planner spreadsheet is available for download at qrtips.com/appendix.

Inserting rows and columns

Insert ▶ Rows
Insert ▶ Columns

As ideas develop it is highly likely that you will think of items that did not make it to the first draft of your *Excel* worksheet. That is why you need to know how to insert rows and columns.

Select the cell below or to the right of the column you want to insert

From the menu, click on Insert ▶ Rows to insert a row above the cell that is currently selected.

From the menu, click on Insert ▶ Columns to insert a column to the left of the cell that is currently selected.

Resize rows and columns

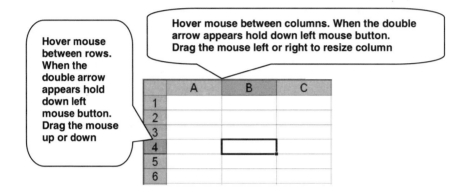

Hover mouse between columns. When the double arrow appears hold down left mouse button. Drag the mouse left or right to resize column

Hover mouse between rows. When the double arrow appears hold down left mouse button. Drag the mouse up or down

Entering formulas

Excel has the power to execute formulas that solve a broad array of problems ranging from basic arithmetic to statistics and finance. Formulas are equations that perform calculations on data in your worksheet cells. I will show you how to perform a few basic formulas and functions just to get you started.

These examples are simply to give you an idea of what can be done with formulas and functions in *Excel*. Functions are pre-programmed formulas and equations that allow you to answer complex questions with relative ease. Use the Microsoft Help system and other references for more assistance with *Excel* functions and formulas.

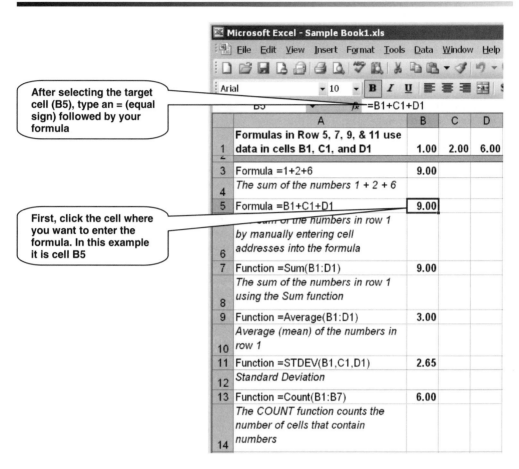

After selecting the target cell (B5), type an = (equal sign) followed by your formula

First, click the cell where you want to enter the formula. In this example it is cell B5

Formulas can be entered manually as shown. Three different formulas that yield the same results are in cells B3, B5, and B7. Data for the formulas in B5 and B7 are in cells B1, C1, and D1.

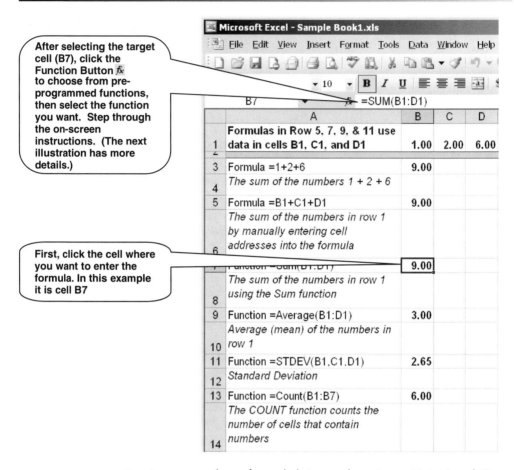

After selecting the target cell (B7), click the Function Button *fx* to choose from pre-programmed functions, then select the function you want. Step through the on-screen instructions. (The next illustration has more details.)

First, click the cell where you want to enter the formula. In this example it is cell B7

Functions were used to perform calculations as shown in rows 7, 9, 11, and 13.

As you can see in cells B3, B5, and B7 in the example above, different formulas and functions can be used to return the same answer.

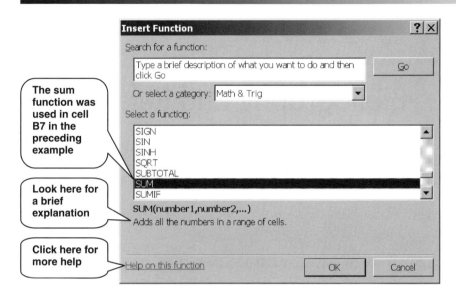

The sum function was used in cell B7 in the preceding example

Look here for a brief explanation

Click here for more help

Many functions are available to perform calculations in *Excel*.

There are many tricks that allow you to copy cells and formulas to greatly hasten the creation of your workbook. Look at online tutorials, books, and Microsoft's Help system to learn more.

Microsoft *Access* basics

Access basics are included at the beginning of Chapter 7.

Bibliography and References

American Psychological Association. (2001). *Publication Manual of the American Psychological Association* (5th edn.). Washington, DC: American Psychological Association.

Baker, L. M. (2006). Observation: A complex research method. *Library Trends, 55*(1), 171–89.

Charmaz, K. (2006). *Constructing Grounded Theory.* Thousand Oaks, CA: Sage Publications.

Creswell, J. W. (2003). *Research Design: Qualitative, Quantitative, and Mixed Methods Approaches* (2nd edn.). Thousand Oaks, CA: Sage Publications.

Eisenhardt, K. (2002). Building theories from case study research. In A. M. Huberman and M. B. Miles (Eds), *The Qualitative Researcher's Companion.* Thousand Oaks, CA: Sage Publications.

Emerson, R. M., Fretz, R. I., and Shaw, L. L. (1995). *Writing Ethnographic Fieldnotes.* Chicago: University of Chicago Press.

Enns, B. (2004). *Technology for Qualitative Coding, thematic analysis, and data reporting.* Paper presented at the Capella Fall Colloquium, Dulles, VA.

Giorgi, A. (1997). The theory, practice, and evaluation of the phenomenological method as a qualitative research procedure. *Journal of Phenomenological Psychology, 28*(2), 26.

Glaser, B. G. (1978). *Theoretical Sensitivity.* Mill Valley, CA: Sociology Press.

Glatthorn, A. A. (1998). *Writing the Winning Dissertation: A Step-by-step Guide.* Thousand Oaks, CA: Corwin Press.

Glicken, M. D. (2003). *Social Research: A Simple Guide.* Boston: Pearson Education.

Haydu, J. (1998). Making use of the past: Time periods as cases to compare as sequences of problem solving, *American Journal of Sociology* (Vol. 104, pp. 339–71): University of Chicago Press.

Huberman, A. M. and Miles, M. B. (2002). *The Qualitative Researcher's Companion.* Thousand Oaks, CA: Sage Publications.

Husserl, E. (1927). Phenomenology (R. E. Palmer, Trans.). In *Britannica article (1927)* (4th edn.). Retrieved from http://www.stanford.edu/dept/relstud/faculty/sheehan.bak/EHtrans/8-eb.pdf: Encyclopedia Britannica.

Johnson, R. B. (1997). Examining the validity structure of qualitative research. *Education, 118*(2), 282.

Kelle, U. (1997, 6/30/1997). *Theory building in qualitative research and computer programs for the management of textual data.* Retrieved June 7, 2007, from http://www.socresonline.org.uk/2/2/1.html.

Kostere, K. (2004). *Research: Qualitative Analysis II: Qualitative Research Methods and Data Analysis.* Paper presented at the Capella Fall Colloquium, Dulles, VA.

Leedy, P. D. and Ormrod, J. E. (2004). *Practical Research: Planning and Design* (8th edn.). Upper Saddle River, NJ: Prentice Hall.

Markham, A. N. (2004). The methods, politics, and ethics of representation in online ethnography (pre-publication draft). In N. Denzin and Y. Lincoln (Eds), *Handbook of Qualitative Research.* Thousand Oaks, CA: Sage Publications.

Mertens, D. A. (2005). *Research and Evaluation in Education and Psychology* (2nd edn.). Thousand Oaks, CA: Sage Publications.

Moustakas, C. (1994). *Phenomenological Research Methods.* Thousand Oaks, CA: Sage Publications.

Neuman, W. L. (2003). *Social Research Methods: Qualitative and Quantitative Approaches.* Boston: Allyn and Bacon.

Northcutt, N. and McCoy, D. (2004). *Interactive Qualitative Analysis.* Thousand Oaks, CA: Sage Publications.

Seidman, I. (1998). *Interviewing as Qualitative Research: A Guide for Researchers in Social Sciences* (2nd edn.). New York: Teachers College Press.

Strauss, A. and Corbin, J. (1998). *Basics of Qualitative Research: Techniques and Procedures for Developing Grounded Theory* (2nd edn.). Thousand Oaks, CA: Sage Publications.

Yin, R. K. (2003). *Case Study Research: Design and Methods* (3rd edn., Vol. 5). Thousand Oaks, CA: Sage Publications.

Index

References to proper names are in small caps. Entries in italics are associated with downloads and links.